FORESTRY COMMISSION BULLETIN 122

Agroforestry in the UK

Edited by Max Hislop and Jenny Claridge

*Silviculture (North) Branch, Forest Research,
Northern Research Station, Roslin,
Midlothian EH25 9SY*

D1492753

Edinburgh: Forestry Commission

ISBN 0 85538 414 X

Hislop, A. Maxwell; Claridge, Jennifer N. 2000. Agroforestry in the UK. Bulletin 122.
Forestry Commission, Edinburgh. xii + 136 pp.

FDC 26:268.1: (410)

KEYWORDS: Agroforestry, Arable crops, Environment, Farm management,
Grazing, Landscape, Pigs, Poultry, Sheep, Silvoarable systems, Silvopastoral
systems

The editors and authors of chapters in this Bulletin should be cited as:

Auclair, D.	Claridge, J.N.	Hooker, J.E.	Sibbald, A.R.
Beaton, A.	Dorward, P.	Incoll, L.D.	Sinclair, F.L.
Bell, S.	Doyle, C.J.	McAdam, J.H.	Thomas, T.H.
Brownlow, M.J.C.	Eason, W.R.	Newman, S.M.	Willis, R.W.
Carruthers, P.	Hislop, A.M.	Sheldrick, R.D.	

Acknowledgements

The editors' thanks are due to all the authors whose contributions have made this
publication possible and for their patience throughout the refereeing process.
Thanks are also due to David Corry (Leeds University), Peter Dennis (MLURI),
Richard Crowe (Greenmount College) for their helpful comments on chapters at an
early draft stage. In addition, many of the authors provided useful suggestions to
other authors' chapters. Many project leaders, scientists, research workers and
research students past and present have contributed to the experiments referred to
in this publication and have given permission for their results to be used. James
Simpson initiated the publication and thanks are due to him for the original concept
and for approaching the authors for their contributions. Numerous helpful
comments have been made by Bill Mason, Paul Tabbush and Jim Dewar. Finally, we
are grateful to the Forest Research typists for typing various drafts, and to the staff
in Communications Branch for their help with photographs, illustrations, editorial
advice and references.

Front cover: Upland silvopastoral
system with larch and sheep at Radnor,
Wales. (FOREST RESEARCH PHOTO LIBRARY 51404)

Back cover: *top* Lowland silvoarable
system with poplar and winter wheat at
Bramham, West Yorkshire. (LYNTON INCOLL,
UNIVERSITY OF LEEDS) *bottom* Pigs at pannage
in Denny Wood, New Forest,
Hampshire. (TERRY HEATHCOTE)

Enquiries relating to this publication
should be addressed to:
The Research Communications Officer,
Forest Research
Alice Holt Lodge
Wrecclesham
Farnham
Surrey GU10 4LH

Contents

List of plates

Plates 1 – 26 between pages 28 and 29.

List of figures

Agroforestry in the UK

Summary

This Bulletin provides advice about the establishment and management of a range of agroforestry systems in the United Kingdom (UK). It is based on a decade of research undertaken by scientists from a number of British and European institutes. The agricultural industry in the UK is going through a major period of change. Health and welfare concerns such as the BSE crisis and the transportation of live animals are affecting the livestock farmer. Environmental concerns over the use of fertilisers and pesticides are affecting arable enterprises. These concerns are just part of the current debate about the future of the countryside in the UK and are encouraging farmers, foresters and policy-makers to explore alternative approaches to rural land use. Agroforestry is one such alternative. The possibility of combining agriculture and forestry on the same unit of land appears attractive. In theory, agroforestry could improve productivity, livestock welfare, wildlife habitats and provide diversification opportunities, as well as reducing fertiliser and feed inputs. The fact that there is little experience of agroforestry systems in the UK may be due to uncertainty about the practicalities of establishment and management and the associated costs and benefits in the short and long term. The objective of this Bulletin is to reduce that uncertainty.

The Bulletin is divided into four sections. Section 1 defines agroforestry, describes the historical and current context for the Bulletin and explains the complexity of agroforestry systems compared to conventional agricultural or forestry systems. Section 2 provides advice on the establishment and management of various agroforestry options and makes recommendations for best practice, based on current research experience. Section 3 considers the impact of agroforestry systems on the environment and gives advice on how to fit agroforestry sympathetically into the landscape. Section 4 considers the social implications of the increased adoption of agroforestry systems in the UK and provides economic assessment of a range of agroforestry scenarios using the best information currently available.

This Bulletin is recommended reading for farmers, farm and forestry advisers, landowners, students and all others with an interest in developing alternative land-use systems in the countryside.

L'agroforesterie en UK

Résumé

Ce bulletin donne des suggestions concernant l'établissement et la gestion d'une diversité de systèmes agroforestiers au Royaume-Uni (UK). Il est basé sur des recherches longues d'une décennie, entreprises par des chercheurs appartenant à plusieurs instituts britanniques et européens. L'agriculture du Royaume-Uni traverse actuellement une période de changement d'importance majeure. Des affaires de santé et de bien-être, telles que la crise de la vache folle et le transport des animaux vivants, se répercutent sur les éleveurs. Des préoccupations environnementales concernant l'utilisation des engrais et des pesticides se répercutent sur les entreprises agricoles. Ces questions, qui occupent une partie des discussions portant actuellement sur l'avenir de la campagne en UK, encouragent fermiers, forestiers et preneurs de décisions à explorer d'autres modes d'utilisation des terres rurales, et parmi ceux-ci se trouve l'agroforesterie. La possibilité de combiner agriculture et forêt sur la même parcelle de terrain paraît séduisante. En théorie, l'agroforesterie pourrait améliorer la productivité, le bien-être du bétail, les habitats sauvages et fournir des possibilités de diversification, tout en réduisant les apports d'engrais et d'aliments. Il existe peu d'exemples d'utilisation des systèmes agroforestiers en UK. Ceci provient peut-être du fait que les détails pratiques de leur établissement et de leur gestion, et leurs coûts et bénéfices à court ou à long terme restent vagues. Ce bulletin a pour objectif de réduire ces incertitudes.

Le bulletin se divise en quatre sections. La Section 1 donne une définition de l'agroforesterie, décrit le contexte (historique et actuel) dans lequel s'insère le bulletin, et explique la complexité des systèmes agroforestiers par rapport aux systèmes agricoles et forestiers conventionnels. La Section 2 fournit un certain nombre de suggestions pour l'établissement et la gestion de diverses options agroforestières, et recommande les méthodes les plus efficaces en s'appuyant sur l'expérience acquise grâce aux recherches en cours. La Section 3 examine les incidences des systèmes agroforestiers sur l'environnement et fait des suggestions pour introduire l'agroforesterie dans le paysage sans défigurer celui-ci. La Section 4 examine les incidences sociales qui résulteraient d'une adoption croissante des systèmes agroforestiers en UK et fournit l'évaluation économique d'une diversité de scénarios agroforestiers, à l'aide des meilleures informations actuellement disponibles.

La lecture de ce bulletin est recommandée aux fermiers, conseillers agricoles et forestiers, propriétaires terriens, étudiants, et à toute autre personne concernée par le développement d'autres systèmes d'utilisation des terres au sein de la campagne.

Agroforstwirtschaft in Großbritannien

Zusammenfassung

Dieses Bulletin informiert über die Etablierung und Verwaltung verschiedener Agroforstwirtschaftssysteme in Großbritannien. Ein Jahrzehnt Forschung in mehreren britischen und europäischen Instituten bildet die Basis für dieses Bulletin. Die Landwirtschaft in Großbritannien durchgeht zur Zeit eine große Umbruchperiode. Gesundheits- und Wohlfahrtsbedenken, wie die BSE Krise und der Lebendtiertransport, betreffen die Viehwirtschaft. Umweltbedenken, wie etwa der Gebrauch von Düngern und Pestiziden, betreffen Feldwirtschaft. Diese Bedenken formen nur einen Teil der gegenwärtigen Debatte über die Zukunft der ländlichen Gebiete in Großbritannien und fördern Landwirte, Forstwirte und Planer, den alternative Gebrauch von Agrarland zu erforschen. Agroforstwirtschaft ist solch eine Alternative. Die Möglichkeit, Land- und Forstwirtschaft auf der gleichen Flächeneinheit zu kombinieren, erscheint sehr attraktiv. Theoretisch könnte dies Produktivität, Tierwohlfahrt und Wildlebensräume verbessern und sowohl Diversifizierung ermöglichen als auch den Gebrauch von Düngern und Futterstoffen verringern. Die Unsicherheit hinsichtlich der praktischen Aspekte von Etablierung und Verwaltung und der damit verbundenen Kosten und Nutzen (lang- und kurzfristig), mag erklären warum es sehr wenig Erfahrung mit Agroforstwirtschaft in Großbritannien gibt. Diese Bulletin versucht diese Unsicherheit zu reduzieren.

Das Bulletin ist in vier Sektionen unterteilt. Sektion 1 definiert Agroforstwirtschaft, beschreibt die historischen und gegenwärtigen Zusammenhänge und erklärt die Verworrenheit von Agroforstwirtschaftsystemen im Vergleich zu herkömmlichen land- und forstwirtschaftlichen Systemen. Sektion 2 informiert über die Etablierung und Verwaltung verschiedener Agroforstwirtschaftmöglichkeiten und macht Vorschläge zur besten Ausführung, die sich auf anerkannte Forschungsergebnisse basieren. Sektion 3 befasst sich mit dem Einfluß den Agroforstwirtschaftsysteme auf die Umwelt haben und gibt Hinweise wie Agroforstwirtschaft der Landschaft harmonisch angepasst werden kann. Sektion 4 betrachtet die sozialen Auswirkungen des zunehmenden Gebrauchs von Agroforstwirtschaft in Großbritannien und benutzt die besten, zur Zeit erhältlichen Informationen um eine Reihe von Agroforstwirtschaftsszenarien wirtschaftlich zu bewerten.

Diese Bulletin ist empfohlener Lesestoff für Landwirte, Land- und Forstwirtschaftsberater, Landbesitzer, Studenten und alle die ein Interesse an der Entwicklung alternativer Landnutzungssysteme in ländlichen Gebieten haben.

Amaethgoedwigaeth yn y Deyrnas Unedig

Crynodeb

Mae'r Bwletin hwn yn rhoi cyngor ar sefydlu a rheoli amryw o systemau amaethgoedwigaeth yn y Deyrnas Unedig (DU). Mae'n seiliedig ar ddegawd o ymchwil a wnaethpwyd gan wyddonwyr o nifer o sefydliadau Prydeinig ac Ewropeaidd. Mae'r diwydiant amaethyddol yn y DU yn mynd drwy gyfnod o newid mawr. Mae pryderon am iechyd a lles cyhoeddus fel yr argyfwng BSE a chludo anifeiliaid byw, yn effeithio ar ffermwyr da byw. Mae pryderon am yr amgylchedd ynghylch y defnydd o wrteithiau a phlaladdwyr yn effeithio ar fusnesau tir âr. Rhan yn unig yw'r pryderon hyn o'r drafodaeth gyfredol am ddyfodol cefn gwlad yn y DU; maent yn annog ffermwyr, coedwigwyr a gwneuthurwyr polisïau i archwilio dulliau eraill o ddefnyddio tir yng nghefn gwlad. Mae amaethgoedwigaeth yn ddewis arall o'r math hwn. Ymddengys y posibilrwydd o gyfuno amaethyddiaeth a choedwigaeth ar yr un uned o dir yn ddeniadol. Mewn egwyddor, gallai amaethgoedwigaeth wella cynhyrchiant, lles y da byw, cynefinoedd bywyd gwyllt a rhoi cyfleoedd i arallgyfeirio, yn ogystal â lleihau'r defnydd o wrtaith a phorthiant. Gallai'r ffaith mai prin yw'r profiad o systemau amaethgoedwigaeth yn y DU ddeillio oherwydd ansicrwydd ynghylch yr agweddau ymarferol o sefydlu a rheoli, a'r costau a'r budd cysylltiedig yn y tymor hir a byr. Amcan y Bwletin hwn yw lleihau'r ansicrwydd yna.

Rhennir y Bwletin yn bedair adran. Mae Adran 1 yn diffinio amaethgoedwigaeth, yn disgrifio'r cyd-destun hanesyddol a chyfredol ar gyfer y Bwletin ac yn egluro cymhlethdod y systemau amaethgoedwigaeth o'u cymharu â systemau amaethyddol neu goedwigol confensiynol. Mae Adran 2 yn rhoi cyngor ar sefydlu a rheoli amryw o opsiynau mewn amaethgoedwigaeth; hefyd mae'n gwneud argymhellion ar gyfer yr arfer gorau, wedi ei seilio ar brofiad ymchwil cyfredol. Mae Adran 3 yn ystyried effaith systemau amaethgoedwigaeth ar yr amgylchedd ac yn rhoi cyngor ar sut i osod amaethgoedwigaeth yn y dirwedd â chydymdeimlad. Mae Adran 4 yn ystyried y goblygiadau cymdeithasol o weld mwy o fabwysiadu systemau amaethgoedwigaeth yn y DU; mae'n rhoi asesiad economaidd o amrywiaeth o senarios amaethgoedwigaeth gan ddefnyddio'r wybodaeth orau sydd ar gael ar hyn o bryd.

Anogir ffermwyr, ymgynghorwyr fferm a choedwigaeth, tirfeddianwyr, myfyrwyr a phawb arall sydd a ddiddordeb mewn datblygu systemau defnydd tir gwahanol yng nghefn gwlad i ddarllen y Bwletin hwn.

List of contributors

Daniel Auclair	Unité de Modelisation des Plantes, INRA-CIRAD, Montpellier, France
Arnold Beaton	Formerly Tilhill Economic Forestry, Tilford, Surrey GU10 2DY. Present address: Pot Common, Red House Lane, Elstead, Surrey GU8 6DS
Simon Bell	Formerly Policy and Practice Division, Forestry Commission, Edinburgh EH12 7AT. Present address: School of Landscape Architecture, Edinburgh College of Art/Heriot-Watt University, Lauriston Place, Edinburgh EH3 9DF
Mark Brownlow	Institute für Agrarokonomik, Universitat für Bodenkultur, Vienna, Austria. Present address: Lobmeyrgasse 7/74, 1160 Vienna, Austria
Peter Carruthers	Centre for Agricultural Strategy, University of Reading, PO Box 237, Earley Gate, Reading RG6 6AR
Jenny Claridge	c/o Forest Research, Alice Holt Lodge, Farnham, Surrey GU10 4LH
Peter Dorward	Department of Agriculture, University of Reading, Reading RG6 6AT
Chris Doyle	Scottish Agricultural College, Auchincruive, Ayr KA6 5HW
Bill Eason	Ecology and Land Use Division, Institute of Grassland and Environmental Research, Aberystwyth SY23 3EB
Max Hislop	Forest Research, Northern Research Station, Roslin, Midlothian EH25 9SY
John Hooker	Formerly Scottish Agricultural College, Aberdeen AB21 9TR. Present address: School of Applied Sciences, University of Glamorgan, Pontypridd, Mid-Glamorgan CF37 1DL
Lynton Incoll	School of Biology, University of Leeds, Leeds LS2 9JT
Jim McAdam	Department of Agriculture and Rural Development for Northern Ireland, Newforge Lane, Belfast BT9 5PX
Steven Newman	Biodiversity International Ltd, Buckingham, Buckinghamshire MK18 1BP
Roger Sheldrick	Institute of Grassland and Environmental Research, North Wyke, Okehampton EX20 2SB
Alan Sibbald	The Macaulay Land Use Research Institute, Aberdeen AB15 8QH
Fergus Sinclair	School of Agricultural and Forest Sciences, University of Wales, Bangor, Gwynedd LL57 SUW
Terry Thomas	School of Agricultural and Forest Sciences, University of Wales, Bangor, Gwynedd LL57 2UW
Rob Willis	Formerly School of Agricultural and Forest Sciences, University of Wales, Bangor, Gwynedd LL57 SUW

Section One

Background

Chapter 1
Introduction

Max Hislop and Fergus Sinclair

Aims of the Bulletin

The main aim of this Bulletin is to provide practical advice about the establishment and management of a range of agroforestry practices derived from a decade of research in the United Kingdom (UK). In addition, the Bulletin describes the interactions of trees with crops and livestock, the environmental, social and economic impacts of these interactions and how best to manage them to meet the objectives of farmers and/or policy-makers. To meet these aims the research findings and recommendations have been brought together in 11 chapters which are grouped into four sections:

- Background.
- Best practice and current research.
- Environmental and landscape impacts.
- Economic and social impacts.

There are few commercial examples of agroforestry systems in the UK. A recent survey in Northern Ireland found that most farmers knew very little about agroforestry, but when shown examples their level of interest was very high (Thomas and Willis, 1997). The Bulletin therefore sets out to raise awareness about the potential of agroforestry as a land-use option in the UK. It is directed at agricultural and woodland advisers, who need to be aware of the potential and practicalities of agroforestry systems, as well as farmers and other landowners.

What is agroforestry?

The generally accepted definition of agroforestry is that adopted by The International Centre for Research in Agroforestry (ICRAF) in the 1980s:

> **Agroforestry** is a collective name for land-use practices where trees are combined with crops and/or animals on the same unit of land and there are significant ecological or economic interactions between the tree and the agricultural components.
> *(After Lundgren and Raintree, 1982)*

Agroforestry practices generally have a number of characteristics that distinguish them from conventional agriculture or forestry (Nair, 1991). These include:

- more structural and functional complexity than monocultures;
- the combination of production of multiple outputs with protection of the resource base;
- emphasis on the use of multipurpose trees and shrubs.

The design and implementation of agroforestry has generally involved consideration of social and cultural factors as well as economic benefits.

Worldwide, agroforestry is a major land use. For example:

- Tree fallows restore fertility on almost a third of the world's arable soils that sustain 300 million of the world's poorest people (Bandy *et al.*, 1993); 2000 million people rely on wood as the major source of heat for cooking food and increasingly obtain it from trees on land that is also farmed (Sinclair, 1997).

3

- Undomesticated trees in farming landscapes are important both for local diets and international commerce. For example, the shea butter tree in sub-Saharan Africa provides the principal source of dietary energy for many rural people as well as industrial raw materials that generate a significant proportion of the foreign exchange income of some African nations (Hall *et al.*, 1996).

- Much of the world's tea, coffee and cocoa is grown beneath timber and shade trees, which are important in cycling nutrients and providing a variety of habitats (Toledo and Moguel, 1997).

- Thirty million hectares of Brazil were seriously degraded following removal of trees and then grazing (World Resources Institute, 1988); agroforestry is now being actively encouraged to rehabilitate land and avoid further degradation.

Agroforestry is also an increasingly attractive land-use option in temperate regions as countryside policy objectives have been broadened (see Chapter 2). In those countries where the agroforestry concept is understood and practised the term has come to cover a wide range of practices. For example:

– In *New Zealand*, where grazing under radiata pine is a widespread silvopastoral practice (Plate 1) (Knowles, 1991).

– In *Australia*, where trees are used to lower salinised water tables on agricultural land (Schofield, 1993).

– In *USA*, where many agroforestry practices are being promoted, including: rows of timber trees in arable fields; windbreaks; forest farming (Merwin, 1997); and the use of trees in integrated riparian management to filter out nitrates and phosphates from water running into streams (Williams *et al.*, 1997).

In the UK, there are two main types of agroforestry that are relevant to our temperate conditions. These are:

- **Silvoarable practices** in which crops are grown between rows of trees and/or shrubs which have been growing at a spacing appropriate for the use of agricultural machinery (Plate 2).

- **Silvopastoral practices** in which trees are grown in grazed pasture (Plate 3) and where the planting pattern can be more varied than for silvoarable systems (Sibbald, 1991).

For over a decade, research carried out under the auspices of the UK Agroforestry Research Forum (see Chapter 2) has focused on these two main practices. This Bulletin presents the lessons learned from these investigations and is written by some of the scientists involved. Of necessity, the research has been focused on rigid experimental design and on a limited set of system variations. However, because the studies have included measurement of interactions (see Chapter 3), the conclusions and recommendations can be extrapolated to a wide range of ways in which trees might be incorporated into farming landscapes.

Why choose agroforestry?

Agroforestry systems are structurally and functionally more complex than pure agricultural or forestry systems. Agroforestry research has provided and continues to develop a knowledge base that makes it increasingly possible to manage these complex systems to satisfy multiple objectives. The objectives may be set by farmers and policy-makers and include the examples shown in Box 1.1.

The extent to which an agroforestry system delivers these objectives depends on the design of the system and how it is managed (see Chapter 3). The complexity of an agroforestry system provides the main advantage to a farmer since, in a time of considerable uncertainty over the future of British agriculture, a land-use system that provides a diversity of options is attractive because of its flexibility (see Chapter 10).

For the policy-maker, agroforestry provides the opportunity to encourage a gradual change in long accepted agricultural practices over a time period that is acceptable to farmers. This approach may well be more successful than trying to 'sell' conventional forestry to farmers which has met with only modest success. While there are some farmers who are enthusiastic about tree planting, for the majority, the benefits of farm forestry appear

• Timber products and farm income	Utilising underdeveloped resources; diversification.
• Environmental benefits	Provision of wildlife habitat; reducing the leaching of nitrogen, phosphate and other pollutants; making lower-input agriculture more profitable.
• Landscape improvement	Improving and enhancing hedgerows, parklands, copses and woods.
• Recreational opportunities	Providing game cover and scope for wildlife observation.
• Livestock welfare	Provision of shelter.

to cater more for the forester than the farmer. Most farmers regard forestry as an inflexible land-use option, an 'inappropriate' use of productive land, and not economically rewarding (Thomas and Willis, 1997). In contrast, the economic analysis presented in Chapter 11 demonstrates that relatively modest support arrangements or a change in relative price structures would make agroforestry competitive with monocultural land-use options. In outline, the analysis shows that:

- **Lowland silvopastoral systems** compare very favourably with agricultural systems.

- **Upland silvopastoral systems** are less competitive with agriculture than in a lowland situation. However, silvopastoral agroforestry provides superior economic returns to a farmer as an alternative land-use option than conversion to forestry.

- **Silvoarable systems** become economically favourable when possible price reductions for crops and changes in compensatory area payments are taken into account.

The future of agroforestry in the UK

The development of agroforestry as a significant land use in the UK will depend upon:

- **Dissemination of information**. This Bulletin is a start in providing relevant information in an accessible form. Experience in Northern Ireland has shown that demonstrations and promotions, such as farm open days, backed up with advice and practical support, have a dramatic effect on the willingness of farmers to adopt agroforestry on part of their holding.

- **Changes in agricultural support mechanisms**. Emerging changes to agricultural support mechanisms in favour of agri-environment objectives are likely to make agroforestry more financially attractive. Chapter 11 explores some potential scenarios.

- **The ability to continue to provide advice and support as the system develops**. Although many questions about agroforestry in the UK have been satisfactorily answered, no system has been studied through a complete rotation. Inevitably assumptions have to be made in the economic analysis about those management interventions and outputs which are expected beyond 10 to 12 years through to final harvest and re-establishment of the tree crop. If landowners are to be confident in adopting agroforestry they will require the reassurance of advice and support based on a continuation of methodical research into later phases of agroforestry rotations.

Assuming that agroforestry research continues and agri-environment support is appropriately structured over the coming years, what is the likely role for agroforestry in the UK landscape? There are many rural policy initiatives that have an increase in woodland cover on farmland as a prime objective. Agroforestry could play an important role in helping to break down the barriers between the farmer and the forester. An 'evolutionary' approach to creating a new generation of farm-foresters may be more successful than expecting a 'revolutionary' change. Whatever the context, agroforestry, no matter whether a broad or a narrow definition of the term is used, could occupy a niche within the agriculture–forestry continuum.

REFERENCES

BANDY, D.E., GARRITY, D.P. and SANCHEZ, P.A. (1993). The world-wide problem of slash-and-burn agriculture. *Agroforestry Today* **5**(3), 2–6.

HALL, J.B., AEBISCHER, D.P., TOMLINSON, H.F., OSEI-AMANING, E. and HINDLE, J.R. (1996). *Vitellaria paradoxa: a monograph.* School of Agricultural and Forest Sciences Publication Number 8, University of Wales, Bangor.

KNOWLES, R.L. (1991). New Zealand experience with silvopastoral systems: a review. *Forest Ecology and Management* **45**, 251–268.

LUNDGREN, B.O. and RAINTREE, J.B. (1982). Sustained agroforestry. In: *Agricultural research for development : potentials and challenges in Asia,* ed. B. Nestel. ISNAR, The Hague, 37–49.

MERWIN, M.L. , ed. (1997). *The status, opportunities and needs for agroforestry in the United States. A national report.* Association for Temperate Agroforestry, Lexington, KY.

NAIR, P.K.R. (1991). State-of-the-art of agroforestry systems. In: *Agroforestry: principles and practices,* ed. P.G. Jarvis. Special issue. *Forest Ecology and Management* **45**, 1–4.

SCHOFIELD, N.J. (1993). Tree planting for dryland salinity control in Australia. In: *The role of trees in sustainable agriculture,* ed. R.T. Prinsley. Kluwer Academic Publishers, Dordrecht, The Netherlands, 1–24.

SIBBALD, A.R. (1991). The UK Agroforestry Forum and the National Network Experiment. In: *Advances in agroforestry: project design, selection and management of components and system evaluation,* ed. F.L. Sinclair. Proceedings of a British Council Short Course, School of Agricultural and Forest Sciences, University of Wales, Bangor, 147–154.

SINCLAIR, F.L. (1997). *A professional update on agroforestry.* Commissioned report for the DFID Natural Resources Advisors Conference, July 1997. Natural Resources International, Chatham, UK.

THOMAS, T.H. and WILLIS R.W. (1997). *Agroforestry research and development in the United Kingdom; progress, perceptions and attitudes. A review.* BEAM Project, School of Agricultural and Forest Sciences, University of Wales, Bangor.

TOLEDO, V.M. and MOGUEL, P. (1997). Searching for sustainable coffee in Mexico: the importance of biological and cultural diversity. In: *Proceedings of the first sustainable coffee congress,* ed. R.A. Rice, A.M. Harris, J. McLean. Smithsonian Migratory Bird Center, USA, 163–173.

WILLIAMS, P.A., GORDON, A.M., GARRETT, H.E. and BUCK, L. (1997). Agroforestry in North America and its role in farming systems. In: *Temperate agroforestry systems,* ed. A.M. Gordon and S.M. Newman. CAB International, Wallingford, 9–84.

WORLD RESOURCES INSTITUTE (1988). *World resources 1988-89: an assessment of the resource base that supports the global economy.* A report by the World Resources Institute, The International Institute for Environment and Development and the United Nations Environment Programme. Basic Books, New York.

Chapter 2
Origins of agroforestry and recent history in the UK

Roger Sheldrick and Daniel Auclair

Introduction: origins and principles

Although agroforestry has been practised for thousands of years, ever since man first started to manage trees, food crops and domestic animals on a particular area of land (Von Maydell, 1985), the scientific study of agroforestry is very young. The International Council for Research in Agroforestry (ICRAF) was founded in 1977 in Nairobi, Kenya and renamed the International Centre for Research in Agroforestry in 1991 when it was incorporated within the CGIAR (Consultative Group on International Agricultural Research). Several other research institutes in the tropics have an interest in agroforestry, including ICRISAT (International Crops Research Institute for the Semi-Arid Tropics), CATIE (Centro Agronómico Tropical de Investigación y Enseñanza) and CTFT (Centre Technique Forestier Tropical) (MacDicken and Vergara, 1990; Jarvis, 1991; Nair, 1993). Many tropical agroforestry systems have been described and investigated in detail (Huxley, 1983; Nair, 1991, 1993).

Ancient systems

A majority of the more ancient agroforestry systems take the form of low intensity subsistence farming, developed to be in balance with relatively fragile environments but giving some limited advantage to the farmer. In the humid tropics, food crops were grown under trees or shrubs yielding fruit or other useful products, so protecting the soil from erosion. In the temperate and Mediterranean regions of Europe and elsewhere, agroforestry was a traditional practice (Evelyn, 1729). Recent advances in agricultural productivity have led to an almost complete separation between forestry and agricultural science, and agroforestry has been seen as an anachronism. The following examples briefly illustrate the variety of systems practised in different countries over many centuries.

Cork oak

One of the better known Mediterranean agroforestry systems is the Spanish *dehesa* (Portuguese *montado*), based on scattered oak trees (*Quercus rotundifolia, Q. suber*) producing wood, charcoal and cork, on shallow stony soils in drought-prone areas. Sheep, goats, pigs and cattle grazed and browsed beneath the trees (Plate 4). Socio-economic pressures on the system have caused overgrazing, halting the natural regeneration of the trees, and some unsuccessful attempts were made to introduce arable cropping. Appropriate management techniques for a sustainable system were researched (Joffre *et al.*, 1988). The situation is closely paralleled in South America by the *espinal* system with *Acacia caven* (Ovalle *et al.*, 1990).

Shelterwoods

In western and northern Europe, cattle or sheep were sheltered in mature woodland in the worst of the winter weather, not deriving much forage or browse from the woodland but fed hay or straw for maintenance. In contrast, farmers in Mediterranean regions may herd cattle in woodland in early summer, providing some browse or forage in a drought period, as well as relief from high temperatures. Such grazing can have a valuable environmental effect by reducing the risk of forest fires in the summer tourist season, as well as helping to maintain the rural population in these areas (Msika and Hubert, 1987). Several woody species, both trees and shrubs, provide browse in the Mediterranean region, and research is directed at the use of such woody species not only in Europe, but in other semi-arid areas (Mansat, 1987; Morandini, 1989). In parts of Europe with more of the land area under forest than in the UK, forest grazing may help relieve the pressure on arable land, and understorey vegetation, fruits, leaves and twigs are still an important feed resource (Lachaux et al., 1987; Bellon and Guérin, 1992).

Pannage
From Roman times pigs in the UK were herded in oak or beech woodland in autumn to eat the acorns or beech mast (Plate 18), and sometimes in fruit orchards to consume fallen fruit. Chickens were also often kept in fruit orchards, to provide some control of insect pests and benefit from their consumption. The possibility of more intensive rearing of pigs in woodland has been re-examined by Brownlow et al. (1993); see Chapter 6.

Hunting forests and parkland
Hunting wild pigs in woodland has been a popular sporting activity in eastern Europe, while the raising of game birds in woodland in Britain and France has been common, thereby greatly increasing the numbers available for shooting. The essentially British concept of grazing cattle and sheep in open parkland with scattered trees probably had more to do with 18th century aesthetic considerations than the complementary interactions between trees and livestock. However, open grown timber with its strongly developed branches was much more valuable then because of the great demand for curved timbers for ship building.

Erosion control and shelter belts
The concept of planting trees to combat soil erosion dates back to at least the 19th century. The French forest administration of that time introduced a programme of planting black pine (*Pinus nigra*) on steep, overgrazed, eroded slopes, and large areas of degraded land were converted to forest. A similar use of trees for soil protection was advocated by Smith (1914) in the USA, early in the 20th century. Planting shelter belts of trees and shrubs to control erosion may be considered an extension of agroforestry (Plate 5).

The importance of windbreaks has long been recognised for checking wind erosion on the French Atlantic coast and on the plains of Jutland in Denmark (Swain, 1987). Removal of hedgerows in the 'bocage' regions of Brittany and Normandy to aid mechanisation in the 1950s and 1960s caused severe wind erosion, and regulations now require shelter belts in these sensitive areas. Some traditional European landscapes are the result of centuries old shelter belt establishment, such as those to reduce the violence of the dry 'Mistral' wind in the Rhône valley. Shelter belts in Britain (Caborn, 1957, 1965; Palmer et al., 1997) are most commonly associated with establishment of orchards, and in exposed sites they have provided protection for arable crops, livestock and buildings. The complex bioclimatic effects of shelter belts in promoting crop yields by reducing evapotranspiration have been investigated (Als, 1986; Guyot et al., 1986). Other aspects have often not been fully evaluated, particularly their ecological value in providing corridors for wildlife movement within an area (Jarvis and Sinclair, 1990).

Modern systems
Within the last two decades, there has been a widespread re-examination of the principles underlying agroforestry, and the development of more intensive forms than practised in the past (Sinclair, 1995). Three main situations can be identified:

- Tropical agroforestry.
- Temperate agroforestry: the Antipodes, the Americas and Asia.
- Temperate agroforestry: Western Europe.

It must be remembered that the precepts and motivations for each type are different and that conclusions relevant to one cannot be applied uncritically to another.

Tropical agroforestry
Tropical agroforestry research and development is typified by the approach adopted by ICRAF in Nairobi, Kenya (Sanchez, 1995). The main requirement is for sustainable small-holder cropping systems, providing food crops as well as

animal forage or browse, fuel wood and poles for construction (Plate 6). The aim is also to assist in the control of soil erosion, so often a major problem on tropical soils with high rainfall when cropping intensifies and trees are cut down for fuel. Typical systems are built on the existing local knowledge about crops and trees, with cropping taking place in alleys between contour plantings of multipurpose trees or shrubs, ideally N-fixing, which are well adapted to the local environment. Labour is usually readily available for cultivation or cutting and carrying forage.

Temperate agroforestry: the Antipodes, the Americas and Asia

Saw-log production is an important output of agroforestry in Chile and New Zealand, and seeks to maximise cash returns from high-grade *Pinus radiata* logs (Fenton and Sutton, 1968). The thinning and high pruning regimes required to obtain top quality logs allow understorey development. To control difficult weeds, improve access for workers and reduce the dry-season fire hazard, cattle and sheep from adjacent farms are grazed through the forest. The livestock may be regarded therefore as a silvicultural tool, though it has been found helpful to raise the nutritional value of the available forage by oversowing with the legume *Lotus uliginosus* (Knowles, 1991). The agroforestry concept has been extended to new, low-density plantings of *P. radiata* into existing pasture. After initial concern over reduced grazing due to pruning debris and needle fall, some 60 000 ha of pasture were being planted annually (Mead, 1994). With a final density of 100–250 stems per ha, the internal rate of return can approach 12% (Dupraz *et al.*, 1992; Knowles *et al.*, 1991).

As an alternative to continuous stands, shelter belts may be planted, and can yield good quality timber (Tombleson and Inglis, 1988; Auclair *et al.*, 1991) or trees may line field margins in dairying areas, though this has a marked visual impact. Soils and climate in Australia are less favourable for tree growth, though farmers there are now adopting the New Zealand practices, but with more emphasis on environmental than economic objectives (Prinsley, 1992), particularly the control of salinity.

Silvopastoral systems similar to those in New Zealand have been developed in the south-eastern United States (US) based mainly on slash pine (*Pinus ellotii*) (Lewis *et al.*, 1983) and further north in the continent with other pines (*P. contorta*, *P. ponderosa*). Silvoarable production systems have also been developed in North America, either based on interculture of crops in fruit and nut orchards or, more recently, widely spaced rows of trees in arable fields, particularly black walnut (*Juglans nigra*) grown for nut production (Garret *et al.*, 1991) and a range of valuable hardwood species (Gordon and Williams, 1991). Environmental considerations are increasingly important in the US and Canada, and trees have been used in integrated vegetation management of riparian zones on agricultural land to improve water quality and wildlife habitat by reducing soil erosion, nutrient leaching and water temperatures (Williams *et al.*, 1997).

There is a wide range of traditional agroforestry systems in China (Zou and Sanford, 1990). Of major interest are the systems based on *Paulownia tomentosa* underplanted with wheat, beans or medicinal plants (Newman, 1994).

Temperate agroforestry: Western Europe

In mainland Europe it is common to find woodland or forests owned by farmers; for example, in France, 16% of the forested area is in farmer ownership (Cavailhes and Normandin, 1993). Such farmers regard the woodland as a source of capital to be realised when investment is required in the farm business (Swain, 1987). Developments in New Zealand outlined above (Mead, 1994) provided the impetus for reconsidering agroforestry systems in a Western European context. Additional reasons included a concern for farm woodland and the large agricultural surpluses generated in the 1980s, which have led to the policy of 'Set-Aside'. Diversification away from both grassland and arable production into non-agricultural enterprises has been promoted by the European Union (EU). Tree planting has seemed particularly appropriate, with broadleaved deciduous species preferred to conifers for amenity and environmental reasons

(Bock and Rondeux, 1990). Initial interest was in silvopastoral systems, stimulated by the beef and butter 'mountains' of the early 1980s, but silvoarable systems are now of more immediate applicability due to the availability of highly productive poplar clones and reduction in arable crop subsidies (Willis *et al.*, 1993).

Bryant and May

The earliest of the new, more intensive agroforestry systems developed in the UK was that practised by Bryant and May (Forestry) Ltd, over 30 years ago. In this system, the alleys between rows of poplars were cropped in rotation with cereals and other crops for 7–8 years, a last cereal crop being undersown with a grass–clover mixture. The poplars were by then above a height where livestock would damage them by browsing, and grazing could continue so long as the sward could support livestock, usually a few years before final felling at 25 years of age. Rising land values and cereal prices coupled with cheap imported poplar timber made the system uneconomic in the 1970s.

Recent developments in the UK

Formation of the Agroforestry Research: UK Discussion Forum

By 1984 several research centres in the UK were developing an interest in agroforestry (see Figure 2.1) and two groups, one Edinburgh-based and the other in southern Britain, were formed to pool experiences.

The first serious research activity in the UK was the construction of two separate computer simulation models of silvopastoral systems. One was based on Douglas fir in the uplands (Tabbush *et al.*, 1985), and the other on ash in the lowlands (Doyle *et al.*, 1986). Both models relied on assumptions about interactions in the system and were not validated. Tabbush *et al.* (1985) made estimates of agricultural revenue based on the assumed reduction of net photosynthesis of grass caused by shading of tree crowns, calculated on the basis of projected crown area. The trees were assumed to be unaffected by the

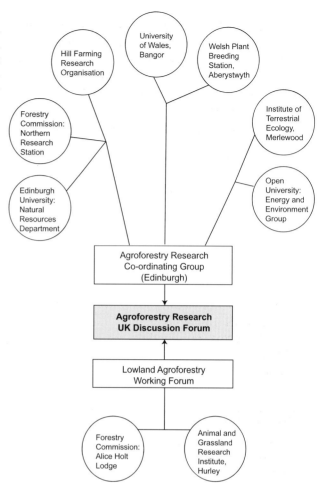

Figure 2.1 Origins of the Agroforestry Research Discussion Forum 1984–1986.

grass and no other interactions were taken into account. Doyle *et al.* (1986) considered competition for nutrients and water as well as shading. Both models suggested that silvopastoral systems in the UK would give similar financial returns to the purely agricultural systems that they might replace, over a 45–50 year production cycle at prevailing prices, costs and levels of support. The results were sensitive to the discount rate and timber price and predicted that grass production would be maintained as a high proportion of that on non-forested land for at least the first 15 years after planting at low tree stocking densities. These models indicated that agroforestry was worth investigating in the field. They also identified knowledge gaps about light, temperature and humidity regimes under widely spaced trees, about tree growth and crown development at wide spacings, also tree rooting patterns in competition with an understorey, and about water and nutrient uptake.

To draw the groups together and formulate priorities for funding, MAFF sponsored a joint meeting at Hurley in 1986. Candidate treatments for a national experiment were proposed and possible sites discussed. It was decided that a national forum was required to discuss research needs and locate the wide range of scientific skills that would be required to support a long-term research programme. Further meetings in 1986 agreed the desirability to establish a multi-site national silvopastoral experiment, together with a working group given the title 'Agroforestry Research: UK Discussion Forum'. Further meetings in 1987 drew up detailed protocols for the National Network Experiment and approved a formal constitution for the Forum.

The Forum has held annual meetings since 1987. Once most national network sites were planted, discussion of protocols and problems was delegated to a subgroup. Other subgroups were also formed to discuss silvoarable research and other topics. The Annual Meeting includes reports from such groups, formal papers, poster sessions and a business meeting. A newsletter, *Agroforestry Forum*, was launched in 1990 by the University of Wales, Bangor, and has now gained recognition as an international scientific bulletin. In 1991 the Forum dropped the word 'discussion' from its title and became the 'UK Agroforestry Research Forum'. In 1998 the title 'UK Agroforestry Forum' was adopted to reflect its wider range of activity.

The National Network Experiment

The major achievement of the early period of the Agroforestry Research: UK Discussion Forum was agreement on the major variables to be included in the 'National Network Experiment'. The decisions were informed by the preliminary trials carried out on treeshelters and other aspects of

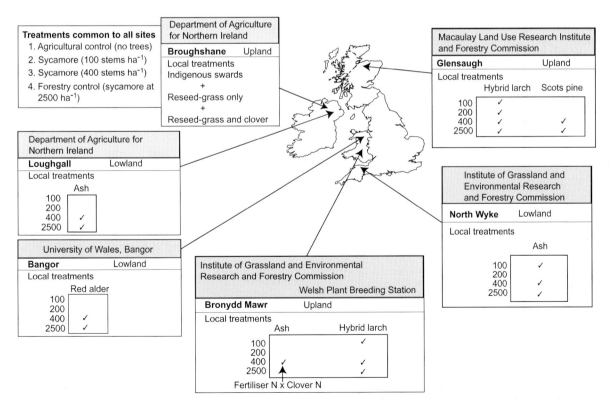

Figure 2.2 The National Network Experiment sites.

establishment practice. Sycamore was eventually chosen as the common tree species and ryegrass swards receiving 160 kg N ha^{-1} annum^{-1} as the common understorey. Other variables included the choice of sheep as the grazing animal and decisions on the tree densities to be investigated and the protection procedures that should be adopted. The statistical layout comprised three replicate blocks to ensure that statistically valid conclusions could be drawn. Original plans were for six sites, namely North Wyke (Devon), Anglesey (Wales) and Loughgall (Northern Ireland) in lowland situations, and Glensaugh (Grampian), Bronydd Mawr (Wales) and Broughshane (Northern Ireland) in upland situations (Sibbald and Sinclair, 1990; see Figure 2.2). The Anglesey site was relocated to Henfaes, near Bangor in 1992. At the new site, certain aspects of the common design were modified in the light of experience at the other sites (e.g. stake and netting protection, trees planted in clumps).

EU ALWAYS project

In a major development in 1993, the Network Experiment became the basis for the EU funded research project on 'Alternative agricultural land-use with fast growing trees' (Auclair, 1993; CEC, 1994). This project provided a major impetus to modelling the biophysical factors interacting in an agroforestry system. This was a serious weakness in earlier economic modelling efforts, but with the extra information gained within the ALWAYS Project (Auclair, 1998), more reliable bio-economic models may be constructed (see Chapter 11). The Network Experiment has also proved a most valuable resource for studying a wide range of factors relating to silvopastoral systems, from changes in avifauna or predatory beetle populations to botanical or hydrological changes (see Chapter 8).

Silvoarable research

In parallel with the establishment of the National Network Experiment, a number of silvoarable trials have been established in various parts of lowland Britain (see Table 2.1). The main tree species have either been high yielding poplar clones or a range of broadleaves with good timber properties and/or nut production, e.g. walnut

(Cutter and Garrett, 1993; Liagre, 1993; Jay-Allemand, 1994).

Bangor Conference 1998

In Northern Ireland in 1997, DANI and Greenmount College organised successful Agroforestry Open Days which resulted in positive uptake of agroforestry systems by local farmers. Encouraged by this response the Agroforestry Research Forum recognised that the time was right to increase work on the transfer of agroforestry technology to practitioners throughout the UK.

Consequently, in July 1998 a conference was held at the University of Wales, Bangor entitled 'Trees in Fields and Farming Landscapes'. This conference marked a departure from previous annual conferences, which had been largely organised by academics for academics. The emphasis was on the dissemination of the practical lessons from a decade of agroforestry research to farm and forestry advisers. The conference attracted a wide range of policy-makers, farm advisers and landowners, and was well received in Wales at a time of crisis in farming.

In recognition of the wider audience now interested in the potential of agroforestry the Forum changed its name to the UK Agroforestry Forum. It continues to hold open annual conferences attracting a wide range of participants, provides advice to landowners and policy-makers and promotes agroforestry systems at shows and conferences.

The future

The availability of clonal poplar material has enabled silvoarable plantings, but the more widespread adoption of silvopastoral agroforestry systems in the UK would be encouraged by the provision of genetically superior, clonal hardwood planting stock. The issues are further discussed and referenced in Chapter 4.

Table 2.1 Recent agroforestry trials in the UK.

Year planted	Silvoarable (SA) or silvopastoral (SP)	Parent organisation	Location	Tree species	Comments	References
1987/88	SA	Open University	Buckingham-shire, Essex	Walnut	Only one site still operational	Newman *et al.*,1991
1988	SA	Open University	Various	Poplar	Farm trials. Site near Milton Keynes very successful	Newman *et al.*,1995
1987	SA	Institute of Terrestrial Ecology, Manchester University	Jodrell Bank, Cheshire	Common alder, ash, poplar	Closed 1990	
1989	SA	Leeds University	Bramham, near Tadcaster, West Yorkshire	Ash, cherry sycamore, walnut	Promising results	Incoll *et al.*, 1997b; Peng *et al.*, 1993; Phillips *et al.*, 1994; Wright, 1994.
1992	SA	Royal Agricultural College, Leeds University, Cranfield University	Cirencester, Leeds, Silsoe, Bed-fordshire	Poplar clones	Good results from silvoarable treatments	Incoll *et al.*, 1997a
1986	SP	Welsh Plant Breeding Station	Bronydd Mawr, near Brecon	Various	Considerable sheep damage	
1987	SP	Long Ashton Research Station	Bristol	Various	Cattle damage	
1987	SP	Hill Farming Research Organisation and Forestry Commission	Cloich, near Edinburgh	Sitka spruce at different spacings	Studies on grass growth and stand microclimate	Sibbald *et al.*, 1991
1987	SP	Forestry Commission	Radnor, Wales	Larch undersown with grass	Sheep damage	
1987–1992	SP	Various	Six sites across the UK	Various (sycamore common to all sites)	National Network Experiment (see Figure 2.2)	Hoppé *et al.*, 1996

REFERENCES

ALS, C. (1986). Planting and establishing of windbreaks in Denmark. In: *International symposium on windbreak technology*, ed. Llintz and Brandle. Lincoln, Nebraska, USA, 93–94.

AUCLAIR, D. (1993). Alternative agricultural land-use with fast growing trees. In: *Agriculture and agro-industry programme of research and technological development (1991-1994): synopsis of projects selected for the first call for proposals*, ed. CEC. Commission of the European Communities, Brussels, 60-61.

AUCLAIR, D., ed. (1998). Alternative agricultural land use with fast growing trees. Final technical report, EC DGVI, Contract AIR-CT290134.

AUCLAIR, D., TOMBLESON, J.D. and MILNE, P. (1991). *Timberbelt growth model.* Agroforestry Research Collaborative Report No. 17. FRI, Rotorua.

BELLON, S. and GUERIN, G. (1992). Old holm-oak coppices: new silvopastoral practices. In: *Quercus ilex L. ecosystems: function, dynamics and management*, ed. F. Romane and J. Terradas. *Vegetatio* **99/100**, 307–316.

BOCK, L. and RONDEUX, J., eds (1990). *Marginal agricultural land and efficient afforestation.* EUR 10841. Commission of the European Communities, Luxembourg.

BROWNLOW, M.J.C., CARRUTHERS, S.P. and DORWARD, P.T. (1993). The integration of pigs and poultry with forestry : practice, theory and economics. *Agroforestry Forum* **4** (3), 51–57.

CABORN, J.M. (1957). *Shelterbelts and microclimate.* Forestry Commission Bulletin 29. HMSO, London.

CABORN, J.M. (1965). *Shelterbelts and windbreaks.* Faber, London.

CAVAILHES, J. and NORMANDIN, D. (1993). Déprise agricole et boisement – État des lieux, enjeux et perspectives dans le cadre de la réforme de la PAC. *Revue forestière Française* **45**, 465–481.

CEC, ed. (1994). *Agriculture and agro-industry, programme of research and technological development (1991–1994): synopsis of projects selected for the first call for proposals.* Commission of the European Communities, Brussels.

CUTTER, B.E. and GARRETT, H.E. (1993). Wood quality in alleycropped eastern black walnut. *Agroforestry Systems* **22**, 25–32.

DOYLE, C.J., EVANS, J. and ROSSITER, J. (1986). Agroforestry: an economic appraisal of the benefits of intercropping trees with grassland in lowland Britain. *Agricultural Systems* **21**, 1–32.

DUPRAZ, C., AUCLAIR, D. and GUITTON, J.L. (1992). Vingt ans de recherche agroforestière en Nouvelle Zélande. *Revue forestière Française* **44**, 523–538.

EVELYN, J. (1729). *Sylva, or a discourse on forest trees and the propagation of timber in his Majesties dominions inc. Pomona*, 3rd edn. Royal Society, London.

FENTON, R. and SUTTON, W.R.J. (1968). Silvicultural proposals for radiata pine on high quality sites. *New Zealand Journal of Forestry* **13**, 220–228.

GARRET, H.E., JONES, J.E., KURTZ, W.B. and SLUSHER, J.P. (1991). Black walnut (*Juglans nigra* L.) agroforestry – its design and potential as a land use alternative. *The Forestry Chronicle* **67**, 213–218.

GORDON, A. M. and WILLIAMS, P.A. (1991). Intercropping valuable hardwood tree species and agricultural crops in southern Ontario. *The Forestry Chronicle* **67**, 200–208.

GUYOT, G., BEN SALEM, B. and DELECOLLE, R. (1986). *Brise-vent et rideaux-abris avec référence particulière aux zones sèches.* Cahier FAO Conservation No. 15, Food and Agriculture Organisation, Rome.

HOPPÉ, G.M., SIBBALD, A.R., MCADAM, J.H., EASON, W.R., HISLOP, A.M. and TEKLEHAIMANOT, Z. (1996). The UK National Network Silvopastoral Experiment – a co-ordinated approach to research. Fourth Congress of the European Society for Agronomy, Book of Abstracts.

HUXLEY, P.A., ed. (1983). *Plant research and agroforestry.* International Council for Agroforestry, Nairobi, Kenya.

INCOLL, L.D., BURGESS, P.J., EVANS, R.J., CORRY D.T. and BEATON, A. (1997a). Temperate silvoarable agroforestry with poplar. *Agroforestry Forum* **8** (3), 12–15.

INCOLL, L.D., CORRY, D.T., WRIGHT, C. and COMPTON, S.G. (1997b). Temperate silvoarable agroforestry with quality hardwood timber species *Agroforestry Forum* **8** (3), 9–11.

JARVIS, P.G., ed. (1991). *Agroforestry: principles and practice.* Elsevier, Amsterdam.

JARVIS, P.G. and SINCLAIR, F.L. (1990). Priorities in farm forestry research. In: *Marginal agricultural land and efficient afforestation*, ed. L. Bock and J. Rondeux. Commission of the European Communities, Luxembourg.

JAY-ALLEMAND, C., ed. (1994). *European development of walnut trees for wood and fruit production as an alternative and extensive system for agricultural crops.* EC project AIR3 - CT920142 third periodic progress report.

JOFFRE, R., VACHER, J., DE LOS LLANOS, C. and LONG, G. (1988). The dehesa: an agrosilvopastoral system of the mediterranean region with special reference to the Sierra Morena area of Spain. *Agroforestry Systems* **6**, 71–96.

KNOWLES, R.L. (1991). New Zealand experience with silvopastoral systems: a review. *Forest Ecology and Management* **45**, 251–267.

KNOWLES, R.L., MANLEY, B. and THOMSON, J. (1991). FRI modelling systems help evaluate profitability of agroforestry. *What's new in forest research?* No. 207. Forest Research Institute, Rotorua.

LACHAUX, M., DE BONNEVAL, L. and DELABRAZE, P. (1987). Pratiques anciennes et perspectives d'utilisation fourragère des arbres. In: *La forêt et r'élevage en région mediterranéenne française*, 99-124.

LEWIS, C.E., BURTON, G.W., MONSON, W.G. and MCCORMICK, W.C. (1983). Integration of pines, pastures and cattle in South Georgia, USA. *Agroforestry Systems* **1**, 277–297.

LIAGRE, F. (1993). *Les pratiques de cultures intercalaires dans la noyeraie fruitière du Dauphiné.* ENGREF, Formation Forestière Supérieure pour les Régions Chaudes/INRA Montpellier.

MACDICKEN, K.G. and VERGARA, N.T., ed (1990). *Agroforestry: classification and management.* Wiley, New York.

MEAD, D.J. (1994). The role of agriculture in industrialized nations – the Southern hemisphere perspective. In: *Proceedings international symposium on agroforestry and land-use change in industrialized nations.* ZALF, Berlin, 30 May–3 June 1994.

MANSAT, P., ed. (1987). *Proceedings of the fifth meeting of the FAO network for rangelands and fodder production.* Montpellier.

MORANDINI, R., ed. (1989). *Programme de recherche agrimed – Les espèces ligneuses à usages multiples des zones arides méditerranéenes.* Commission of the European Communities, Luxembourg.

MSIKA, B. and HUBERT, B., ed. (1987). *Colloque agriculture et forêt en région méditerranéenne.* INRA, Avignon.

NAIR, P.K.R. (1991). State-of-the-art of agroforestry systems. *Forest Ecology and Management* **45**, 5–29.

NAIR, P.K.R. (1993). *An introduction to agroforestry.* Kluwer, Dordrecht.

NEWMAN, S.M. (1994). An outline comparison of approaches to silvoarable research and development with fast growing trees in India, China and the UK with emphasis on intercropping with wheat. *Agroforestry Forum* **5**(2), 29–31.

NEWMAN, S.M., WAINWRIGHT, J., OLIVER, P.N. and ACWORTH, J.M. (1991). Walnut and agroforestry in the UK: Its history and current research in relation to experience in other countries. *Agroforestry in the UK* **2** (3), 14–27.

NEWMAN, S.M., WAINWRIGHT, J., HUTTON. N., WU, Y., MARSHALL, C., AMATYA, S.M., RANASINGHE, D.M.S.H.K. and MORRIS, R.M. (1995). Spacing and variety effffects on poplar silvoarable systems in the UK. *Agroforestry Forum* **6** (2), 37–43.

OVALLE, C., ARONSON, J., DEL POZO, A. and

AVENDANO, J. (1990). The espinal: agroforestry systems of the mediterranean-type climate region of Chile. *Agroforestry Systems* **10**, 213–239.

PALMER, H., GARDINER, B., HISLOP, M., SIBBALD, A. and DUNCAN, A., eds. (1997). *Trees for shelter*. Forestry Commission Technical Paper 21. Forestry Commission, Edinburgh.

PENG, R.K., INCOLL, L.D., SUTTON, S.L., WRIGHT, C. and CHADWICK, A. (1993). Diversity of airborne arthropods in a silvoarable agroforestry system. *Journal of Applied Ecology* **30**, 551–562.

PHILLIPS, D.S., GRIFFITHS, J., NAEEM, M., COMPTON, S.G. and INCOLL, L.D. (1994). Responses of crop pests and their natural enemies to an agroforestry environment. *Agroforestry Forum* **5**(2): 14–20.

PRINSLEY, R.T., ed. (1992). *The role of trees in sustainable agriculture*. Kluwer, Dordrecht.

SANCHEZ, P.A. (1995). Science in agroforestry. In: *Agroforestry: science, policy and practice*, ed. F.L. Sinclair. Kluwer, Dordrecht, 5–55.

SIBBALD, A.R., GRIFFITHS, J.H. and ELSTON, D.A. (1991). The effects of the presence of widely spaced conifers on under-storey herbage production in the U.K. *Forest Ecology and Management* **45**, 71-77.

SIBBALD, A.R. and SINCLAIR, F.L. (1990). A review of agroforestry research in progress in the UK. *Agroforestry Abstracts* **3**, 149–163.

SINCLAIR, F.L., ed. (1995). *Agroforestry: science, policy and practice*. Kluwer, Dordrecht.

SMITH, J.R. (1914). Soil erosion and its remedy by terracing and tree planting. *Science* **39**, 858–862.

SWAIN, P.J. (1987). *A study of aspects of farm forestry in New Zealand, Denmark, Sweden, Finland and California*. ADAS/WOAD, Aberystwyth.

TABBUSH P.M., WHITE, I.M.S., MAXWELL, T.J. and SIBBALD, A.R. (1985). *Tree planting on upland sheep farms – study team report*. Forestry Commission and Hill Farming Research Organisation, Edinburgh.

TOMBLESON, J.D. and INGLIS, C.S. (1988). Comparison of radiata pine shelterbelts and plantations. In: *Agroforestry symposium proceedings*, ed. P. Maclaren. Bulletin 139. FRI, Rotorua, 261–278.

VON MAYDELL, H.J. (1985). The contribution of agroforestry to world forestry development. *Agroforestry Systems* **3**, 83–90.

WILLIAMS, P.A., GORDON, A.M., GARRET, H.E. and BUCK, L. (1997). Agroforestry in North America and its role in farming systems. In: *Temperate agroforestry systems*, ed. A.M. Gordon and S.M. Newman. CAB International, Wallingford, 9–84.

WILLIS, R.W., THOMAS, T.H. and VAN SLYCKEN, J. (1993). Poplar agroforestry: a re-evaluation of its economic potential on arable land in the UK. *Forest Ecology and Management* **57**, 85–97.

WRIGHT, C. (1994). The distribution and abundance of small mammals in a silvoarable agroforestry system. *Agroforestry Forum* **5**(2), 26–28.

ZOU, X. and SANFORD, R.L. Jr. (1990). Agroforestry systems in China: a survey and classification. *Agroforestry Systems* **11**, 85–94.

Chapter 3

Understanding and management of interactions

Fergus Sinclair, Bill Eason and John Hooker

Introduction

When farmers practise agroforestry, they obtain products and environmental benefits from trees in addition to those they obtain from agricultural crops or animals. Because the trees and agricultural components affect each other, the management of these interactions lies at the heart of successful agroforestry practice.

This chapter begins with an illustration of the complexity inherent in interactions in agroforestry systems because they vary over space and may change in their nature and magnitude through time. This is followed by a section that discusses the need to understand the various interactive effects that influence the yield and environmental impact of agroforestry practices. Different types of interactions are then described and the remaining sections deal with the following aspects:

- **Resource capture:** how to minimise competition for light, water and nutrients among different components growing in the same environment.

- **Biodiversity:** how mimicking the diversity and structure of natural ecosystems may improve stability, sustainability and animal welfare.

- **Succession:** how trees may modify the soil and aerial microclimate over time leading to a succession of different opportunities for intercropping.

- **Scale:** how to scale up the impacts of individual trees on soil, water and climate to predict the effects of integration of agroforestry practices at a landscape level.

Finally, examples are given of management interventions that farmers can use to control interactions and so obtain the desired mixture of outputs from their agroforestry practice.

Complexity inherent in managing interactions

The importance of some interactions is well understood, while others have been less intensively studied and their effects remain difficult to predict. For example, trees planted into agricultural fields will cast increasingly heavy shade on the understorey crop or pasture as their crowns develop (Figure 3.1). The extent of this interaction can be directly influenced by management, as outlined in Box 3.1.

However, actions taken to reduce shade may have other consequences and understanding their impact is complicated by the number of factors involved. For example, the simple operation of pruning trees, while reducing the shade cast by the tree, may lead to an increase in the photosynthetic efficiency of the remaining leaves. It may also promote shoot regrowth and affect root growth and so increase competition with crops or pasture for nutrients and water (Singh and Thompson, 1995). Furthermore, the crop may compete with young tree seedlings for nutrients and water, affecting tree growth and development of their crowns. Crop husbandry such as cultivation and the use of fertilisers, pesticides and herbicides may also affect the trees. Animals may damage trees either directly by browsing, rubbing or bark stripping or indirectly by congregating around the trees and compacting the soil. Higher humidity levels and lower temperatures under tree shade may favour the spread of fungal disease. Trees

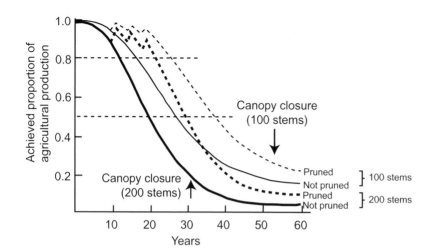

Figure 3.1 Decline of pasture productivity over time for upland silvopastoral rotations with and without tree pruning. Source: Maxwell (1986).

Box 3.1 How tree management can affect shading

Which tree species to plant?

Some tree species develop more dense crowns than others, some only have leaves for part of the growing season while others always have leaves.

At what density?

Higher tree densities will lead to more rapid development of the shaded area of the crop.

In what arrangement?

For any given overall density of trees in the field, a clumped arrangement would result in rapid development of shaded islands of woodland-like habitat in the field. Much of the crop area would not be affected by tree shade for some time, with consequences both for crop productivity and biodiversity.

What timing, extent and method of thinning and pruning is used?

In general, thinning and pruning will result in reducing the shading effect and hence favour crop productivity. Many different pruning strategies may be followed (see Figure 3.2) depending largely on what the tree is producing, with different consequences for shading of the crop.

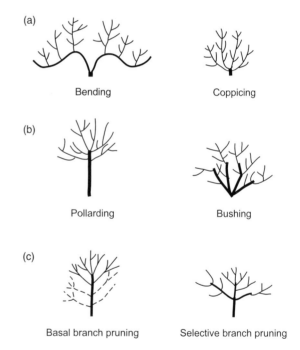

Figure 3.2 Different tree pruning strategies: (a) pruning operations that spread tree crowns; (b) lopping operations and (c) removal of branches. Source: Cannell (1983).

may be a host environment for overwintering crop pests or, conversely, may host predators of crop pests, facilitating biological pest control. The issues described above make it apparent that the decision about tree planting and subsequent management in a particular farm context is a complex one, involving a large number of factors.

The need to understand interactions

There is no single blueprint for agroforestry in the UK but there are many different niches for trees in farming landscapes. These may be occupied by different tree species that will be grown to satisfy various objectives set by farmers and policy-makers, across a wide range of site types (see Chapter 1). It is not feasible to measure tree, crop and animal productivity for all of the possible agroforestry permutations that may be established by farmers in the UK. Understanding interactions, however, allows prediction of the effects of different trees on the environment and system productivity and of how various management actions can be used to manipulate these effects to meet farmers' objectives.

This contrasts with New Zealand where a widespread and successful agroforestry practice was based on combining just one tree species, radiata pine (*Pinus radiata*), with grazed pasture (Knowles, 1991). Trials were conducted across New Zealand with trees planted into pastures at various densities and then subjected to different thinning and pruning regimes. Empirical functions were derived from these trials relating pasture production to the sum of the green crown length per hectare (Figure 3.3). These relationships were used within a simulation model to help farmers to decide on planting densities, thinning and pruning, on the basis of predicted effects on tree and agricultural production. In this example, the predictions derived from these data were only valid for the species and conditions under which they were collected. This strategy is not appropriate in the UK which has a wider range of tree planting options. The approach here is based on understanding the fundamental processes that determine yield and environmental impact, allowing extrapolation to a broad range of species and sites.

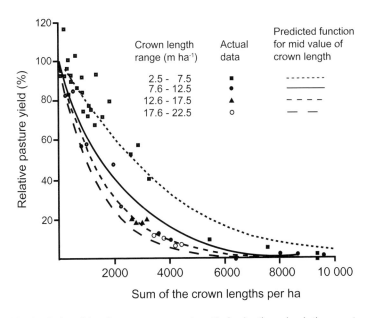

Figure 3.3 Empirical relationships between crown length (m ha⁻¹) and relative pasture yield for *Pinus radiata* in New Zealand. Source: Percival and Knowles (1988).

Types of interactions

Interactions between two species may be *direct*, for example where an animal eats a tree, or *indirect* where the interaction is mediated via the environment, for example where animals congregate around trees to gain shelter benefits and consequently compact soil close to trees, thereby reducing tree growth (Sibbald *et al.*, 1996).

Trees and agricultural crops *respond to the environment* in which they are growing but also *affect the environment* as they grow. For example, trees may grow faster if there is a higher temperature or more light available, but in doing so, they create shade which reduces light and temperature by intercepting solar radiation. One species affecting the environment of another is known as the response–effect principle (Figure 3.4) and may involve:

- the capture of limiting growth resources (light, water and nutrients) by one species reducing their availability to another species;

- the alteration of the microclimate in other ways (including effects on temperature, humidity, wind speed and soil structure);

- influence on the action of other organisms (principally pests and their predators, diseases and soil fauna);

- the release of chemicals by one plant which are toxic to another (known as allelopathy).

Interactive effects of one species on another may be *positive*, for example, shelter from evergreen trees buffering understorey temperatures in spring and autumn in the uplands, increasing the growing season of pasture. Alternatively, they may be *negative*, where shade from the same trees in midsummer reduces understorey light levels and thereby limits pasture productivity (Sibbald *et al.*, 1991). Positive and negative interactions may occur simultaneously. It is useful, therefore, to distinguish individual interactions and the net effect of all the interactions that occur when particular species are mixed, which is expressed in the overall yield of the species mixture.

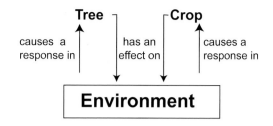

Figure 3.4 The response–effect principle. Source: Goldberg and Werner (1983), redrawn from Anderson and Sinclair (1993).

Resource capture

One of the key principles underlying agroforestry is that by combining plant species that have very different patterns of resource use, the overall productivity of the mixture may be higher than would be obtained if the same species were grown as monocultures. This is exploiting the natural phenomenon of *niche differentiation*, where different species obtain resources from different parts of the environment. Where it occurs, the species are said to have a high *ecological combining ability*. Plants capture light via their leaf area, and water and nutrients via their root surface area and associated mycorrhizal hyphae. The extent of niche differentiation exhibited when species are mixed can be estimated from knowledge of:

- the amount of leaf area and root length of each species;

- their distributions in space and time;

- the rate at which each unit of leaf area or root length captures resources.

Differences in the timing or spatial distribution of leaf area and root length development by tree and crop can be exploited to increase overall system productivity. Ash, for example, does not come into leaf in southern Britain until late May, largely avoiding the period of maximal grass growth rates from mid April to mid June. On a spatial basis, trees may root more deeply than crops and thus have access to soil nutrients and water that are not available to crops. This creates the possibility of trees taking up leached nitrogen below the crop rooting zone and subsequently depositing it on the soil surface via leaf fall or in surface soil via fine root turnover (Scroth, 1995). This may result in greater overall nutrient capture by the tree–crop system than that achieved by tree or crop monocultures as well as nutrient transfers among species.

Niche differentiation may be more pronounced when trees are grown in combination with competitive crops than would be expected from their root distribution in monoculture. For example, experiments have shown that more biomass was allocated to roots in wild cherry (Campbell *et al.*, 1994) and that the vertical profile of root distribution was downwardly displaced in ash (Tomlinson and Eason, 1990) when they were grown in competition with aggressive grass swards (Figure 3.5). These changes in tree rooting pattern are consistent with a response to lower nutrient and water levels in upper soil layers as a result of resource consumption by the sward, demonstrating the plasticity of tree root systems in response to microenvironmental changes. There is also evidence that the degree of plasticity of tree root systems is a heritable trait that can be selected for (Dassanayake, 1996), creating the possibility of breeding trees specifically to have a high ecological combining ability with crops.

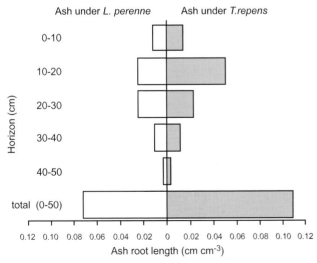

Figure 3.5 Root length (cm cm⁻³) at different soil depths of an ash tree *(Fraxinus excelsior)* with a grass sward on one side of the tree and a clover sward on the other side. Source: Tomlinson (1992).

Biodiversity

The idea that more diverse agroecosystems are more stable and sustainable than less diverse ones stems from a belief that mimicking the structure of natural ecosystems with many interacting species will confer advantages (Ewel, 1986). This hypothesis, while not unreasonable, has not yet been fully tested. Most agroforestry experiments have involved simple mixtures of one tree and one crop, with intensive management of both components, rather than exploring more extensive diversity. Specific ways in which enhanced biodiversity and mimicry of natural ecosystems might be important in UK agroforestry are shown in Box 3.2.

Enhanced biodiversity may also be perceived to have a value over and above effects on the productivity of components. A more heterogeneous environment created in an agroforestry system is likely to encourage greater diversity of flora and fauna. There is evidence of greater diversity of insects associated with the introduction of trees to both arable land (Peng *et al.*, 1993) and pasture (Dennis *et al.*, 1996) in the UK, as well as a larger number and diversity of small mammals (Wright, 1994) and birds (Agnew and Sibbald, 1996) in agroforestry plots as opposed to agricultural controls (see Chapter 8). Reintroduction of trees into agricultural landscapes may also have high aesthetic and amenity values, particularly where traditional landscape features, such as parklands (spaced trees in fields), copses (clumps of trees in fields) and hedgerows are recreated.

Succession

In ecology, succession describes the directional change of species composition at a site. In agroforestry, where trees are introduced to agricultural land, they modify the soil and aerial microclimate over time, leading to a succession of different opportunities for intercropping. If trees are used to improve soil, then agroforestry may be a transitional practice.

A classic example of successional phases of intercropping in UK agroforestry is the poplar agroforestry promoted in the UK by the match manufacturers Bryant and May in the 1950s and 1960s (see Chapter 2). This involved arable cropping between rows of trees for about the first seven years of the rotation followed by sowing to grazed pasture when shade had become too intense to permit ripening of arable crops (Beaton, 1987).

Opportunities for intercropping and land utilisation may, therefore, change as an agroforestry rotation progresses and may be influenced by management. While there is considerable flexibility, possibly through use of thinning and pruning operations to alter the intensity of tree influence at a site, future land utilisation should be considered at the outset of any agroforestry initiative.

Scale

Interactions occur at different scales. These include the level of the organism, the crop or forest stand, the landscape or watershed and, with respect to carbon sequestration, the global climate. Most of this Bulletin focuses on the management of individual trees or stands of trees at a field scale but it is also important to consider the impact of tree planting at larger scales (see Chapter 9). This is complicated because fundamental differences in the way interactions occur in agroforestry, as opposed to conventional forestry, make it impossible to predict the impact of a sparse tree stand on the environment by simply scaling relationships for forest cover by tree density or leaf area (van Noordwijk and Ong, 1996).

Shelter

Until recently, the effect of overhead shelter provided by widely spaced tree crowns with pruned stems could not be predicted from studies either in dense forest stands or with windbreaks. Measurements in Scotland, however, among widely spaced Sitka spruce trees, demonstrated substantial reductions in mean wind speed under the tree crowns that could then be modelled using mathematical simulation of the fluid dynamics of air flow (Green *et al.*, 1995). Wind speeds less than half those in the open were measured under trees that were 8 m tall, pruned to 1.3 m and spaced 8 m apart on a square grid, with larger reductions at closer tree spacings.

Hydrology

At the landscape level, tree cover may have considerable impact on the hydrology of catchments, affecting both the quantity and quality of water flowing into watercourses (Newson and Calder, 1989). Recent research in the UK has shown that isolated trees have different effects on the hydrological balance when compared with trees in closed forest stands. Interception loss per unit of leaf area, for example, was higher for trees in sparse than in closed stands in Scotland. This was as a result of higher rates of wet canopy evaporation caused by the trees in sparse stands having a higher boundary layer conductance than those in forest stands (Teklehaimanot and Jarvis, 1991).

Carbon sequestration

At a global scale, introducing trees to farmland in Europe could help in reducing carbon dioxide levels in the atmosphere by contributing to long-term storage of carbon. The structural carbon in trees themselves, grown for productive purposes, may only be temporarily removed from the atmosphere since it may be liberated again when the trees are eventually harvested and used (Sibbald and Hutchings, 1994). However, the presence of trees in fields may raise soil organic carbon levels more durably (Dixon, 1995), particularly where vegetation cover is maintained when trees are felled, thus avoiding the high levels of carbon liberation that occur with clearfelling of forests.

Managing interactions to meet objectives

This section looks at how current knowledge of component biophysical interactions can be used to help achieve particular objectives. In some circumstances a negative interaction may be prevented, such as root competition from grass swards during tree establishment or direct herbivore damage to trees. Prevention of all tree–agriculture interactions is neither possible nor desirable. Most management objectives in agroforestry seek to optimise outcomes from the various interactions that may occur.

Knowledge about UK agroforestry is largely confined to the first 10 years of the rotation for which research results are available. This covers a period during which trees are established in agricultural fields and environmental benefits are achieved without the trees impacting substantially on agricultural productivity. Further research is needed to be able to understand more mature systems.

Choice of species

Species choice impinges on most decisions made about the design and management of an agroforestry system. Fundamental characteristics of a tree species such as evergreen or deciduous habit, crown shape, leaf area density and leaf area duration, and the distribution and dynamics of the root system will determine the magnitude of interactive effects on productivity and environment.

In order to make the fullest possible use of available growth resources (light, nutrients and water) niche differentiation of the tree and crop should be maximised. Evergreen species are likely to have a greater impact on crop production than deciduous ones, at least in terms of competition for light. If the aim is to maximise agricultural production for as long as possible, deciduous species with short leaf duration may be most appropriate. However, in exposed upland conditions, shelter from evergreen trees may buffer temperatures and improve agricultural productivity in the spring and autumn. Preferred agroforestry tree species should root deeply and so utilise nutrients and water unavailable to agricultural crops or pasture. They should have a crown which either is in leaf when the agricultural crop is not growing or has a sparse, spreading form that casts a light, even shade across the understorey rather than creating areas of intense shade. Measurements of the pattern of light interception by seven-year-old tree crowns of ash, sycamore and larch at 400 stems ha[-1] growing at different sites, show that the larch crowns which were larger (10 times greater crown cover) reduced the amount of light received by the sward by more than twice as much as the broadleaved species (Bergez et al., 1997). The ideal agricultural crop for an agroforestry system will be tailor-made to the tree it is to complement; that is, it would be shallow rooted, have a contrasting phenology and be shade tolerant. Tree and crop species exhibiting all such attributes are not yet available (Sinclair, 1996) so decisions about what tree and agricultural species to select are compromises.

Some tree species may be more palatable than others to livestock in silvopastoral systems, which may aggravate the problem of herbivore damage. For example, when exposed to periods of sheep grazing, ash was shown to suffer more bark damage than sycamore (Eason et al., 1996) but sheep appear to eat the foliage of young sycamore trees more voraciously than alder. The relative fodder value of tree foliage, as litterfall or in slash from prunings, has not been quantified in UK studies although it may add significantly to animal diet (Thomas, 1988). The chemical composition of leaf litter of different tree species varies both qualitatively and quantitatively and decomposes at different rates, thereby having different impacts on the ground vegetation. For example, it was shown that large, slowly decomposing leaves of sycamore affected a grass–clover sward more than smaller hybrid larch needles (Eason, 1991). The sycamore leaves had a smothering effect on the sward, reducing yield and affecting botanical composition. By contrast, ash leaves in silvopastoral systems have been found either to decompose very quickly or to be eaten by grazing animals after they fall and so have no effect on sward composition or production.

Tree spacing and arrangement

Spacing and planting arrangements will be dictated by specific species requirements and management objectives. Tree spacing is often governed by the requirements of existing agricultural machinery while arrangement of trees may be determined as much by aesthetic and environmental considerations. For example, buffer strips of trees may be used in strategic places in farming landscapes to reduce the transport of nitrates and phosphates to watercourses. Different planting arrangements with trees at the same overall planting density will have contrasting impact on agricultural activities, the landscape and the extent of development of woodland-type habitat (Figure 3.6). The key to a good agroforestry system is one that is built around the land user's requirements. An advantage of planting trees at relatively low densities in agroforestry is the flexibility that this allows in terms of how trees are arranged on the farm and in maintaining the option to revert to pure agricultural use of land should this become desirable.

Tree planting density affects the survival and early growth of trees in silvopastoral systems and the speed of decline of agricultural production in most agroforestry practices. Low initial tree stocking densities may result in lower survival and growth rates of trees in silvopastoral systems because there is a higher level of attention from

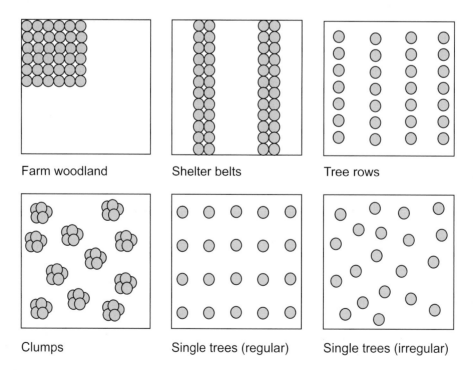

Farm woodland   Shelter belts   Tree rows

Clumps   Single trees (regular)   Single trees (irregular)

Figure 3.6 Different tree arrangements that cover one-quarter of a field.

24

livestock (see Chapter 5). The timing and extent of reductions in light available to the understorey will be a function of species, planting arrangement and density (Plate 7).

Pruning and thinning

Tree pruning and thinning will increase light levels at ground level and improve timber quality. Palatable pruned material can be left on the site so reducing overall labour costs and providing additional nutrition to grazing animals (Plate 8). Thinning will also prolong the period of agricultural production under the trees and allow removal of individual trees that are slow growing or of poor form.

Establishment

Measures to protect trees from being browsed (treeshelters or stockades) and to eliminate competition from ground vegetation (mulch or herbicide) are discussed in Chapter 4. In addition to protecting the trees, however, these measures may influence tree root development during the critical establishment phase. Root:shoot ratios have been lower in young trees in silvopastoral systems than in conventional forestry (Eason *et al.*, 1994). This is caused by several factors. Firstly, when root competition from ground vegetation is prevented, the tree roots are likely to take up sufficient nutrients with a small root system and so tree root growth may be reduced. Furthermore, when in treeshelters, the movement of young tree stems in response to wind is restricted, which reduces stem thickening and possibly lateral root development.

Tree roots may also be damaged directly by livestock. Increased animal activity in positions close to trees damages tree roots, especially of shallow rooted species, and may be aggravated further if there is a bare soil region adjacent to the tree perhaps as a result of herbicide application to control weed competition.

Fertilisation and nutrient cycling

The ability of systems to retain and cycle nutrients is very important to both productivity and sustainability; the largest losses are likely to be through leaching and can have undesirable environmental impacts through increasing the nitrogen and phosphorus in solution in watercourses. Natural woodlands are often considered to be effective at retaining nutrients because of the diversity of plant species present and their different nutrient foraging strategies. Adding trees to a farm either in fields or as buffer strips may help to improve nutrient recycling and reduce leaching losses.

Where a major management objective is to maximise productivity of one or more components in an agroforestry system, it is important to ensure that nutrients are available when needed and supply does not limit the growth of the components of interest. Individual species, however, vary in their requirements for nutrients, largely because they have different thresholds for nutrient uptake by roots, or a preference for nutrients in a particular form, such as uptake of nitrogen as nitrate (NO_3) rather than ammonium (NH_4), and have different prevailing growth rates.

The tree component usually has a lower demand for nutrients than the understorey because of a slower growth rate. Fertiliser application rates are, therefore, usually adjusted to maintain the growth of the understorey at satisfactory levels and may initially be similar to those used in monoculture. As tree shading limits potential growth rate of the understorey, optimal fertiliser rates will decline. Growth rates are not constant throughout the year and more frequent applications of smaller amounts of fertiliser will usually result in a greater uptake of applied nutrients. In an agroforestry context the amount to be applied in each split dressing needs to take into account temporal differences in the growth of different components and how these are influenced by competition. Water availability, for example, may limit uptake of nutrients and the potential for plant growth and be influenced by competitive uptake of water by several components.

The presence of trees may allow fertiliser additions to be lowered without a reduction in agricultural yield, through improved nutrient cycling or biological nitrogen fixation. For example, alders fix atmospheric nitrogen by means of an association with *Frankia*, a micro-organism which forms root nodules, and this has been shown to transfer nitrogen to a grass understorey (Wheeler *et al.*, 1986). Red alder (*Alnus rubra*) has been mixed with grass/clover swards in experimental silvopastoral systems in the UK that receive no nitrogen fertiliser (Teklehaimanot and Sinclair, 1993). Potential benefits include maintaining sward clover content, the implications of which are discussed in Chapter 5, and reducing purchased inputs.

A summary of how managing interactions can help in meeting objectives is given in Box 3.3.

Box 3.3 Key points in the management of interactions

- **Species choice.** Select tree species which are suited to site and climatic conditions. To maintain agricultural production for as long as possible, select tree and agricultural species with complementary phenology. Consider the properties of individual tree provenances and crop cultivars.

- **Spacing and arrangement.** Tree spacing and planting arrangements are flexible and should meet the land user's requirements, subject to the needs of individual species chosen. Very low planting densities may not be suitable as there is increased pressure on individual trees from agricultural activities, which may affect growth and performance and there is little scope for tree selection after planting.

- **Pruning and thinning.** Agricultural production can be maintained for longer by thinning out trees and reducing tree crown size by pruning, which will also have a positive influence on tree form and timber quality. Pruned material provides extra nutrition for grazing animals.

- **Establishment.** Control of competition from agricultural components is essential for rapid tree growth during the early establishment period. Caution is advised in the use of individual treeshelters which may affect tree stability in some species on exposed sites. Overstringent control of competition among trees and vegetation, and the prevention of stem movement, may lead to inappropriate tree root development.

- **Fertiliser and nutrient cycling.** Introducing trees to agricultural fields can increase nutrient recycling, improving nutrient use efficiency and reducing pollution of watercourses. Nitrogen fixing trees can transfer nitrogen to associated pasture and when combined with a grass/clover sward can constitute a low input silvopastoral system. Fertiliser can be applied in small frequent amounts that match the growth and nutrient demand of the component of the system for which it is intended.

REFERENCES

AGNEW, R.D.M. and SIBBALD, A.R. (1996). The avifauna of the Glensaugh silvopastoral site 1995–96. *Agroforestry Forum* **7**(3), 20–21.

ANDERSON, L.S. and SINCLAIR, F.L. (1993). Ecological interactions in agroforestry systems. *Agroforestry Abstracts* **6**(2), 57–91.

BEATON, A. (1987). Poplars and agroforestry. *Quarterly Journal of Forestry* **81**, 225–233.

BERGEZ, J-E., DALZIEL, A.J.I., DULLER, C., EASON, W.R., HOPPÉ, G. and LAVENDER, R.H. (1997). Light modification in a developing silvopastoral system in the UK: a quantitative analysis. *Agroforestry Systems* **37**, 227–240.

BROWNLOW, M.J.C., CARRUTHERS, S.P. and DORWARD, P.T. (1993). The integration of pigs and poultry with forestry: practice, theory and economics. *Agroforestry Forum* **4**(3), 51–57.

CAMPBELL, C.D., ATKINSON, D., JARVIS, P.G. and NEWBOULD, P. (1994). Effects of nitrogen fertiliser tree/pasture competition during the establishment phase of a silvopastoral system. *Annals of Applied Biology* **124**, 83–96.

CANNELL, M.G.R. (1983). Plant management in agroforestry. In: *Plant research and agroforestry*, ed. P.A. Huxley. ICRAF, Nairobi, 455–488.

DASSANAYAKE, K.B. (1996). Differential responses of perennial root systems to change in soil moisture. PhD Thesis, University of Aberdeen.

DENNIS, P., SHELLARD, L.J.F. and AGNEW, R.D.M. (1996). Shifts in arthropod species assemblages in relation to silvopastoral establishment in upland pastures. *Agroforestry Forum* **7**(3), 14–17.

DIXON, R.K. (1995). Agroforestry systems – sources or sinks of greenhouse gases. *Agroforestry Systems* **31**, 99–116.

DORWARD, P.T. AND CARRUTHERS, S.P. (1990). *The potential for integrating livestock with trees on farms in the UK*. Farm Animal Care Trust, London.

EASON, W.R. (1991). The effect of tree leaf litter on sward botanical composition and growth. *Forest Ecology and Management* **45**, 165–172.

EASON, W.R., GILL, E.K. and ROBERTS, J.E. (1996). Evaluation of anti-sheep tree-stem-protection products in silvopastoral agroforestry. *Agroforestry Systems* **34**, 259–264.

EASON, W.R., HOPPÉ, G., BERGEZ, J-E., ROBERTS, J.E., HARRISON, C., CARLISLE, H., SIBBALD, A.R., MCADAM, J., SIMPSON, J. and TEKLEHAIMANOT, Z. (1994). Tree root development in agroforestry systems. *Agroforestry Forum* **5**(2), 36–44.

EWEL, J.J. (1986). Designing agricultural ecosystems for the humid tropics. *Annual Review of Ecology and Systematics* **17**, 245–271.

GOLDBERG, D.E. and WERNER, P.A. (1983). Equivalence of competitors in plant communities: a null hypothesis and a field experiment approach. *American Journal of Botany* **70**, 1098–1104.

GREEN, S.R., GRACE, J. and HUTCHINGS, N.J. (1995). Observations of turbulent air-flow in 3 stands of widely spaced Sitka spruce. *Agricultural and Forest Meteorology* **74**, 205–225.

KNOWLES, R.L. (1991). New Zealand experience with silvopastoral systems: a review. *Forest Ecology and Management* **45**, 251–268.

MAXWELL, T.G. (1986). Agro-forestry systems for hills and uplands. In: *Agro-forestry. A discussion of research and development requirements*. Ministry of Agriculture, Fisheries and Food, London, 30–38.

NEWSON, M.D. and CALDER I.R. (1989). Forests and water resources: problems of prediction on a regional scale. *Philosophical Transactions of the Royal Society of London, Series B* **324**, 283–298.

PENG, R.K., INCOLL, L.D., SUTTON, S.L., WRIGHT, C. and CHADWICK, A. (1993). Diversity of airborne arthropods in a silvoarable agroforestry system. *Journal of Applied Ecology* **30**, 551–562.

PERCIVAL, N.S. and KNOWLES, R.L. (1988). Relationship between radiata pine and understorey pasture production. In: *Proceedings of the agroforestry symposium*, ed. P. Maclaren. FRI Bulletin No. 139. Ministry of Forestry, Rotorua, 152–164.

PHILLIPS, D.S., GRIFFITHS, J., NAEEM, M., COMPTON, S.G. and INCOLL, L.D. (1994). Responses of crop pests and their natural enemies to an agroforestry environment. *Agroforestry Forum* **5**(2), 14–20.

SCROTH, G. (1995). Tree root characteristics as criteria for species selection and systems design in agroforestry. *Agroforestry Systems* **30**, 125–143.

SIBBALD, A.R. and HUTCHINGS, N.J. (1994). The integration of environmental requirements into livestock systems based on grazed pastures in the European Community. In: *Proceedings of the 2nd international symposium on the study of livestock farming systems in a research and development framework*, Zaragoza, Spain, September, 1992, ed. A. Gibbon and J.C. Flamant. CEC, Brussels, 86–100.

SIBBALD, A.R., ELSTON, D.A., IASON, G.R. and DICK, J. (1996). *Agroforestry Forum* **7**(3), 26–28.

SIBBALD, A.R., GRIFFITHS, J.H. and ELSTON, D.A. (1991). The effects of the presence of widely spaced conifers on under-storey herbage production in the UK. *Forest Ecology and Management* **45**, 71–78.

SINCLAIR, F.L. (1996). The emergence of associative tree ideotypes from ecophysiological research and farmers' knowledge. *Agroforestry Forum* **7**(4), 17–19.

SINGH, K.A. and THOMPSON, F.B. (1995). Effect of lopping on water potential, transpiration, regrowth, ^{14}C-photosynthate distribution and biomass production in *Alnus glutinosa*. *Tree Physiology* **15**, 197–202.

TEKLEHAIMANOT, Z. and JARVIS, P.G. (1991). Direct measurement of evaporation of intercepted water from forest canopies. *Journal of Applied Ecology* **28**, 603–618.

TEKLEHAIMANOT, Z. and SINCLAIR, F.L. (1993). Establishment of the silvopastoral network experiment site, Henfaes, Bangor. *Agroforestry*

Forum **4**(2), 18–21.

THOMAS, R.J. (1988). A review of the use of nitrogen-fixing shrubs and trees in agroforestry and farm forestry systems in N. Europe. *Research and Development in Agriculture* **5**, 143–152.

TOMLINSON, H.F. (1992). The mineral nutrition of isolated trees in pasture. PhD Thesis, Bristol University.

TOMLINSON, H.F. and EASON, W.R. (1990). Sward type affects tree root distribution. *Agroforestry in the UK* **1**(2), 17–18.

VAN NOORDWIJK, M. and ONG, C.K. (1996). Lateral resource flow and capture – the key to scaling up Agroforestry results. *Agroforestry Forum* **7** (3), 29–31

WHEELER, C.T., HOOKER, J.E., CROWE, A. and BERRIE, A.M.M. (1986). The improvement and utilization in forestry of nitrogen fixation by actinorhizal plants with special reference to *Alnus* in Scotland. *Plant and Soil* **90**, 393–406.

WRIGHT, C. (1994). The distribution and abundance of small mammals in a silvoarable agroforestry system. *Agroforestry Forum* **5**(2), 26–28.

(a)

Plate 1 *Radiata pine planted on steep slopes as an erosion prevention measure on a farm in the Bay of Plenty area of North Island, New Zealand. (a) Sheep grazing in a young silvopasture; (b) a more mature silvopasture being rested from sheep grazing.* (ALAN SIBBALD, MLURI)

(b)

Plate 2 *Lowland silvoarable system with poplar and winter wheat at Bramham, near Tadcaster, West Yorkshire.*
(LYNTON INCOLL, UNIVERSITY OF LEEDS)

Plate 3 *Upland silvopastoral system with sheep and 19-year-old larch at Radnor, Wales.*
(FOREST RESEARCH PHOTO LIBRARY 50525)

Plate 4 *Adult fighting bulls grazing on a Spanish dehesa with holm oaks.*
(JOSÉ MANUEL GÓMEZ-GUTIÉRREZ)

Plate 5 *Single row of white pine acting as a windbreak on a prairie farm in Nebraska, USA.*
(MAX HISLOP)

Plate 6 *Alley cropping in Cameroon:* Leucaena *hedge (at right) about to be cut and nutrient-rich foliage placed between maize, as indicated by research scientist.* (JULIAN EVANS)

Plate 7 An experiment at Glentress, Peebleshire to assess sward growth under different densities of tree cover. (a) Sward boxes under tall trees at medium spacing. (b) View showing different spacing arrangements.

Plate 8 Tree pruning in a lowland silvopastoral system with sheep and ash at Loughgall, Co. Armagh, Northern Ireland; sheep browsing pruned foliage.
(JIM McADAM, DARDNI)

Plate 9 Unrooted hybrid poplar set 1.5 m long and cylindrical steel bar used for drilling holes in soil prior to planting.
(FOREST RESEARCH, SILVICULTURE AND SEED RESEARCH BRANCH)

Plate 10 Laying a black plastic mulch strip prior to inserting a row of poplar cuttings at Old Wolverton, Milton Keynes.
(BIODIVERSITY INTERNATIONAL LTD)

Plate 11 *Line of first-year poplar planted as unrooted sets through plastic mulch using a tractor-mounted spike.*
(ARNOLD BEATON)

Plate 12 *A newly planted tree in a silvopastoral system protected from grazing sheep by a treeshelter with one robust stake and a short secondary stake to prevent turning.*
(FOREST RESEARCH PHOTO LIBRARY 38594)

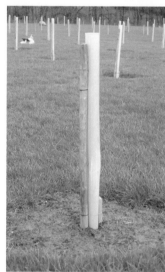

(b)

(a)

Plate 13 *(a) and (b) Red alder planted at the Henfaes, Bangor NNE site (400 trees ha^{-1}) protected against sheep by an individual fence and against rabbits by a spiral guard. A mulch mat has been used to assist in weed control.*

Plate 14 *(a) and (b) Sycamore at the Glensaugh NNE site 8 years after planting (400 trees ha^{-1}) protected against sheep by 1.8 m plastic mesh guard.* (FOREST RESEARCH PHOTO LIBRARY (a) 50878, (b) 50877)

Plate 15 *Sheep grazing in a deciduous silvopastoral system with sycamore at Loughgall, Co. Armagh, Northern Ireland.* (JIM McADAM, DARDNI)

Plate 16 *Exclusion cages to monitor sward growth. (a) In a 400 tree ha^{-1} sycamore plot at Glensaugh, Grampian, Scotland. (b) In a mature poplar silvopasture, Ballywalter, Co. Down, Northern Ireland.*
((a) ALAN SIBBALD, MLURI; (b) JIM McADAM, DARDNI)

Plate 17 *Tractor application of fertiliser to encourage good pasture growth, ash silvo-pasture, Loughgall, Co. Armagh, Northern Ireland.* (JIM McADAM, DARDNI)

Plate 18 *Pigs at pannage in Denny Wood, New Forest, Hampshire.* (TERRY HEATHCOTE)

Plate 19 *Free-range turkeys in a commercial forest enterprise in northern England.* (MARK BROWNLOW)

Plate 20 *Shade from 4-year-old poplar over a germinating spring crop at Old Wolverton, Buckinghamshire.*
(BIODIVERSITY INTERNATIONAL LTD)

Plate 21 *Thinning of 4-year-old, 1 m spaced poplar trees at Old Wolverton, Buckinghamshire.*
(BIODIVERSITY INTERNATIONAL LTD)

Plate 22 *Harvesting of winter wheat in a silvoarable trial at Silsoe, Bedfordshire.*
(P. BURGESS, CRANFIELD UNIVERSITY)

Plate 23 *Build up of weeds at the edges of mulch strip, and in areas of strip damaged by wild animals, round 4-year-old poplar at Old Wolverton, Buckinghamshire.*
(BIODIVERSITY INTERNATIONAL LTD)

Plate 24 *Side pruning of poplar in a silvoarable trial at Silsoe, Bedfordshire.*
(JIM McADAM, DARDNI)

Plate 25 *(a) The carabid beetle* (Pterostichus niger), *commonly found in silvopasture on lowland sites in Northern Ireland.*
(ROY ANDERSON, DARDNI)

(b) The fieldfare (Turdus pilaris) *is particularly attracted to silvopasture in upland and sites across the UK.*
(T. A. WADDELL)

Plate 26 *The necessarily regular layout of this experimental site at Bronydd Mawr (NNE site) has resulted in poor landscape impact. Compare with Figure 9.6(a).*
(FOREST RESEARCH PHOTO LIBRARY 51409)

Best Practice and Current Research

Chapter 4
Trees in agroforestry systems

Arnold Beaton and Max Hislop

Introduction

This chapter considers the silvicultural aspects peculiar to agroforestry systems, in particular: species choice, establishment, protection and pruning. Where the silviculture of trees in agroforestry systems is regarded as the same as in forestry systems, references have been given or further reading advised. The advice is based on experience and research which started with the Bryant and May (Forestry) Limited silvoarable system in the 1960s through to the recent MAFF silvoarable trials and the silvopastoral National Network Experiment (NNE) (see Chapter 2).

The complex interactions between the various elements in an agroforestry system are discussed in Chapter 3. The management of livestock or crops between trees is discussed in Chapters 5, 6 and 7.

Species choice for agroforestry systems

In an agroforestry system where timber production is one of the main objectives, the selection of appropriate species should be based on:

- good timber producing potential;
- relatively fast growth;
- a dominant leading shoot and a single straight stem (apical dominance);
- a light branching habit.

Table 4.1 assesses a range of species that have been tested in agroforestry experiments in the UK against the selection criteria mentioned above. Some additional species are listed which have not been tested in UK conditions.

It is particularly important to select agroforestry tree species based on the prevailing site conditions if the fastest growth rates and timber yields are to be realised. Forest Research's Ecological Site Classification (ESC) (Pyatt and Suárez, 1997) provides foresters and agroforesters with a powerful aid in making this crucial decision. ESC will also assist in species selection for other criteria, such as deciding on which National Vegetation Classification woodland community is best suited to site conditions.

Agroforestry systems have relatively low densities of trees in comparison to more conventional woodland establishment (see section on Spacing and layout, page 37). There is less opportunity, therefore, to select better performing trees through successive thinning operations, and a lesser margin for poor establishment. The aim should be to produce high quality timber from each tree planted. A well-adapted provenance should be chosen. Genetically improved material is desirable (seed from seed-orchards, or as clonal material) but is not available for most hardwood species in the UK, apart from poplar.

Clones of *Prunus avium* are commercially available in France and work at HRI will lead to commercial release of some micro-propagated cherry clones in 2000. Forest Research has established extensive provenance trials of oak, ash, beech and sycamore in recent years which will facilitate choice of seed sources of good form and vigour (Cundall, 1999). Breeding Seedling Orchards of ash and oak are being established under the auspices of the British Hardwood Improvement Programme (BHIP, 1999) but it will be at least a decade before even small quantities of improved seed are available. Information on the best planting stock for four of the recommended agroforestry species is given below.

Table 4.1 Species which have been tested in UK agroforestry systems and some with potential for use in the UK.

Species	Potential for valuable timber production	Potential growth rate in UK - Yield Class[a]	Apical dominance	Light branching habit	Success in UK systems trials	Notes
Alder (grey)	**	14	**	**	Untested	Potential alternative to red alder in northern Britain
Alder (red)	**	14	**	**	** SP	Nitrogen fixing of root nodules may benefit grass productivity. Avoid frost hollows
Ash	***	12	***	***	*** SP, **SA	Recommended for lowland silvopastoral systems. Avoid frost hollows
Beech	**	10	**	*	Untested	Consider use for amenity and environmental benefits
Hazel	*	Not known (coppice yield ≅ 2.5 t ha⁻¹ yr⁻¹)	*	*	*SA	Potential nut producer between timber species in silvoarable systems
Oak	**	8	**	*	Untested	Consider use for amenity and environmental benefits
Poplar	***	26	***	***	**SP, *** SA	Highly recommended for silvoarable systems
Sweet chestnut	**	Not known (coppice yield ≅ 5 t ha⁻¹ yr⁻¹)	***	*	Untested	Potential nut and timber producer in silvoarable systems in southern Britain
Sycamore	***	12	***	**	*** SP, **SA	Recommended for upland silvopastoral systems
Walnut	***	Not known (saleable 30 cm dbh in 40 years)	**	**	* SA	Potential nut and timber producer in silvoarable systems in southern Britain
Wild cherry	***	9	***	*	** SP, **SA	Wide spacing leads to heavy branching. Pruning is essential (see 'Formative pruning')
Hybrid larch	**	14	**	***	* SP	Establishment in treeshelters in exposed conditions not recommended
Scots pine	**	14	***	**	** SP	Establishment in treeshelters in exposed conditions not recommended

[a]Maximum mean annual increment over bark (m^3), based on traditional forest spacing. These Yield Classes are the highest achievable on the best sites in the UK.
SP: silvopastoral, SA: silvoarable.

Poplar

Poplar has been the principal species to be used in silvoarable systems in Europe and is believed to be the only species of commercial significance at the present time in the UK (Beaton, 1988). Most commercially grown poplars in the UK are hybrids between one or more of four species of poplar widely used in breeding programmes in Europe (Beaton, 1993). Commercial hybrid poplars have typically been selected for fast growth rates, good form and good disease resistance. The history of poplar breeding and the description of important hybrids are described in Forestry Commission Bulletin 92 (Jobling, 1990). Eight new clones from the Poplar Research Station at Geraardsbergen in Belgium, released to growers in the UK from 1985 onwards, are of particular importance (Tabbush, 1995).

Under the Forest Reproductive Materials Regulations 1977 (FRMs), it is a legal requirement that any reproductive material of listed species (including poplar) marketed for the production of wood is produced from a registered source described in a master certificate issued by the Forestry Commission. Information on approved poplar clones is provided in Forestry Commission Information Note 21 *Approved poplar varieties* (Tabbush, 1999), which lists currently approved clones and gives brief information on origins, relative performance and silviculture. This information is periodically updated as new clones become available or the risk of disease in older clones is found to be unacceptable.

The poplar hybrids eligible for grant under the Woodland Grant Scheme in Britain at the time of publication are listed in Table 4.2; those planted in any quantity are starred *. All clones starred in Table 4.2 may be considered suitable for agroforestry use – particularly for silvoarable systems – subject to good site selection.

Sycamore

Sycamore was selected as the common tree species in the NNE (see Chapter 2, page 9) and has performed well even on exposed upland sites. Early results from recent Forest Research provenance trials suggest that on fertile lowland sites most British seed-sources will perform well (Cundall *et al.*, 1998). Of just four continental sources tested, one

from Denmark was outstanding, and this will be evaluated further in grower-managed trials.

Ash

The performance of ash is strongly site related. It demands a sheltered site and prefers a moist but well-drained deep calcareous loam. Frost hollows and exposed situations are not suitable. This has been borne out by the use of ash in the NNE sites where it has performed extremely well on the lowland sites at Loughgall, Bangor and North Wyke (less exposure and good soil conditions) and less well on the upland site at Bronydd Mawr in mid-Wales.

Recent Forest Research ash provenance trials are evaluating 12 British and 10 continental seed-sources at eight sites. Few meaningful results are yet available. It is expected that British material will generally prove to be well adapted. After four years' growth there is already evidence that material from eastern Europe is significantly slower growing, whereas some sources from France are promising.

Cherry

Cherry has been successfully established in a silvopastoral experiment by the Macaulay Land Use Research Institute (MLURI) at Glensaugh Research Station in north-east Scotland using commercially available stock. However, cherry is not subject to EU regulations on the registration of seed stands. There is thus no guarantee of the origin of the seed used by nurseries and consequently no guarantee of timber quality and stem form (Pryor, 1988). A recent research programme at Horticulture Research International (HRI) is developing genetically improved clonal cherry which has the potential to ensure better form and yield (Russell, 1996). One clone is now commercially available from forest nurseries.

Establishment

Planting stock

Poplars
Poplars have an important advantage over most other broadleaved trees in their ability to produce roots from young dormant shoots when inserted into the ground. All the commercial poplar hybrids

Table 4.2 Poplar clones acceptable for registration under the Forest Reproductive Materials Regulations (1977).

Parent group	Clone
D x N (*P. deltoides* x *nigra*)	Older varieties
	'Robusta' *
	'Serotina'
	'Gelrica'
	'Heidemij'
	'Casale 78'
	Introduced since 1985
	'Primo'
	'Ghoy' *
	'Gaver' *
	'Gibecq' *
T x D (*P. trichocarpa* x *deltoides*)	Introduced since 1985
	'Beaupré' *
	'Raspalje'
	New release under test
	'Hoogvorst'
	'Hazendans'
T (*P. trichocarpa*)	Older varieties
	'Fritzi Pauley' *
	'Scott Pauley' *
	Introduced since 1985
	'Trichobel' *
	'Columbia River'
P. trichocarpa x *balsamifera*	'Balsam Spire' *
	(formerly TT32)
P. alba x *tremula*	*P.* x *canescens*

*Hybrids planted in any quantity.

listed in Table 4.2, except for *P.* x *canescens*, can be propagated vegetatively from one-year-old wood. This facility has largely determined poplar nursery practice and in recent years has led to the widespread use of unrooted planting material in preference to rooted plants.

Poplars can be successfully established using rooted plants, unrooted sets or cuttings, and there are advantages and disadvantages for each type of material (Jobling, 1990). Rooted plants are generally one year or two years old and are lifted with a cut back root system. They may be from 1 m to over 3 m in height. Unrooted sets are one year or two year shoots of similar size range taken from rooted nursery plants and have a terminal bud. They may also be taken from selected straight prunings from established trees. Cuttings are portions cut from a one year shoot, usually between 15 cm and 25 cm in length, and having a good sized bud just below the top cut end. They have additional buds below the top but these are less important.

Other species
Planting material for other broadleaved species with agroforestry potential will be rooted, usually one- or two-year-old transplants. These will probably range in height from 20 cm to 90 cm and be bare rooted. Container grown plants or bare-root stock larger than 90 cm are more expensive than bare-rooted transplants, but this additional expense might be justified when small schemes are being established. Full details of best practice are contained in Forestry Commission Bulletin 121 *Forest tree seedlings* (Morgan, 1999).

In silvoarable systems the choice of planting material and the method of planting may have to be decided after considering first the method of weed control to be applied (see section on Weed control, pages 35–37). In practice, the field space should be considered as divided into narrow strips of trees (the tree row) and alternate broad strips of arable cultivation (the alleys). To a very large extent the work done in these two distinct areas of the field are independent of each other although the one must not compromise the other.

In silvopastoral systems the choice of size of planting material is determined by the method of protection from grazing animals. Where treeshelters are used (see section on Protection, pages 38–40) bare-rooted transplants of 20 cm to 30 cm will be appropriate. Where fenced enclosures are used for protection, bare-rooted transplants ranging from 30 cm to 90 cm in height may be used, depending on whether a spiral rabbit guard is necessary. There is no evidence that larger planting material confers any lasting advantage: larger plants can stagnate for several years and are more expensive (Kerr and Evans, 1993).

Planting

Tree planting should not begin until full dormancy has occurred and the plants have been subjected to cold conditions. In most years this will preclude any planting until late November or early December. Thereafter planting may continue throughout the winter months up to the end of March.

Poplars

Early leafing clones of poplar should be planted not later than mid-March in the south of England but may be planted up to a month later in southern Scotland, depending on the season. Poplar cuttings and sets taken from the nursery in winter can be stored for several months in cold store at between 2 and 3°C but the planting of freshly cut material is greatly preferred. The longer such planting material is stored the greater the moisture loss and consequent risk of infection by organisms likely to weaken or kill the plant. 'Cut and plant in the same week' is a good maxim.

Planting methods vary with the material used. Poplar cuttings are inserted by hand. The soil must be well cultivated to the full depth required for the cutting to be inserted vertically so that the top bud is level with the soil surface. It is essential to plant with buds pointing upwards. Unrooted sets of poplar should be planted with approximately one-third of the total length in the ground. For sets of 1.2 m in length it is possible to plant into deep ploughed, friable soils by hand to 30–40 cm. Sets longer than this need to be pit planted, using a soil auger, or can be inserted into pre-drilled holes made with a cylindrical steel bar having a diameter close to the average basal diameter of the sets to be used (Figure 4.1, Plate 9). The set is inserted to the required depth in the hole and since these are tapered there will be a gap between the top of the set and the side of the hole. This gap must be filled with dry sand to provide a firm medium for the newly developing root hairs to colonise and also to maintain the set in a firm position during this early period of rooting. The new root hairs that develop in March and April will be easily broken if there is any movement of the set during this period. Loosely inserted sets subjected to wind rock may lead to partial or complete failure of the planting. Rooted plants of poplar should also be planted to approximately one-third of their length to encourage a new root system to develop coincidentally with the existing nursery root and to ensure that rooting development is in moist soil even in hot dry summers. Planting holes are usually best dug with a tractor mounted auger having a wide bit, preferably not less than 25 cm, to accommodate the cut back root system. For sets and rooted plants of poplar, deep planting cannot be overstressed. Success depends on the root system developing into moist soil that will remain moist throughout the driest summers. Deep planting also helps to maintain stability during the initial phase of establishment.

Other species

The planting of bare-rooted transplants of other tree species is generally undertaken during the dormant season. However it is possible to delay the planting of cold-stored transplants until late spring should conditions dictate. The roots of all bare-rooted stock must be carefully handled and kept in planting bags, away from drying winds and hot sunshine, until the moment of planting. Full details of best practice are contained in Forestry Commission Handbook 6 *Forestry practice* (Hibberd, 1991) and Forestry Commission Bulletin 121 *Forest tree seedlings* (Morgan, 1999).

Weed control

Weeds, particularly grasses, are fast growing and compete aggressively with newly planted trees for moisture and nutrients. Severe competition can cause the death of recently planted trees and will certainly reduce health and growth. Careful and well-timed weed control can greatly benefit tree survival and growth and is crucial to the successful establishment of any agroforestry system. Whatever method is used to kill weeds, trees must be freed from competition around their rooting zone until rooting is extensive and deep enough for the tree to compete with weeds. In practice this usually means planning for weed control for the first two or three growing seasons.

Silvoarable systems

Lines of trees with arable cropping on either side cannot be cultivated effectively to control weed

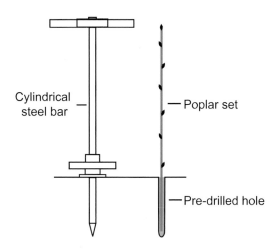

Figure 4.1 Planting techniques for unrooted poplar sets.

growth unless the distance between trees and the edge of the cropping zone is at least as wide as a small tractor and rotovator. In practice this would take up too great a proportion of field space. Since the choice of a weed control method in the tree row influences the choice of planting material and planting method, it is appropriate to consider weed control options at this point.

Mulches. Silvoarable trials with poplars (Newman and Wainwright, 1989) have relied on the use of approximately 1 m wide 500 gauge black plastic mulch for weed control. This is laid as a continuous strip using a tractor mounted roll dispenser and layer (Plate 10). Plastic is best laid on clean cultivated land and it is essential for the edges to be turned and buried during the laying operation. Widths of between 1 m and 2 m have been used successfully; the wider the strip the greater the weed-free zone around each tree. Once the plastic strip is laid trees have to be planted through the plastic. Since cuts in the plastic must be made for each tree this system is not recommended for large rooted plants. Both cuttings and unrooted sets can be planted through the plastic with ease. Large sets will require holes to be forced with a cylindrical spike (Plate 11) and for such planting material the recommendation to infill gaps with dry sand or soil must be carried out under dry conditions. The use of 1.2 m unrooted

sets which can be directly inserted by hand may therefore be the most convenient size of poplar to use in this planting system. Trials indicate that 500 gauge plastic may last five or more years before beginning to break up. Well-laid, black, UV stable plastic provides an excellent mulch, conserving moisture and maintaining a weed-free environment during the critical years of establishment (Plate 11). Other broadleaves have been successfully planted through plastic mulch, including small transplants of ash, oak, wild cherry, hazel, field maple and sweet chestnut. Cuts are made in the plastic to expose a sufficient area of soil and after planting the cut pieces are folded back close to the tree. The use of other mulches, such as straw, appears to be too costly to consider for large scale application and cannot be recommended.

Herbicides. The cultivated tree row can be maintained weed free by the use of pre-emergent and contact herbicides. If individual tree guards providing an effective barrier against herbicides are used, both contact and pre-emergent herbicides can be applied after planting. In trials to date, hand-operated knapsack sprayers have been used. However, in theory it should be possible to fit an additional small spray tank and two offset jets on a tractor mounted spray boom so as to allow tree rows to be treated obliquely coincidentally with herbicide applications to the adjacent arable crops. Poplars are particularly susceptible to glyphosate while in leaf and young trees may be severely affected by this herbicide. Weed control in tree rows may have to be maintained for at least five years until trees are well established. Thereafter weed infestation to neighbouring land may require control of specific weed species in the tree row. Costs of repeated herbicide applications over several years should be compared against the once-only cost of plastic mulch. Details of approved herbicides and their use in these situations is given in Forestry Commission Field Book 14 *Herbicides for farm woodlands and short rotation coppice* (Willoughby and Clay, 1996) and Technical Paper 28 *Herbicide update* (Willoughby and Clay, 1999).

Ground cover plants. Establishment of ground cover plants to prevent noxious weed invasion and provide only minimum competition with the tree crop is seen as a possibly acceptable method of controlling weeds in the tree row. During the period of tree establishment, perennial broadleaved ground cover species are seen as possible alternatives to mulch provided the chosen composition can be maintained. Clover and lucerne are plants that may be used effectively under certain conditions. It is believed that all grass species used as a ground cover will compete strongly with a newly planted tree crop. However, once trees are fully established and growing strongly a grass mixture may be a suitable ground cover. It should be emphasised that maximum tree growth will be obtained under weed-free conditions and the presence of a competitive weed spectrum in the tree row may very severely inhibit the early growth of the tree crop. For this reason the possible use of ground cover plants as a means of weed control should be considered with caution.

Silvopastoral systems
Where grazing animals can gain access to the base of widely spaced trees in silvopastoral systems, the use of mulches or ground cover plants cannot be recommended. This is because any effective weed control will be lost due to the destruction of the mulch layer, or eating of the cover crop by the animals. The only effective weed control regime in these situations is the use of herbicides. In the silvopastoral NNE both residual (propyzamide) and systemic (glyphosate) herbicides were applied for three years after planting to maintain a 1 m diameter vegetation-free zone (Sibbald *et al.*, in press). The use of treeshelters on these sites made the application of herbicide straightforward. At the Henfaes NNE site some plots were planted in groups and fencing used as protection from grazing sheep. Here plastic mulch was used successfully as a weed control because the fencing prevented access to the mulch by the sheep (Plate 13 (a) and (b)).

Spacing and layout in agroforestry systems
Under forestry plantation conditions trees are planted at close spacing to reduce the period required for the trees to dominate all other vegetation. Once the tree crop has totally dominated the site the forestry manager may adjust thinning regimes to meet certain objectives. However, in an agroforestry system the land manager is striving to achieve the best compromise between efficient and effective tree growth while maintaining economical agricultural production. Agroforestry systems present many management options so the land manager needs to appreciate the impacts of the various options on the whole system (see Chapter 3 for discussion of these impacts). One of the most obvious management options is the spacing and layout of the trees in the system. The various options for silvoarable and silvopastoral systems are discussed below. The spacing and layout of an agroforestry system has immediate and long-term impacts on the local landscape. Chapter 9 discusses these impacts and gives guidance on designing a sympathetic system.

Silvoarable systems
Under a silvoarable system the initial spacing of the trees is not dictated by silvicultural objectives but by timber and agricultural requirements. Considerations of alley width for arable cultivation are given in Chapter 7, in which the spacing of trees in the row and the possibility of mixtures are discussed.

Single lines of trees will be pruned at an early age to facilitate the movement of tractors and machinery in adjacent alleys. If production of poplar sawlog and veneer log timber is the sole objective, trees may be planted at the 'final crop spacing' of between 6 m and 8 m so as to achieve this objective in the shortest time. If it is required to produce an intermediate return from one or more thinnings then any spacing from 2 m can be chosen. On good poplar sites, and allowing for regular pruning, poplars may grow nearly 2 m in height annually and achieve crown diameters of between 4.5 and 5 m in the first 10 years. At a 3 m spacing crowns will be touching from 5 to 6 years after planting and at an initial spacing of 8 m crowns will be touching at about the 15th year. Once the crowns in a tree line are touching, diameter increment will be progressively reduced thereafter unless the trees are subsequently thinned. Under plantation conditions there is a strong relationship between spacing and the ultimate average diameter the crop trees will reach at that spacing, depending on clone and site. With single rows of trees this relationship is less clear.

The best markets for poplar timber are likely to be for mature well-pruned boles of 6 to 9 m and approximately 50 cm dbh. This should be achieved in 20 to 40 years depending on the site and clone. Wide spacing in the tree row is necessary to achieve maximum timber value in the minimum time. A spacing of between 6 m and 8 m in the row is recommended but if it is intended to plant at closer spacing so as to allow intermediate thinnings, it is suggested that initial spacings should allow alternate trees to be removed on one or two occasions. Thus planting at 2 m will allow one thinning to 4 m and a second to the final crop spacing of 8 m. Alternatively a 3 m initial spacing will allow one thinning to 6 m.

Rows of trees, even when separated by wide alleys, will impose some shading on arable crops. The shading will increase marginally with increase in latitude but more significant factors are the density of tree planting and row alignment. Shading effect will be least with rows aligned north to south and with widely spaced, well-pruned trees. The most uneven shading of arable crops will occur with closely spaced, underpruned trees in rows aligned east–west.

At wide spacing, mixtures with other broadleaved trees may be made. On land suitable for poplars no other species will compete in rate of growth and the poplars will always be dominant. Mixtures of poplar and hazel or hazel with some other valuable timber tree seem entirely feasible. However, any other broadleaved tree grown in mixture with poplar will extend the silvoarable tree rotation from about 25 years to between 50 and 75 years.

Silvopastoral systems
Silvopastoral systems have fewer constraints on the spacing and layout of the trees compared to silvoarable systems because the requirements to provide access for large agricultural machines for tending and harvesting are not the same. Consequently, the layout can be more easily matched to the landowner's management objectives.

The NNE has shown that poorer growth and lower survival rates are associated with the widest spacing (10 m x 10 m, 100 trees per ha) when compared to higher density planting under the same grazing regime. At lower planting densities there will be more grazing animals per tree than at higher planting densities and consequently more soil compaction and tree damage (see Grazing pattern in Chapter 5). This presents the landowner with several options:

- plant at a higher density (the NNE found that 5 m x 5 m, 400 trees per ha, gave satisfactory results);
- reduce livestock numbers per ha;
- change grazing regime to a rotational grazing system (see Grazing pattern in Chapter 5);
- provide individual fencing to single trees to keep livestock away from the base of the trees;
- plant the trees in clumps and protect each clump with fencing.

Because of the flexibility of a silvopastoral system any number of combinations of spacing and layout can be employed to suit the landowner and site requirements. A mixture of clump and individual planting with varying protection options suited to the situation can be used. A planting density greater than 400 trees per ha might be planted with the intention of early selection or thinning. Clearly, the greater the planting density the greater the cost of establishing the system, and the earlier the impact of trees on the grazing sward (see Pasture growth in Chapter 5).

Protection

Silvoarable systems
Young trees are liable to be severely damaged by rabbits and hares eating bark and cambium on the lower stem and by rubbing and browsing by deer. Protection against rabbits and hares can be provided by a number of methods including fencing, treeshelters, plastic mesh guards and spiral tree guards. Of these methods spiral tree guards have proved to be effective on poplar sets. They are relatively cheap and easy to apply but

can fail to expand with radial growth, causing the tree to be strangled, and may not give sufficient protection with high rabbit populations. If herbicides are to be used close to the tree row more reliable protection will be provided by 1.2 m treeshelters secured with a stake to give protection against both careless herbicide application and rabbits. These will also protect against roe deer. Protection against fallow deer requires a 1.5 m tree guard. All tree guards must be removed before the tree grows to fill their internal diameter. For fast growing poplars this may only take two growing seasons. Young poplars provide good perches for pigeons, crows and rooks attracted to the food available within cropped alleys. Crows are the main offenders, visiting poplars during the summer period and being sufficiently heavy to break vigorous leading shoots. The provision of stable wooden perches, the destruction of crows and their nests and the use of bird scarers and similar devices are all mitigating possibilities.

Silvopastoral systems

A major factor in the economics of silvopastoral systems is the cost of protecting young trees, initially from browsing damage and later from bark stripping. Unprotected trees are damaged and often killed by browsing, and protection will normally be required for some time following planting (Nixon *et al.*, 1992). Various ways in which this protection can be provided are discussed below.

Treeshelters

Treeshelters offer a potentially cost-effective method of protecting young trees. A series of tree protection trials was set up in 1987 under the auspices of the Agroforestry Forum. The effectiveness of various methods of staking treeshelters in protecting trees from sheep and cattle was tested (Eason *et al.*, 1996). The results showed that:

- Animals tend to rub and crush treeshelters. The damage that occurs can significantly reduce the lifespan of the shelters to as little as 2 or 3 years. They will require renewal or replacement with an alternative system of protection.

- One robust supporting stake and a short secondary stake or pin at the front of the shelter to prevent turning has been shown to be a minimum requirement to protect trees from sheep (Plate 12). However, the use of two full-sized stakes can help reduce the rubbing and crushing damage and prolong the life of the shelters.

- Where cattle are being grazed, a single strand of barbed wire wrapped around the treeshelter also appears necessary to give adequate protection.

- Treeshelters need to be at least 1.5 m or 2.2 m tall to protect trees from sheep or cattle respectively.

In the NNE sites treeshelters have proven effective protection against sheep in the early years but appear to have modified the stem development of the conifer species (hybrid larch and Scots pine). These species have put on rapid height growth in the early years without commensurate girth. Consequently when the trees have emerged from the protection of the treeshelters and developed a crown the trees have become unstable in windy conditions leading to stem failure. Once bent or fractured in the stem the trees are accessible to the sheep which rapidly browse and strip the branches. On this evidence alternative protection systems should be used for conifer species in agroforestry systems.

Elaborate individual tree protection

Robust individual fences erected around each tree will obviously provide protection but they can be prohibitively expensive. Experiments have shown that attempts to reduce costs can lead to the use of materials that can be rendered ineffective by the heavy pressure they receive from sheep and cattle. An example is the use of rabbit netting. Even where strong supporting posts are used, sheep are quite capable of breaking through the net to obtain access to young trees. Although the cost of robust individual tree protection is high, the initial expenditure may be justified for low density planting because it will remain effective over a long time period (Plate 13 (a) and (b)).

Plastic mesh guards

Plastic mesh guards can be used to provide individual tree protection from planting or as a replacement for treeshelters to protect trees from sheep in the later stages of the establishment period. Guards of this material have been adopted for use in the NNE. Guards 1.5 m tall, 35 cm in diameter and with a mesh aperture size of approximately 3.5 cm x 2 cm were used to replace the original treeshelters as these became degraded. The net guards were staked with a large main stake and a smaller secondary stake (Plate 14). In use it became clear that the rough upper edge of the mesh guard was damaging the bark of the trees as they moved in the wind. Mesh guard material has been developed, and is recently available, which ensures a non-abrasive upper edge. This should help to reduce the problem.

Electric fencing
The use of electric fencing can be very cost-effective under circumstances where the reliability of the system can be ensured. However, individual tree protection is difficult and this form of protection is more appropriate for trees planted in groups, rows or belts. The main disadvantage of electric fencing is that, without a physical barrier, any failure in the power supply may lead to immediate catastrophic damage to trees.

Animal repellents
There are a number of products on the market, mainly originally developed for use against deer or other 'wild' animals. The use of a glue-based substance, impregnated with sharp sand particles ('Wobra') has proven effective in preventing damage from sheep to larch, ash and sycamore stems. A more comprehensive assessment of 'Wobra' was undertaken at the NNE site, Bronydd Mawr (Eason *et al.*, 1996) on 4-year-old ash and sycamore. This study indicated that 'Wobra' is effective at preventing damage from grazing livestock but its use would be limited to established trees. It may also not prove cost-effective on fast growing trees where frequent reapplication is required. However, it could form part of an integrated strategy for the protection of trees against herbivore damage in silvopastoral systems.

Animal husbandry
Whichever system of tree protection is employed, the management of the grazing animals can have an important role to play in minimising damage.

Such considerations as the choice of animal breed, the timing of release of the animals into the agroforestry areas, the duration and intensity of grazing, and supplementary feeding during harsh weather or periods of reduced pasture growth, are all important factors about which our knowledge is currently limited. Trials are currently being established in Northern Ireland by DARDNI to study some of these factors.

Formative pruning

The objective of formative pruning in agroforestry systems is to produce a single straight stem at least 5 m in height and free of branches, leaving it virtually defect free and able to attract a high market price (Kerr and Evans, 1993). This operation is important in agroforestry systems as a remedial treatment because wide spacing encourages poor form of many timber species. As every tree in an agroforestry system is potentially a final crop tree, an investment in this operation in the early years will significantly affect the marketability of the timber at harvest.

In general, species which lack apical dominance (e.g. oak, walnut) will require more formative pruning than those which are more apically dominant (e.g. poplar, ash, sycamore). Wild cherry has strong apical dominance but at wide spacing forms low, heavy branches that should be removed. However, all species will require formative pruning if damage occurs to the leading shoot. Such damage can occur from frost, strong winds and perching birds and can lead to double leaders and vigorously competing side branches.

The main priority is to remove forks and hence favour the best leader (see Figure 4.2). This will reduce the chances of a low, weak fork developing. The second priority is to remove disproportionately large branches from the tree crown. A large branch is one which at the point of connection with the main stem has a diameter of greater than 50% of the main stem diameter (see Figure 4.2). Ideally, branches removed in formative pruning should not be allowed to become too large to cut with a knife or a pair of secateurs; early intervention will prevent large wounds which can allow defects and decay to develop.

40

The treatment should start soon after establishment, and ideally be continued annually until the objective of a single straight stem of at least 5 m in height is satisfied. Figure 4.3 indicates for three potential agroforestry species, the times of year when it is best to prune (grey shading), e.g. cherry in July, and times when it is inadvisable to prune (no shading), e.g. ash in December. For further guidance on pruning of broadleaved species refer to Forestry Commission Handbook 9 *Growing broadleaves for timber* (Kerr and Evans, 1993).

Pruning of poplars

Poplars should be pruned progressively to develop a clean, branch-free lower stem of between 7 m and 10 m. Most poplars produce epicormic shoots on the main stem (especially *P. trichocarpa*) and these also must be removed during each pruning operation. In this way clean, knot-free timber is produced around a knotty core of between 5 cm and 15 cm diameter. The higher the pruning is taken up the stem the costlier each operation may become for progressively less knot-free timber. The upper limit of pruning will depend on management objectives: 6 m is the minimum, 8–9 m is the normal upper limit, but poplar can be pruned to 10 m to good effect.

Commercial hybrids of poplar develop a

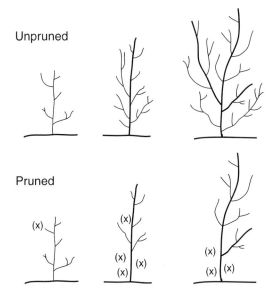

Unpruned

Pruned

Figure 4.2 Formative pruning; (x) indicates branch removed at pruning.

pronounced main whorl of up to seven branches at the beginning of each growing season with generally much smaller branches from mid-summer onwards, known as the interwhorl branches. Pruning can readily be related to this whorled branch formation by pruning to leave a specific number of whorls at about half the total tree height. The distance between whorls frequently varies and some degree of judgement is required. Only one whorl and interwhorl branches above it should be pruned in one season. As a rough guide, poplars may be pruned to leave two whorls in the third and fourth seasons, three whorls in the sixth and seventh seasons and four whorls in the ninth season. With very fast growing poplars some modification of this schedule may be required to maintain a reasonable crown depth to total height (never less than one-third).

It may also be beneficial to anticipate the development of very large branches in the next whorl above at each operation and to shorten or remove these in advance. The tendency is to prune too late and this should be strongly resisted. Delayed pruning of widely spaced poplars will lead to larger branch diameters at the time of pruning and consequently to higher costs, a reduction in the proportion of knot-free timber and a longer time for pruning wounds to heal.

Pruning may be carried out during the dormant season, when branch whorls are clearly visible, or from mid-June onwards throughout the rest of the growing season. The spring period from March through May should be avoided as poplar bark tissue peels away very easily at that time and strips of bark may be torn away from the stem immediately below the branch that is being pruned. Under silvoarable conditions pruning can most conveniently follow shortly after the adjacent arable crop harvest. Pruned branches are racked in the centre of each alley (or in alternate alleys) and can be chopped up by a tractor and haulm pulveriser, which is driven over the racks before autumn or winter ploughing. Pruning at other seasons may compromise arable cropping practices as branches can become lodged in standing crops.

Timely and regular pruning of poplars cannot be overstressed if the maximum potential of the tree crop is to be obtained. Higher pruning above 6 m

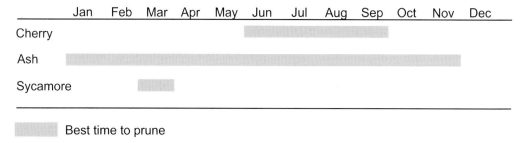

	Jan	Feb	Mar	Apr	May	Jun	Jul	Aug	Sep	Oct	Nov	Dec
Cherry							▓	▓				
Ash	▓	▓	▓							▓	▓	▓
Sycamore				▓								

▓ Best time to prune

Figure 4.3 Time to prune (adapted from Kerr and Evans, 1993).

requires the use of a hydraulic lift platform mounted on a tractor so that the operator can safely use a small petrol or hydraulic chain saw. From head height up to about 6 m, hand-held pruning saws with extending handles are probably the most efficient tool available (Plate 24). At each operation any development of epicormic shoots on the pruned section of the tree should also be removed. For maximum timber value epicormic shoots should never be allowed to grow beyond one year.

Key points on poplar pruning

- Prune poplars early, starting in second or third year.
- Never prune less than half or more than one-third of the total height of the tree.
- Never remove more than one whorl in a season.
- Prune to a minimum height of 6 m, maximum 9 m.
- Avoid pruning from March through May.

Pruning of conifer species

Conifer species grown at wide spacing will develop low heavy branches which will reduce timber quality. Though it has been shown that any removal of live branches reduces conifer increment (Møller, 1960), it is generally accepted that up to one-third of the green crown can be removed without significant reduction in growth. Any reduction in growth from pruning will be compensated by the improvement in timber quality.

REFERENCES

AUCLAIR, D. and CAILLIEZ, F. (1994). Les besoins de recherche en agroforesterie. *Revue forestière Française* **46**, Special Issue, 141–151.

BEATON, A. (1987). Poplars and agroforestry. *Quarterly Journal of Forestry* **81** (4), 225–233.

BEATON, A. (1988). *A new look at poplars and their role in agroforestry.* ICF Proceedings Broadleaves - Changing Horizons. Heriot Watt University, Edinburgh, 4–8.

BEATON, A. (1993). *A poplar revolution.* Shell Agriculture No. 17. Shell International Chemical Co. Ltd, London, 25–27.

BHIP (1999). Annual Conference. Proceedings of the British Hardwoods Improvement Programme, 9th November 1999, HRI, Wellesbourne, Warwickshire.

CUNDALL, E.P., CAHALAN, C.M. and PLOWMAN, M.R. (1998). Early results of sycamore (*Acer pseudoplatanus L.*) provenance trials at farm forestry sites in England and Wales. *Forestry* **71** (3), 237–245.

CUNDALL, E.P. (1999). Evaluation and selection of seed sources in British broadleaves. In: *Forest Research Annual Report and Accounts 1998–1999.* The Stationery Office, Edinburgh, 26–33.

EASON, W.R., GILL, E.K. and ROBERTS, J.E. (1996). Evaluation of anti-sheep tree-stem-protection products in silvopastoral agroforestry. *Agroforestry Systems* **34**, 259–264.

HAMMATT, N. (1995). Progress in HRI's genetic and propagation research with broadleaved farm woodland trees. *Agroforestry Forum* **6**(1), 40–45.

HIBBERD, B.G. (1991). *Forestry practice.* Forestry Commission Handbook 6. HMSO, London.

JOBLING, J. (1990). *Poplars for wood production and amenity*. Forestry Commission Bulletin 92. HMSO, London.

KERR, G. and EVANS, J. (1993). *Growing broadleaves for timber*. Forestry Commission Handbook 9. HMSO, London.

MØLLER, C.M. (1960). The influence of pruning on the growth of conifers. *Forestry* **33** (1), 37–53.

MORGAN, J. (1999). *Forest tree seedlings*. Forestry Commission Bulletin 121. Forestry Commission, Edinburgh.

NEWMAN, S.M. and WAINWRIGHT, J. (1989). An economic analysis of energy from biomass: poplar silvoarable systems compared to poplar monoculture. In: *Euroforum new energies*, vol. 3, Proceedings of International Congress at Saarbrucken, 1988. Stephens, Bedfordshire, 456–458.

NEWMAN, S.M., WAINWRIGHT, J., OLIVER, P. and ACWORTH, J.M. (1991a). *Walnut in the UK: History and current potential*. Proceedings 2nd North American Conference on Agroforestry, Missouri, USA, 95–115.

NEWMAN, S.M., WAINWRIGHT, J., OLIVER, P. and ACWORTH, J.M. (1991b). *Walnut in the UK: Research (1900-1991) assessed in relation to experience in other countries*. Proceedings 2nd North American Conference on Agroforestry, Missouri, USA, 74–94.

NIXON, C.J. ROGERS, D.G. and NELSON, D.G. (1992). *The protection of trees in silvopastoral agroforestry systems*. Research Information Note 219. Forestry Commission, Edinburgh.

PRYOR, S.N. (1988). *The silviculture and yield of wild cherry*. Forestry Commission Bulletin 75. HMSO, London.

PYATT, D. G. and SUÁREZ, J.C. (1997). *An ecological site classification for forestry in Great Britain*. Technical Paper 20. Forestry Commission, Edinburgh, UK

RUSSELL, K. (1996). *Progress in wild cherry improvement at Horticulture Research International, East Malling*. Woodland Heritage News, No. 2, Winter 1996, 20–21.

SIBBALD, A.R., EASON, W.R., MCADAM, J.H. and HISLOP, A.M. (in press). The establishment phase of a silvopastoral national network experiment in the UK. *Agroforestry Systems*.

TABBUSH, P. (1995). *Approved poplar clones*. Research Information Note 265. Forestry Commission, Edinburgh.

TABBUSH, P. (1999). *Approved poplar varieties*. Information Note 21. Forestry Commission, Edinburgh.

WILLOUGHBY, I. and CLAY, D. (1996). *Herbicides for farm woodlands and short rotation coppice*. Forestry Commission Field Book 14. HMSO, London.

WILLOUGHBY, I. and CLAY, D. (1999). *Herbicide update*. Technical Paper 28. Forestry Commission, Edinburgh.

FURTHER READING

Species choice
EVANS, J. (1984). *Silviculture of broadleaved woodland*. Forestry Commission Bulletin 62. HMSO, London.

Maintenance
WILLOUGHBY, I. and CLAY, D. (1996). *Herbicides for farm woodlands and short rotation coppice*. Forestry Commission Field Book 14. HMSO, London

Protection
POTTER, M.J. (1991). *Treeshelters*. Forestry Commission Handbook 7. HMSO, London.

NIXON, C.J., ROGER, D.G. and NELSON, D.G. (1992). *The protection of trees in silvopastoral agroforestry systems*. Forestry Commission Research Information Note 219. Forestry Authority, Edinburgh.

Pruning
KERR, G. and EVANS, J. (1993). *Growing broadleaves for timber*. Forestry Commission Handbook 9. HMSO, London.

JOBLING, J. (1990). *Poplars for wood production and amenity*. Forestry Commission Bulletin 92. HMSO, London.

Pests and diseases
HIBBERD, B.G., ed. (1988). *Farm woodland practice*. Forestry Commission Handbook 3. HMSO, London.

Chapter 5
Grazing livestock management

Jim McAdam and Alan Sibbald

Introduction

If silvopastoral systems are to be adopted, detailed information on output and quality of livestock must be available for all stages of maturity of the trees. This chapter looks at current practice, research results and experience from temperate silvopastoral systems with respect to sward establishment, grassland management and grazing systems. The overall impact of agroforestry systems on the level of animal production, both predicted and demonstrated are also presented.

Many of the guidelines on grazing livestock management have emerged from the Silvopastoral National Network Experiment (NNE) (see Chapter 2 and Hoppé *et al.*, 1996). In this experiment a common set of treatments was used to quantify all aspects of the output of the system (Sibbald and Sinclair, 1990; Hoppé *et al.*, 1996). These were sycamore (*Acer pseudoplatanus*) planted at two spacings (5 m x 5 m: 400 trees ha^{-1} and 10 m x 10 m: 100 trees ha^{-1}; Plate 15) compared with a woodland (2500 trees ha^{-1}) and an agricultural control (no trees) using common management protocols (sheep-grazed pasture managed to a constant sward height profile, trees given standard stock protection and pruning) and integrated measurement, recording and analysis programmes.

Sward establishment

The advantages of reseeding pastures in terms of yield and quality of herbage produced have been clearly documented. However, at low levels of fertiliser application, permanent pastures containing a complex mixture of indigenous grassland species can give yields comparable to perennial ryegrass (*Lolium perenne*) pastures (Frame,

1992). In this case, the inclusion of white clover (*Trifolium repens*) is recommended to enhance herbage quality through fixing atmospheric nitrogen (see the section on grass–clover below).

Sward duration

In the first eight years of a ryegrass-based reseed under a silvopastoral system (5 m x 5 m: 400 trees ha^{-1}) pasture composition and production were unchanged by the presence of the trees (McAdam and Hoppé, 1996a, 1996b). At this stage the vertical projection of the tree canopy on the sward was 15–22% of the total area.

In older, permanent pastures, juvenile tree cover has little effect on sward composition other than to provide naturally occurring bare areas which can act as foci for successional invasion by a range of species. Levels of livestock production from pastures within the NNE can be compared. Two lowland sites with the highest output were reseeded immediately prior to the establishment of the trials and have a high proportion of ryegrass, whereas on another site, the trees were planted into an older permanent pasture and production was lower.

There is little information available on the long-term performance of swards in mature silvopastoral systems. However, in a 35-year-old, mature poplar stand planted at 8 m x 8 m spacing (156 trees ha^{-1}) into grazed, permanent pasture, species composition was significantly different under the tree canopy than in an open sward (Crowe and McAdam, 1992; Plate 16). Species such as perennial ryegrass, rough-stalked meadow grass (*Poa trivialis*), white clover and creeping thistle (*Cirsium arvense*) were prevalent in the open pasture whereas creeping bent (*Agrostis capillaris*), Yorkshire fog (*Holcus lanatus*) and annual meadow grass (*Poa annua*) performed better under the tree canopy. Of particular interest was the alteration in seasonal pattern of growth of these grass species under the trees, with increased production before tree leaf appearance and after fall. This 'compensation' and adaptation resulted in annual levels of production being maintained at a relatively high level. This result is important as it gives some indication of the likely responses of mixed-species pasture in mature silvopastoral systems and shows that criteria for grassland management to maximise herbage production will need to be different to those used in conventional pasture.

In New Zealand, both reseeded and permanent pastures have been used in silvopastoral systems involving radiata pine (*Pinus radiata*). In most reported trials (e.g. Percival and Knowles, 1988) trees were planted into permanent pasture, but in other examples (e.g. Pollock *et al.*, 1994), pastures were established simultaneously with tree planting. In some situations in Chile, poplar plantations are first established, then the soil is cultivated and an oversown grass crop established. This is cut for forage for 2–3 years after sowing and subsequently grazed by cattle. Levels of utilisation of the pastures are lower in this system than if the new grass had been grazed from the start.

The two upland sites in the NNE, at Glensaugh (north-east Scotland) and Bronydd Mawr (mid-Wales), are on pasture reseeded a considerable time (12 to 20 years) before the trees were planted. On a third upland site affiliated to the NNE at Broughshane (Northern Ireland), reseeded grass/clover pasture with low N and grass-based pasture with moderate/high N were compared. There were no significant differences in annual pasture production between the agricultural control treatment and agroforestry treatments after eight years of tree cover at either Bronydd Mawr or Glensaugh with 160 kg N ha^{-1} year^{-1}. Hence there was no indication that permanent pasture responded any less well under an agroforestry system than in open pasture. At Broughshane, the benefits of reseeding were only seen where levels of fertilisers were relatively high (160 kg N ha^{-1} year^{-1}). At low levels of nitrogen application, output was similar from both the reseeded and unimproved permanent pasture.

However there is evidence that pasture change will occur at a different rate where trees are present. Such a change may not be wholly detrimental as pasture species appear to exhibit flexibility in seasonal patterns of growth which may make mixed swards more adaptable within a silvopastoral system.

Species selection

Although not specifically examined in species or variety trials of grasses or legumes under shade conditions in the UK, it appears that conventional seed mixtures involving ryegrass as the primary constituent are suitable for use in silvopastoral systems. Where broadleaved trees are planted consider the inclusion of seeds of early-flowering varieties in the mixture to exploit the period before the tree leaf canopy emerges and shading becomes a potential constraint to pasture growth. However such varieties are often difficult to manage in the early season. Grass mixtures should be sown at approximately 35 kg ha^{-1}.

Grass–clover

Clover has the ability to fix atmospheric nitrogen which can be transferred to the grass component of a mixed sward. Clover is higher in protein than grass. Currently, there is an increasing trend towards low-input systems and, in the case of grassland, the inclusion of clover in seeds mixtures is seen as a more environmentally friendly and sustainable system than the regular application of nitrogen fertiliser. Clover forms a significant component of the upland pastures at Glensaugh and at Bronydd Mawr despite the application of 160 kg N ha^{-1} year^{-1} and relatively high levels of animal production have been achieved at both sites. At Broughshane, where direct comparisons are possible, clover-based swards receiving 60 kg N ha^{-1} support less grazing than pure grass swards receiving 160 kg N ha^{-1} and without clover (McAdam, 1996a). There are indications from Chile (Balocchi, personal communication) that legumes such as *Trifolium subterranean* and *Lotus corniculatus* can perform well and persist under a mature radiata pine/sheep silvopastoral system. In a New Zealand radiata pine system, for the first three years after sowing, yields of ryegrass and ryegrass– clover pasture were similar (Pollock et al., 1994).

There is no information on the most suitable variety to use but because of their distribution in the sward canopy, small-leaved white clovers are more likely to perform better under shade conditions. A minimum sowing rate of $2^1/_2$–3 kg ha^{-1} is recommended for clover.

Cultivation

If the sward is to be renovated or upgraded, it is better to carry out cultivation before the trees are planted. Cultivation was carried out on two of the lowland NNE sites at Loughgall and Bangor (University of Wales) and no problems were encountered with sward establishment when trees were planted in the following season. Evidence from the silvoarable network trials with poplar (*Populus* spp.) showed that cultivation can be carried out each season to within 0.75 m of the tree without any adverse effects (Beaton *et al.*, 1996). In Chile, rotary cultivation and surface seeding of grass under 3-year-old poplar to be used for a silvopastoral system has proved successful. In Radnor Forest, Wales, pasture was successfully introduced (after cultivation and undersowing of grass with forage kale) under re-spaced semi-mature larch, although establishment was slow (Danby, personal communication). On the other hand, there are indications from the NNE sites that soil compaction reduces tree root growth and Eason *et al.* (1994) reported that roots of young sycamore and ash trees are concentrated in the top 10 cm of soil for up to 5 years after planting. Hence the number of cultivation and vehicle passes should be minimised, but there is no indication that a moderate amount of root pruning causes any harm and indeed may help the firm establishment of trees. Techniques such as strip seeding or direct drilling would merit investigation in this situation.

Sowing and early management

If the pasture is being established before tree planting, normal, clearly defined rules for pasture establishment can be followed. These have been well summarised by Frame (1992); see Table 5.1. If sowing is carried out in autumn, provided sward

Table 5.1 Essential guidelines for sward establishment before tree planting.

- Soil pH (5.8–6.0) and soil P status should be satisfactory.
- Apply water-soluble P_2O_5 at sowing.
- Seedbed should be fine and firm.
- Direct sowing gives the best results.
- If undersowing, preferably cut cover crops for arable silage.
- Avoid midsummer sowing since soil moisture will be limiting.
- If sowing in late season, adhere to mid August deadline.
- Control any problem weeds as soon as possible.
- Graze down to 3 to 6 cm at intervals during early establishment phase.
- Grazing is better than cutting in the year following sowing.
- Aim for about 6000 tillers m^{-2} in spring of year after sowing.

establishment is satisfactory, tree planting should be delayed as late as possible into the winter to minimise trampling and wheel damage to the sward.

Application of lime to correct low pH is best carried out well in advance of both sward establishment and tree planting. A prior, representative soil analysis of the area to be reseeded should be carried out. The normal target pH for grassland is 5.8–6.0 and lime should be applied to achieve this. A typical seedbed fertiliser application for direct sowing into moderately fertile soil would be 60 kg N, 75 kg P_2O_5 and 60 kg K_2 kg ha^{-1} (Frame, 1992).

The nitrogen application should be reduced with later sowing and omitted if clover is to be included in the mixture. Phosphorus is the key nutrient for grass sward establishment and there are indications from foliar analyses of trees on the NNE sites that it may become limiting to trees early in their life cycle (see Establishment in Chapter 4). The eventual achievement of a densely tillered, leafy sward canopy is facilitated by light grazing rather than cutting and by avoiding poaching or trampling damage.

Grassland management

Defoliation and fertility are the key factors in the management of grassland swards and this is no different for swards in silvopastoral systems. In a mature tree stand, factors such as shading, moisture status and tree-induced animal behaviour modifications may change pasture composition and the resultant species mixture should be exploited by greater utilisation in spring and autumn than in summer (Crowe, 1993).

Defoliation

In establishing silvopastoral systems, the guidelines for sward defoliation are essentially the same as for any grass crop. Grass can be cut for hay or silage if the topography and tree planting configuration will permit it, although swards which are only cut and not grazed at any time in the year will have a low tiller density and are likely to deteriorate in quality and yield.

To avoid a decline in grass yields, the continual removal of nutrients from the system in hay or silage must be matched with regular fertiliser application. Removing the grass crop by cutting would circumvent some of the problems of tree protection and interactions between livestock and trees (see Cultivation, page 46), but the lack of flexibility in the system for small livestock farmers and the effects on sward deterioration are adverse. As previously mentioned, in Chile pasture is cut for 2–3 years following oversowing and prior to extensive grazing. In New Zealand, Pollock *et al.* (1994) showed that forage harvesting in young pine plantations is possible on land of suitable topography, provided tree spacings and headlands are planned carefully to suit the machinery used. Timber growing with cut forage is also a land-use option in conditions where the soil is contaminated with high levels of undesirable chemicals, as on spoil heaps and industrial waste sites.

Extensive research has been carried out on the management of pasture under livestock grazing. Much of this research has been synthesised into a series of pasture management guidelines based on maintaining a predetermined sward height profile throughout the grazing season (see Figure 5.1). This may differ slightly between upland and lowland swards but is essentially based on the concept of maintaining the maximum leaf area of the sward while minimising losses through senescence, particularly by retaining the sward in a vegetative state. The derived guidelines for target sward heights throughout the season (see Table 5.2) for sheep grazing have been successfully adopted in the NNE on upland and lowland sites.

Adherence to these guidelines has resulted in the maintenance of swards with productive plant species which are giving highly satisfactory levels of output (e.g. individual lamb growth rates from birth to weaning of 290 and 250 g head^{-1} day^{-1} for lowland (Northern Ireland) and upland (north-east Scotland) sites respectively (Sibbald and Agnew, 1996), and no evidence of significant change in species composition up to eight years after planting (McAdam and Hoppé, 1996b).

The duration of the grazing period is very dependent on the soil type, the natural drainage of the site and the prevailing weather conditions, however, poaching of the sward by animals should be avoided. It is also desirable to graze swards down in the autumn to encourage clover stolon development and to prevent the accumulation of a fund of grass over winter which subsequently senesces, creates conditions which encourage pests and diseases, and reduces pasture growth in the following spring.

Fertiliser application

There is a wealth of information on the effect of fertilisers on pasture growth and composition, but almost none on the effect on trees in agroforestry systems. With increasing rates of fertiliser N applied to a grass sward, herbage production increases linearly in a response of about 15–25 kg

Table 5.2 Target range of sward surface heights for continuous stocking systems.

Stock	Sward surface height (cm)
Sheep (spring and summer)	
Dry ewes	3–4
Ewes and lambs (medium growth rate)	4–5
Ewes and lambs (high growth rate)	5–6
Sheep (autumn)	
Store lambs	4–6
Finishing lambs	6–8
Flushing ewes	6–8
Cattle	
Dry cows	6–8
Store cattle	6–8
Dairy replacements	6–8
Finishing cattle	7–9
Cows and calves	7–9
Dairy cows	7–10

Source: Hodgson *et al.* (1986).

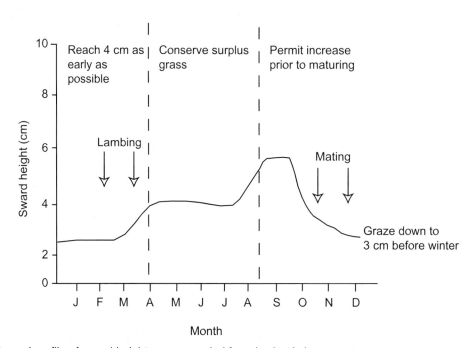

Figure 5.1 Annual profile of sward height recommended for a lowland sheep system.

DM kg N^{-1} applied up to an annual rate of 250–350 kg N ha^{-1} (Morrison *et al.*, 1980; Plate 17). The magnitude of the response is largely determined by soil and climatic conditions and assumes no limitation due to lack of water. The seasonal distribution of the response of pasture to applied N has been calculated for south-west Scotland (Frame *et al.*, 1989) and ranges from 5–15 kg DM kg N^{-1} in April and October to 30–40 kg DM kg N^{-1} in June. Levels of P, K and S applied to pasture are best determined following a soil analysis.

There is little information on the growth and nutrition of trees growing on relatively fertile sites and how they might interact with grass in fertilised silvopastoral systems. In the NNE, 160 kg N ha^{-1} yr^{-1} is applied in four applications and levels of dry matter output in the order of 6–8 t ha^{-1} (McAdam and Hoppé, 1996a) are possible. At these fertiliser levels, considered to be at the upper range of application for hill swards and at the lower range for lowland swards, there appear to be no adverse effects on tree growth although levels of P in the foliage of ash and sycamore are lower than that recommended by the Forestry Commission as optimum for tree growth (Binns *et al.*, 1989). However, these recommendations are not for widely spaced trees in a silvopastoral situation and relatively little is known about the reponse of broadleaved trees to nutrients.

In the upland NNE site at Broughshane, agroforests (400 sycamore trees ha^{-1}) received either 60 kg N ha^{-1} (grass/clover) or the NNE standard 160 kg N ha^{-1}. Total livestock carrying capacity was approximately 29% and 35% greater at the higher fertiliser level in both 1994 and 1995 respectively, although individual lamb growth rates were almost 18% lower in both years (McAdam, 1996b). Tree growth was unaffected by the fertiliser application.

At Glensaugh, a field study of the growth and nutrition of widely spaced wild cherry trees planted into a continuously grazed pasture under different fertiliser N treatments was carried out (Campbell *et al.*, 1994). In a dry year, tree growth was significantly reduced by high N application and in a wet year, trees appeared to respond to high N supply only when grass competition was

controlled by herbicide in a 1 m diameter spot around each tree. Higher grass growth in the high N treatments resulted in greater soil moisture deficits. Hence, there may be scope to use fertilisers to optimise tree growth and account should be taken of prevailing weather conditions before applying fertiliser. At Bangor red alder (*Alnus rubra*), a nitrogen fixing tree species, has been used in conjunction with a grass/clover sward. Hence, at this site, a low-input system relying on biologically fixed nitrogen is being compared with fertilised pasture under sycamore (Teklehaimanot and Sinclair, 1996). The experiment started in 1992 and by 1995 the performance of the system relying on biological N-fixation was not significantly inferior to the higher input system.

In other temperate countries where silvopastoral systems are practised, fertiliser is generally not applied as the livestock components of the system are secondary to the trees. In silvoarable systems in the UK, normal fertiliser applications to cereal crops do not appear to affect the tree growth form, but an evaluation of yield and timber quality has yet to be made (Beaton *et al.*, 1996).

Analyses of foliage from the NNE experiment (Table 5.3) have shown mean foliar nutrient levels to be unaffected by treatment. Also in comparison to a zero fertiliser treatment (woodland control), the evidence is that even with consistent, relatively high levels of fertiliser applied to silvopastoral systems, nutrients from fertilisers are not being taken up by the trees and are not causing adverse effects on tree growth form.

Weed control

The maintenance of weed-free zones around the trees and the reduction of competition between the tree and pasture are described in Chapter 4. The maintenance of this weed-free zone for a period of several years after planting could be seen to act as a focus for reinvasion by aggressive pasture weed species though this may occur to varying extents (McAdam and Hoppé, 1996b). This reinvasion appears to depend on the age of the pasture and possibly the buried seed bank, with 'younger' pasture (as at the Loughgall NNE site) resulting in recolonisation by the aggressive

Table 5.3 The effect of two agroforestry treatments (100 and 400 trees ha-1) all receiving 160 kg N ha-1 yr-1 and a woodland control (2500 trees ha-1) receiving no fertiliser on foliar concentrations of nutrients (4–8 years after planting) of ash and sycamore. Data are from all NNE sites (except ash* which are from Loughgall and North Wyke only) and represent a wide spread of locations.

Treatment (trees ha-1)	%N	%P	%K	%Mg	%Ca	%Na
100 Sycamore	2.29	0.16	1.02	0.25	1.59	0.05
400 Sycamore	2.34	0.17	1.05	0.27	1.73	0.04
2500 Sycamore	2.13	0.20	1.06	0.26	1.80	0.03
Mean sycamore	2.25	0.18	1.04	0.26	1.71	0.04
*Mean ash	1.65	0.18	1.32	0.40	2.27	0.04

and persistent sown species. As with most grassland, weeds may occur in the sward at a level where their impact on production is considered such that they should be controlled. The use of foliar acting herbicides would need to be carried out with caution as spray drift could affect the trees. The use of a wick applicator (the 'Weed Wiper') should be considered and if chemicals must be sprayed, spot spraying or application early in the season before bud-break occurs is recommended. Residual, soil-acting herbicides such as those based on atrazine or simazine should not be used. Leaving a weed-free zone encourages early, rapid tree growth (e.g. Culleton *et al.*, 1996). The guidelines for herbicide application to agricultural crops should be followed at this stage though some reference to forestry practice is advised (e.g. Willoughby and Clay, 1996) to consider tree species susceptibility.

Pasture deterioration

As stated earlier in the section on sward duration, over the life history of silvopastoral systems, there is every likelihood that pasture change will occur (Crowe, 1993). There is no evidence that this change would not have occurred as part of the normal successional dynamics of grazed pasture and the NNE is at too early a stage to detect such changes, although the experimental design will allow such a comparision to be made. It has already been shown that only limited pasture change is occurring in swards in the NNE (McAdam and Hoppé, 1996b), and there is some

evidence that these changes are induced by the presence of the trees.

Silvopastoral systems offer more options for management of the understorey vegetation either directly through sward and livestock management or indirectly through tree species selection and canopy manipulation than with conventional grazing livestock systems. Guidelines on grassland management for nature conservation are being researched (Haggar and Peel, 1994) and these can be adapted to suit silvopastoral systems though the imposition of a tree canopy will create further ecological conditions which will influence sward management decisions.

The extent and duration of maintenance of the weed-free zone around the tree base represents an area to manipulate vegetation diversity to some extent, though early results on the efficacy of this are variable. Tree species have specific characteristics of shade, branch and leaf architecture which will affect light reaching the pasture and which can be manipulated by pruning. The variable quality and effect of leaf litter can also be considered in relation to sward effects. From the very limited work carried out on animal behaviour and on mature systems, it is clear that pasture changes are likely to occur and that animal effects may well be a major determinant of these changes. Many of these aspects are being monitored and researched within the current NNE experiment, but there is a need to extend the range of configurations of tree planting, tree species, pasture types and grazing animals so that the likely effect of systems on understorey vegetation can be predicted and management approached on a more objective basis.

Grazing systems

Stock type

Most research on establishing silvopastoral systems in temperate regions has been carried out using sheep as the grazing animal. This choice is largely because of the necessity to protect trees in the early stages of the system and the difficulty of protection against larger stock, such as horses or cattle. Protection of individual trees against cattle has been demonstrated (Nixon *et al.*, 1992) but is costly and should probably only be considered in the context of widely-spaced specimen trees. The use of rows of trees protected from cattle by electric fencing might also be considered, but any such system would need to be completely reliable. The use of pigs and poultry has been considered (Brownlow *et al.*, 1993) and geese represent a further possibility. Pigs would be best considered in relation to an established system or for woodland grazing as they could cause disruption of root systems through their grubbing and a permanent form of protection against bark stripping might have to be considered.

As with the grazing system adopted, the choice of species or breed of grazing animal should not be seen as a permanent feature for the lifetime of the system. Restrictions in choice are likely during establishment, but once the trees are established, the available range of grazing species becomes greater. Some herbivores may not bark-strip trees as readily as others and this might have a bearing on the overall decision. Based on current knowledge and research, it seems best to establish systems using sheep as the grazing animal with the possibility of cattle being introduced at a later stage. The benefits of mixed grazing systems involving sheep and cattle grazing pasture have been clearly demonstrated (Nolan and Connolly, 1989).

Grazing pattern

A continuous grazing system has been adopted in the NNE. This involves grazing throughout the season with the date of stock going onto and coming off the grazed areas being dictated by the prevailing soil and weather conditions and the availability of pasture. This system has worked reasonably well in the NNE, although there have been no scientific comparisons with other grazing systems. One of the consistent observations from this series of trials has been that trees at the wider spacing (10 m x 10 m, 100 trees ha^{-1}) have grown and survived less well than those planted at closer spacing (5 m x 5 m, 400 trees ha^{-1}) and, therefore, greater density. Preliminary research (Sibbald *et al.*, 1995, 1996) indicates that this reduced growth is due to factors resulting from the modification of animal behaviour by the presence of the trees. Sheep will congregate around trees, rest under them, defecate and urinate around them to a greater degree than in the inter-tree areas (Sibbald and Agnew, 1996). This increases soil compaction around the base of the trees (Laws *et al.*, 1992; Wairiu *et al.*, 1993; Eason *et al.*, 1994). At the lower planting density (10 m x 10 m, 100 trees ha) compaction is significantly greater than at 5 m x 5 m, 400 trees ha^{-1} because there are more sheep per tree than at the higher planting density and this is probably a contributing factor to reduced growth. Another problem is the greater extent of damage to treeshelters at lower tree planting densities.

When the same group of animals is grazing a sward continuously and to a constant sward height, the opportunity for the development of such modifications to behaviour is far greater than, for instance, in a rotational grazing system. In rotational grazing, livestock graze down accumulated herbage to a predetermined height in a particular area before being moved to another, previously rested area. The livestock would be present in a particular field for a relatively short period of time and may not develop particular behavioural patterns in relation to the trees there. There is evidence from New Zealand that rotational grazing, which is practised much more than in the UK, can be carried out with minimal impact on the trees by stock, possibly through the short time available to the sheep to become 'familiarised' with the trees. Such a rotational grazing system would require more intensive stock management but could be economically viable if reduction in damage to treeshelters and enhanced tree growth resulted in greater tree survival.

Pasture growth

Most research into pasture production in temperate agroforestry systems has found a limited effect of trees at low to moderate spacings (50–400 trees ha^{-1}) on pasture production, until the trees are about 8–10 years old (Knowles, 1991; Percival and Knowles, 1988; Sibbald and Agnew, 1996). In computer-based predictions for lowland sites, Doyle *et al.* (1986) estimated that at 400 trees ha^{-1}, pasture production would have decreased to about 50% of that in an 'open' sward without trees by about year 20. This prediction was more pessimistic than the predictions of a computer model of an upland silvopastoral system (Sibbald *et al.*, 1987) which showed a reduction of less than 20% in pasture production after 20 years. A more recent model of the biophysical and bioeconomic components (Bergez *et al.*, 1999), and based partly on the findings from the NNE, has indicated no decrease until years 10–12 and a total reduction over 20 years of less than 15% of production in an 'open' sward.

At wide spacings, 250 trees ha^{-1} thinned to 50 trees ha^{-1} in New Zealand, pasture production under radiata pine was only reduced by 15% after 13 years. At closer spacings (500 trees ha^{-1} thinned to 100 trees ha^{-1} and 1000 trees ha^{-1} thinned to 200 trees ha^{-1}) production was reduced by 50% and 82%, respectively (Percival and Knowles, 1988).

Levels of pasture production in silvopastoral systems in the NNE have not declined over the first five or six years after establishment (Table 5.4) in either a very wet year (year 5) or a very dry year (year 6) at Loughgall. During the drier year (1995, year 6) pasture yields were reduced in the vicinity of the trees in the 10 m x 10 m, 100 trees ha^{-1} treatment (McAdam and Hoppé, 1996a). The previously described effect of animal behaviour on tree growth may additionally apply to swards when conditions are dry. Campbell (1989) found a different result at Glensaugh where growth of grass around trees was enhanced in dry periods. The pasture was cut and not grazed in this trial, highlighting the importance of the animal–tree interaction on the biology of the system.

In New Zealand, Pollock *et al.* (1994) found that in a high density planting of radiata pine (3.2 m x 3.2 m, 1000 trees ha^{-1}), pasture production was not reduced in the first 3 years of the trial, other than that accounted for by the 14% loss in area due to the weed-free planting strips. In the third summer pasture growth was reduced by as much as 40% within 1 m of trees. A model relating relative pasture yield to crown length of radiata pine has been produced by Percival and Knowles (1983 and 1988).

In a mature agroforestry system, Crowe (1993) found that pasture production under 25-year-old *Populus euramericana 'Serotina'* growing at 240 trees ha^{-1} (on a uniform diagonal spacing) was 50% of the value in the open pasture. The trees had also induced significant changes in pasture botanical composition and in the seasonal pattern of pasture production. Seasonal variation in

Table 5.4 Annual pasture production (t DM ha^{-1}) measured in areas protected from grazing in agroforestry and agricultural treatments at the NNE site, Loughgall in 1994 (year 5) and 1995 (year 6)

Treatment	Tree age (years)	
	5 (wet)	6 (dry)
100 trees ha^{-1}	8.12	6.3
400 trees ha^{-1}	10.8	5.0
Agricultural control	8.0	5.9

pasture production has been measured in another experiment in the UK. This research demonstrated greater pasture production below silvopastoral tree canopies than in the open in early spring and late autumn (Sibbald *et al.*, 1991). If these seasonal increases can be shown to be a general feature of silvopastoral systems in the UK, there may be advantages to sheep farmers through provision of extra herbage at lambing in spring and around mating in the autumn in addition to the direct benefits of shelter to livestock which the trees can confer (Fenn *et al.*, 1991; Pritchard, 1992) at these times (Green *et al.*, 1990; McArthur, 1991; Sibbald, 1992; Sibbald, 1996).

Livestock production

The clear indication from the NNE silvopastoral experiment is that up to 9 years after planting of trees, livestock production (Sibbald and Agnew, 1996) and quality (carcass composition) of output (McAdam and Hoppé, 1997) are unaffected by the presence of trees at spacings up to 5 m x 5 m, 400 trees ha^{-1}.

On both lowland and upland sites, approximate stocking rates of 15–20 ewes ha^{-1} can result in annual liveweight carried over the grazing season of approximately 250 tonne-days ha^{-1}. Stocking densities of this order can lead to individual lamb growth rates of 270 g day^{-1}, which are highly acceptable levels of agricultural production.

Bergez *et al.* (1999) has predicted the fall-off in livestock carrying capacity as broadleaved trees mature from recent models synthesising data from EC-wide sources (Figures 5.2 and 5.3). In predictions from New Zealand based on rapidly growing radiata pine, the effect on livestock carrying capacity is more extreme (Percival and Knowles, 1988), although the primary aim of these systems is sawlog production and pastures are not managed as intensively as those upon which the Bergez *et al.* (1999) prediction is based.

Behavioural aspects

Modification of the behaviour of grazing stock by the presence of trees has been observed (Sibbald *et al.*, 1995; Sibbald *et al.*, 1996) and is related to the density of the trees. The use of the trees for shelter and the greater number of sheep per tree at low planting densities have reduced tree growth and survival. This effect probably operates through greater soil compaction around the trees caused by increased animal foot pressure. Another effect of change in animal behaviour appears to be a spatial redistribution of soil nutrients, probably through returns of dung and urine (Nwaigbo *et al.*, 1995; Nwaigbo, 1996). These effects are likely to increase as the trees mature and further stress will be placed on the sward surrounding the trees. Changes in the pattern of distribution of soil nutrients may result

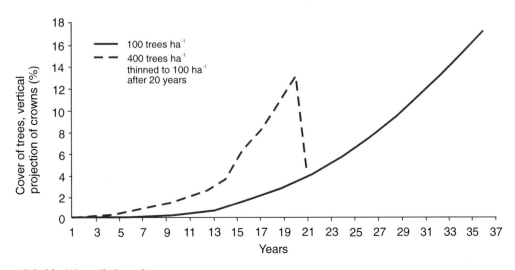

Figure 5.2 Model prediction of tree cover.

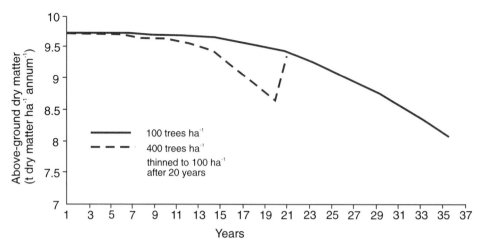

Figure 5.3 Model prediction of pasture production.

in further changes in patterns of species composition and pasture production. These changes may be ameliorated by the adoption of alternative grazing systems (e.g. rotational grazing) which will modify patterns of animal behaviour.

The shelter effect of the trees and their protective guards on the NNE sites, although not substantial at present, will enhance the environment within the system by reducing wind speed and by increasing shading from the sun. A reduction of 15% in wind speed at sheep body height in a 7-year-old agroforestry system planted at 400 trees ha[-1] (Hoppé, *et al.*, 1997) was found on a lowland site. On an upland site with 19-year-old (7.7 m average height) Sitka spruce (*Picea sitchensis*) pruned up to 1.5 m, reductions in wind speed of 54%, 71% and 84% at 156, 278 and 625 trees ha[-1] respectively were measured (Green *et al.*, 1995). The potential benefits of shelter on mature sites, and particularly on upland sites where the reduction in wind speed could make a significant contribution to livestock welfare and performance (Fenn *et al.*, 1991; McArthur, 1991; Pritchard, 1992) may become an important factor in encouraging the uptake of silvopastoral systems.

Integration into farming systems

One of the strengths of silvopastoral systems is their flexibility compared to conventional farm woodland planting. The concept of multipurpose use of land with the added flexibility of selective and uneven aged harvesting and planting make the system adaptable to a wide range of scenarios. The value of mixed-species planting leading to the early harvest of the more rapidly growing tree species is a further advantage. The option to cut grass for hay or silage, perhaps in the early stages of the system, and to graze either continuously or rotationally with a wider range of stock types in more mature systems means that silvopastoral systems can be integrated into most livestock and mixed farms with little inconvenience. The use of a silvoarable system (see Chapter 7) in the tree establishment phase of the cycle to alleviate tree protection and tree–animal interaction problems is a further measure of flexibility and could facilitate integration into a wider range of systems over a wide range of site types.

Key points in grazing systems

- The type of grazing system adopted should not be seen as fixed throughout the life span of the system. During the tree establishment phase a wide variety of alternatives such as rotational grazing, zero grazing, silvoarable and fallow, might be implemented. Once the trees are mature, the system becomes more robust and the range of stock types and grazing options become greater.

- The levels of pasture production in deciduous silvopastoral systems can be expected to be maintained at comparable levels to 'open' pasture for 10–15 years provided the tree density is in the order 100–400 trees ha^{-1}. With evergreen conifers, a greater reduction might be expected.

- High levels of livestock production under intensive management are possible in silvopastoral systems. A range of factors, such as tree species, moisture regime and planting density will determine the rate at which livestock carrying capacity will decline with time.

- Stock will be attracted to the trees in silvopastoral systems and this will affect tree growth, pasture composition and production in a variety of ways.

- The objectives for agroforestry on any farm unit must be clearly defined. Once this has been done, the range of options available and the flexibility demonstrated by even the limited range of systems currently tested indicate that silvopastoral systems can be integrated into most farming systems.

Conclusions

Although silvopastoral systems have been tried and tested on only a very limited scale and the knowledge of their complex biology and their outputs is limited, it is clear that they can offer a viable land-use option. It is also clear that the skills and expertise involved in successful grassland management are applicable to silvopastoral systems and that the presence of the tree component offers an additional level of flexibility which a system manager could exploit to maximise output from all components of the system.

REFERENCES

BEATON, A., BURGESS, P.J., STEPHENS, W., INCOLL, L.D., CORRY D.T. and EVANS, R.J. (1996). Silvoarable trial with poplar. *Agroforestry Forum* 7 (1), 18–19.

BERGEZ, J-E., ÉTIENNE, M. and BALANDIER, P. (1999). ALWAYS: a plot-based silvopastoral system model. *Ecological Modelling* 115, 1–17.

BINNS, W.O., INSLEY, H. and GARDINER, J.B.H. (1989). *Nutrition of broadleaved amenity trees. 1. Foliar sampling and analysis for determining nutrient status.* Arboricultural Research Note 50/89/555. DOE Arboricultural Advisory and Information Service, Forestry Commission, Edinburgh.

BROWNLOW, M.J.C., DORWARD, P.T. and CARRUTHERS, S.P. (1993). The integration of pigs and poultry with forestry: practice, theory and economics. *Agroforestry Forum* 4 (3), 51–57.

CAMPBELL, C.D. (1989). The importance of root interaction for grassland trees in a silvopastoral system. *Aspects of Applied Biology* 22, 155–161.

CAMPBELL, C.D., ATKINSON, D., JARVIS, P.G. and NEWBOULD, P. (1994). Effects of nitrogen fertiliser on tree/pasture competition during the establishment phase of a silvopastoral system. *Annals of Applied Biology* 124:83–96.

CROWE, S.R. (1993). The response of *Lolium perenne* and *Holcus lanatus* to shading in relation to a silvopastoral agroforestry system. PhD Thesis. Department of Applied Plant Science, Queens University of Belfast.

CROWE, S.R. and MCADAM J.H. (1992). Some effects of grazing management on a mixed species sward poplar-sheep agroforestry system. In: *Proceedings of the 14th General Meeting of the European Grassland Federation, Lahti, Finland,* 655–656.

CULLETON, N., MURPHY, W.E. and HICKS, R.R. Jnr (1996). Competition control for establishment of ash *(Fraxinus excelsior)* on lowland soils in Ireland. *Irish Forestry* 52 (1 and 2), 88–94.

DOYLE, C.J., EVANS, J. and ROSSITER, J. (1986). Agroforestry: an economic appraisal of the benefits of intercropping trees with grassland in lowland Britain. *Agricultural Systems* **21,** 1–32.

EASON, W.R., SIMPSON, J., SHELDRICK, R.D., HAGGAR, R.J., GILL, E.K., LAWS, J.A., JONES, D., ASTERAKI, E., BOWLING, P., HOUSSAIT-YOUNG, J., ROBERTS, J.E., ROGERS, D.G. and DANBY, N. (1994). Experimental silvopastoral systems; the first five years. In: *The future of the land: mobilising and integrating knowledge for land use options,* ed L.O. Fresco *et al.* Wiley, Chichester, 123–128.

FENN, P.D., COLGROVE, P.M., SIM, D.A., IASON, G.R. and FOREMAN, E. (1991). The effect of shelter on the energy expenditure of two breeds of sheep in winter. *International Congress on Farm Animals and the Environment, Bangor.*

FRAME, J. (1992). *Improved grassland management.* Farming Press, Ipswich. 351.

FRAME, J., HARKESS, R.D. and TALBOT, M. (1989). The effect of cutting frequency and fertiliser ntirogen rate on herbage productivity from perennial ryegrass. *Research and Development in Agriculture* **6,** 99–105.

GREEN, S.R., HUTCHINGS, N.J., GRACE, J. and GREATED, C. (1990). Shelter in agroforestry. *Agroforestry in the UK* **1**(2): 20–21.

GREEN, S.R., GRACE, J. and HUTCHINGS, N.J. (1995). Observations of turbulent air flow in three stands of widely spaced Sitka spruce. *Agricultural and Forest Meteorology* **74**: 205–225.

HAGGAR, R.J. and PEEL, S. (1994). *Grassland management and nature conservation.* Occasional Symposium No. 28. British Grassland Society, Reading.

HODGSON, J., MACKIE, C.K. and PARKER, J.W.G. (1986). Sward surface heights for efficient grazing. *Grass Farmer* **24,** 5–10.

HOPPÉ, G.M., DUNBAR, P.A. and MCADAM, J.H. (1997). Wind profiles in a developing silvopastoral system. *Agroforestry Forum* **8** (1), 20–22.

HOPPÉ, G.M., SIBBALD, A.R., MCADAM, J.H., EASON, W., HISLOP, A.M. and TEKLEHAIMANOT, Z. (1996). The UK Silvopastoral Agroforestry National Network Experiment – a co-ordinated approach. In: *Proceedings of the European Society for Agronomy, 4th Congress, Veldhoven,*

The Netherlands, 7-11 July 1996, vol. 2, eds M.K.van Ittersum, G.E.G.T. Venner, S.C. van de Geijn and T.H. Jetten, 630–631.

KNOWLES, R.L. (1991). New Zealand experience with silvopastoral systems: a review. *Forest Ecology and Management* **45**: 251–268.

LAWS, J.A., GILL, E.K. and SHELDRICK, R.D. (1992). The effect of tree density on soil compaction in a sheep grazed silvopastoral system. *Proceedings 3rd Research Conference, British Grassland Society,* Northern Ireland, 81–82.

MCADAM, J.H. (1996a). Broughshane; Performance of stock and trees. *Agroforestry Forum* **7** (1): 16–17.

MCADAM, J.H. (1996b). Vegetation change and management in temperate agroforestry systems. *Aspects of Applied Biology* **44,** 245–250.

MCADAM, J.H. AND HOPPÉ, G.M. (1996a). Pasture production between trees in a silvopastoral system. In: *Grassland and land use systems,* ed. G. Parente, J. Frame and S. Orsi. Proceedings 16th meeting of the European Grassland Federation, Grado, Italy, 119–122.

MCADAM, J.H. and HOPPÉ, G.M. (1996b). The effect of tree spacing on pasture composition in a silvopastoral system. *Agroforestry Forum* **7** (2), 30–33.

MCADAM, J.H. and HOPPÉ, G.M. (1997). Sheep production and performance in a lowland silvopastoral system. *Agricultural Research Forum. 23rd Meeting of Irish Grassland and Animal Production Association,* Dublin, 229–230.

MCARTHUR, A.J. (1991). Forestry and shelter for livestock. *Forest Ecology and Management* **45,** 93–108.

MAXWELL, T.J. and TREACHER T.T. (1987). Decision rules for grazing management. In: *Efficient sheep production from grass,* ed. G.E. Pollott. Occasional Symposium No. 21. British Grassland Society, Reading 67–78.

MORRISON, J., JACKSON, M.V. and SPARROW, P.E. (1980). The response of perennial ryegrass to fertilizer nitrogen in relation to climate and soil. *Report of the joint GRI/ADAS Grassland manuring Trial GM20.* Technical Report No. 27. Grassland Research Institute, Hurley.

NIXON, C.J., ROGERS, D.G. and NELSON, D.G. (1992). *The protection of trees in silvopastoral agroforestry systems.* Research Information Note 219. Forestry Commission, Farnham.

NOLAN, T. and CONNOLLY, J. (1989). Mixed vs mono-grazing by steers and sheep. *Animal Production* **48,** 519–533.

NWAIGBO, L.C. (1996). Spatial variation of tree growth and site factors in a silvopastoral system in North East Scotland. PhD Thesis, University of Aberdeen.

NWAIGBO, L.C., HUDSON, G. and SIBBALD, A.R. (1995). Tree-scale trends in available soil nutrients and cone penetration resistance in a grazed hybrid larch (*Larix eurolepis*) silvopastoral system. *Agroforestry Forum* **6**(2), 48–50.

PERCIVAL, N.S. and KNOWLES, R.L. (1983). Combinations of *Pinus radiata* and pastoral agriculture on New Zealand hill country. In: *Foothills for food and forests*, ed. D.B. Hannaway, Oregon State University, College of Agricultural Sciences, Symposium No.2, 185–202.

PERCIVAL N.S. and KNOWLES R.L. (1988). Relationship between radiata pine and understorey pasture production. In: *Agroforestry symposium proceedings 24-27 Nov 1986*, ed. P. Maclaren. Bulletin No. 139. Forest Research Institute, Rotorua, 152–164.

POLLOCK, K.M., LUCAS, R.J., MEAD, D.J. and THOMSON S.E. (1994). Forage–pasture production in the first 3 years of an agroforestry experiment. *Proceedings of the New Zealand Grassland Association* **56,** 179–185.

PRITCHARD, K.M. (1992). Shelter, microclimate and heat loss from sheep. PhD Thesis, University of Nottingham.

SIBBALD, A.R. (1992). Current research in agroforestry. In: *Farm and small scale forestry*, ed. D.A. Greig. Institute of Chartered Foresters, Edinburgh, 105–122.

SIBBALD, A.R. (1996). Silvopastoral systems on temperate sown pastures: a personal perspective.

In: *Western European silvopastoral systems*, ed. M. Étienne. INRA Editions, Science Update, Paris, 23–36.

SIBBALD, A.R. and SINCLAIR, F.L. (1990). A review of agroforestry research in progress in the UK. *Agroforestry Abstracts* **3,** 149–164.

SIBBALD, A.R. and AGNEW, R. (1996). Silvopastoral National Network Experiment. Annual Report 1995. *Agroforestry Forum* **7** (1), 7–10.

SIBBALD, A.R., DICK, J. and IASON, G.R. (1995). The effects of widely spaced trees on the behaviour of sheep. *Agroforestry Forum* **6**(2), 22–25.

SIBBALD, A.R., GRIFFITHS, J.H. and ELSTON, D.A. (1991). The effects of the presence of widely spaced conifers on under-storey herbage production in the UK. *Forestry Ecology and Management* **45,** 71–77.

SIBBALD, A.R., ELSTON, D.A., DICK, J. and IASON, G.R. (1996). Spatial analysis of sheep distribution below trees at wide spacing: a reappraisal. *Agroforestry Forum* **7**(2), 26–28.

SIBBALD A.R., MAXWELL T.J., GRIFFITHS J.H., HUTCHINGS N.J., TAYLOR C.M.A., TABBUSH P.M. and WHITE I.M.S. (1987). Agroforestry research in the hills and uplands. In: *Agriculture and conservation in the hills and uplands*, ed. M. Bell and R.G.H. Bunce. Institute of Terrestrial Ecology, Grange-Over-Sands, 74–77.

TEKLEHAIMANOT, Z. and SINCLAIR, F. (1996). Henfaes: trees in clumps and red alder as a source of nitrogen for pasture. *Agroforestry Forum* **7** (1), 13–14.

WAIRIU, M., MULLINS, C.E. and CAMPBELL, C.D. (1993). Soil physical factors affecting the growth of sycamore (*Acer pseudoplatanus* L.) in a silvopastoral system on a stony soil in north-east Scotland. *Agroforestry Systems* **24**: 295–306.

WILLOUGHBY, I. and CLAY, D. (1996). *Herbicides for farm woodlands and short rotation coppice.* Forestry Commission Field Book 14. HMSO, London.

Chapter 6

Alternatives to grazing livestock

Mark Brownlow, Peter Carruthers and Peter Dorward

Introduction

Most silvopastoral systems tested in recent years in the UK have used ruminant livestock as the pastoral component. However, a number of factors prompt interest in using non-ruminant species. First, woodland is the natural habitat of the ancestors of pigs, chickens and turkeys. Domestic pigs are descended primarily from the Eurasian wild boar (*Sus scrofa scrofa*), a species most often found in mixed, predominantly deciduous woodland. The chicken is derived from the red jungle fowl (*Gallans gallans*) of India, China and Southeast Asia, an inhabitant of indigenous woodland and scrub. The domestic turkey comes from the wild turkey of North America (*Meleagris gallopavo*), also traditionally found in wooded environments. Second, history provides precedents for Agroforestry involving non-ruminants (see Chapter 2). Seasonal fattening of pigs on beech and oak mast achieved particular agricultural and cultural importance as *denbera* in Anglo-Saxon times and as *pannage* thereafter (Brownlow, 1992). Although pannage persists in the New Forest, the practice had declined to insignificance by the 1800s. This disappearance was caused by a general reduction in forest area, the increase in value of woodland products which might be damaged by pig activity, changes in woodland management that precluded mast production (e.g. coppicing) and the progressive intensification of pig-keeping and silviculture. The integration of poultry and forestry was less common. However, agricultural manuals written in the earlier part of the 20th century observed and discussed the use of wooded areas (particularly of orchards) for chicken, turkey and geese husbandry.

Use of these practices effectively ended with the advent of industrial agriculture in the second half

of the 20th century, particularly the move to indoor pig and poultry production. Recent interest arises from the factors prompting interest in agroforestry of all types (see Chapters 10 and 11) and from changes in agricultural and social priorities for pig, poultry and tree husbandry (related, for example, to animal welfare), and specifically from the following:

1. The growth in outdoor (free-range) pig and poultry enterprises, leading to increased demands on land resources.

2. Recognition of the possibility of using tree cover to improve the husbandry conditions and welfare of pigs and poultry kept outdoors.

3. The possibility of identifying and promoting specific markets for 'forest-reared' animal products.

4. Increasing demands on forest managers to find new uses for forest resources and alternative methods for the silvicultural treatment of tree crops.

Current practice in the UK

Pigs

An informal survey in 1994 (Brownlow, 1994) revealed few (less than 10) enterprises featuring *significant* integration of domestic pigs with trees, compared with the total number of outdoor herds (approximately 380 in 1992). Enterprises involving wild boar were similar in number, but relatively more frequent, and accounted for about 20% of the total number of herds. There were no significant patterns in enterprise characteristics other than an expected dominance of mature woodland as the forestry component (see Plate 18).

The integration of pigs with forestry is subject to two basic constraints – uncertainty and space. Uncertainty over enterprise design and performance is inevitable given the scarcity of existing practical models to follow or field research to validate theoretical advice and management guidelines. Wild boar enterprises are less constrained by uncertainty since managers tend to be less risk-averse. Continental enterprises, where wild boar are traditionally integrated with woodland, also act as demonstrations. Uncertainty also extends to regulatory and institutional bodies. As a consequence, institutional support and promotion have been largely absent and new enterprise proposals have been treated sceptically.

The pattern of pig production in the UK does not always lend itself to integration with trees. The space required by an average outdoor pig herd (c. 21 ha) would usually be greater than the available woodland area on a farm, or the agricultural area which an average farmer might be prepared to plant with trees. Many such herds are on rented land and/or part of an arable rotation, further limiting the possibilities for introducing a tree element. Again, this is less of a problem for wild boar, where herds are smaller and rarely part of a cropping cycle. It is not yet clear whether the new interest cited earlier, or further research, will be sufficient to overcome these problems.

Poultry

There are many more poultry/tree businesses. Practitioners appear to fall into three groups:

1. **Large, independent, commercial poultry specialists.** Here, integration is essentially opportunistic, usually with pre-existing mature trees, and often in a parkland landscape. Essentially, there is no reason to remove the trees from poultry paddocks, and there are some reasons (e.g. shade/shelter) for them to be kept. The need to protect the image of free-range production has also encouraged retention of tree cover and supplementary planting for shelter and landscaping.

2. **Corporate poultry producers.** Large corporations with poultry interests have encouraged private contract growers to plant trees. Motivations include the promotion of greater ranging of the birds, landscape improvements in response to planning concerns and improved shelter. Trial enterprises have also been established to produce meat specifically to be promoted as forest-reared. Unlike independent producers, large corporations have sufficient stock and resources to develop and support such a planned marketing strategy.

3. **Smallholders.** In most of the smallholder examples, integration has been inevitable given the size of the farm structure, the relative lack of labour constraints and the need to optimise use of space. The resultant opportunism has usually been reinforced post-establishment by recognition of some net benefits of integration, particularly shade and shelter.

The greater occurrence of agroforestry involving poultry, as against pigs, is because there are relatively fewer constraints to integration. Poultry enterprises are usually independent of other agricultural activities. Agroforestry would, therefore, rarely affect the management of other enterprises. In addition, poultry units are generally small in area compared with domestic pig units, with average ranges of less than 6.5 ha. The popularity of small poultry enterprises among organic and small-scale farmers is another factor, since such enterprises demand only modest areas of trees, which are often an existing part of such less-intensive farming systems.

The uncertainty element is also reduced as there is considerably less perceived risk involved in integrating poultry with trees, particularly in terms of physical damage to trees or woodland vegetation. There is also a lower opportunity cost when integrating new tree plantings with poultry, rather than pigs, since the former are perceived to be compatible immediately with such plantings.

Key considerations in design and management

The most important potential advantages and disadvantages of using non-ruminant alternatives

Table 6.1 The main advantages and disadvantages which might accrue to agroforestry enterprises featuring pigs or poultry.

Advantages (conditional on enterprise design)	Disadvantages (conditional on enterprise design)
Reduced aggression, stress and mortality	Stock inspection, moving and record-keeping less efficient
Improved animal health	Higher site preparation costs
Sales premia and marketing advantages for animal products	Increased fencing demands and maintenance costs
Lower land rental for animal enterprises	Increased demand for labour and land
Positive climatic effects on feed costs and health	Negative climatic effects on feed costs and health
Natural livestock fodder	Increased predator, scavenger, disease vector and parasite populations
Intermediate revenue from afforested land	Poor carcass grading
Some insect pest control	Restricted access to trees for labour and public
Additional forest revenue and products from agricultural land	Restricted use of biocides
Improved animal welfare	Tree damage
Diversification opportunity	Loss of sporting value in woodlands
Reduced pesticide requirements	Loss of regeneration material in natural woodlands
Reduced leaching from agricultural land	Soil nutrient overloads
	Weed flushes
	Ecological disturbance to animal/plant communities in natural woodlands
	Negative climatic effects on animal welfare
	Increased leaching from forest soils
	Deterioration in pasture quality

Poultry only	**Poultry only**
Increased ranging of birds	None

Pigs only	**Pigs only**
Positive climatic effects on pig fertility	Negative climatic effects on fertility
Some small mammal pest control	Soil compaction
Some weed control	
Improved soil aeration, fertility and structure	

in agroforestry are given in Table 6.1. Guidelines for design and management can only be tentative, since there is little scientific research or practical experience on which to base them. Recommendations are based primarily on manipulating key characteristics of these systems in order to maximise the benefits and minimise the problems.

Diversity in the tree component

The main benefits dependent on tree layout are improvements in microclimate and animal welfare. Tree-induced changes in microclimate can have both positive and negative impacts on animal production. Under canopy cover, for example, temperature extremes are ameliorated and wind speeds reduced, but at the expense of a fall in average temperature. Microclimatic influences on pigs and poultry are expressed primarily through animal health/welfare and feeding efficiency (via appetite and the partitioning of digested energy between growth and heat production). In addition, climatic stress (particularly high temperatures at service) has been strongly implicated in seasonal reductions in the fertility of domestic pigs (Greer, 1983).

The overall impact of a uniform tree layout would be uncertain since the resultant changes in microclimate would have both undesirable and desirable consequences. Animal housing, local climates and breed differences (particularly in feather and skin characteristics) will also interact with these changes. Shelter effects might, for example, actually encourage animals to leave a more desirable (from a feed conversion perspective) indoor temperature and use up more energy in exercise. The value of any microclimate change is, therefore, not so clear cut as for grazing animals.

In contrast, a diverse tree layout, combining conventional and wide spacings, with a woodland edge and open spaces, would offer a range of microclimates. An animal would then be able to move to the area most conducive to its own welfare under the prevailing conditions. However, this may still not necessarily coincide with the climate which maximises economic performance, although efficiency of feed utilisation by pigs, for example, occurs at a temperature similar to those recommended on welfare grounds (Close, 1987).

Tree heterogeneity could also be temporal, with animals being moved to the appropriate environment as the season determines.

Trees have other welfare benefits apart from microclimatic influences on animal fitness, behaviour and physiology. Depending on the relative sizes and numbers of trees and animals, the former can provide cover and isolation, giving a means of escape from aggressive encounters and reducing the visual stimuli that provoke aggression. For example tree cover could allow new animals to be integrated into established groups without an excessive risk of bullying. This is particularly valuable in pigs where an individual has a high unit value and culling practices often demand the replacement of single animals from sow batches.

An increase in environmental stimuli (behavioural enrichment) also raises welfare where it allows expression of hitherto frustrated behavioural motivations. The stimuli most appropriate to the evolved behavioural needs of an animal are those it chooses when faced with a range of possible habitats (Broom, 1988). Studies of feral or free-living populations of pigs, chickens and turkeys reveal a clear preference for habitats which include woodland (e.g. Graves, 1984), particularly forest edges (e.g. Stolba and Wood-Gush, 1989).

The recommended spatial variation in tree layout (desirable from a microclimatic viewpoint) applies equally, therefore, to welfare benefits for pigs, turkeys and chickens (though the birds would benefit from wider tree spacing at the expense of a dense or tall overstorey). Although trees would provide some appropriate stimuli for ducks and geese, a wooded landscape would be inferior when compared to an open environment. Scattered trees or young plantations would allow a positive contribution in terms of general stimulation, without a reduction in the value of the open space.

Tree damage and protection

In general, tree damage is unlikely to be a significant factor in agroforestry systems involving poultry, although some browsing on young seedlings can be expected, and tree roots may be undermined by dust bathing and foraging. The only clear problem is with geese, which strip and eat tree bark.

This issue is far more complex when dealing with pigs. In existing forests, the introduction of pigs would damage or even destroy natural regeneration. However, pigs can be used as biological scarifiers to prepare the site to promote natural regeneration in commercial forests. Deliberate tree damage results from scratching, marking and tusking of stems, and consumption of roots and foliage. Incidental damage arises from mechanical disturbance or exposure of roots and small stems through foraging and other activities. The specific factors contributing to this damage have not been examined scientifically, but anecdotal evidence has been accumulated. An understanding of these factors (some of which are interrelated) carries implicit recommendations for the design and management of appropriate enterprises. Some of these may also be applicable to geese.

1. **Bark type.** Rubbing for skin maintenance is a universal phenomenon in pigs, and trees may simply be a convenient substrate. Unsurprisingly, rough-barked trees are favoured targets, while loose-barked trees are more susceptible to actual damage. A suggested explanation for deliberate bark chewing of some conifers is that the resin produced is used for protection against skin parasites (Graves, 1984).

2. **Tree species.** On a pig enterprise where differences in tree damage between mature tree species were observed, the chronological order in which trees suffered bark damage was: oak and ash (most damaged), Scots pine and larch, birch, Corsican pine (completely undamaged). Similar observations from a wild boar enterprise were: Scots pine, Lawson's cypress, beech, Norway spruce, larch. Scots pine appears to be the only species which can be definitively stated to be incompatible with pigs without protection, its bark often being completely removed to a height of 60-80 cm.

3. **Tree size.** The vulnerability of trees to browsing and incidental damage is clearly related to their size.

4. **Pig:tree ratio.** The stocking rate can affect the pattern of damage. On an enterprise where stocking was at 2.5 pigs to the hectare for 6 months, there was no observable damage to any of the trees present, which included all the major broadleaved species. Damage was near universal on another enterprise stocked at 37–49 pigs to the hectare for up to two years.

5. **Other vegetation.** Tree damage increases as vegetation cover decreases.

6. **Temperature.** Debarking is more prevalent during cold weather, suggesting it may be a nutritional or stress response.

7. **Feeding.** Feeding itself can lead to incidental and rooting damage if ground feeding takes place adjacent to trees. Such damage is also increased where wet or weak soils encourage deeper rooting by pigs. Damage also increases if feed supplies drop.

8. **Pig size.** The size of a pig clearly affects its capacity to inflict both deliberate and incidental damage on trees. Piglets, weaners and finishing stock cause less damage than adult sows and boars.

9. **Pig type.** Sows approaching farrowing seem most damaging, which suggests a response to restlessness or perhaps nesting motivations. It seems likely that there will be differences between pig breeds.

10. **Pig behaviour.** To all these factors can be added an element of apparent randomness concerning the predilection of any one pig towards damaging behaviour. Pigs are individuals!

The relevance of these potential problems would depend on their impact on the ability of the trees to fulfil their role in the agroforestry system. Where tree damage would be unacceptable, unrestricted integration of chickens, ducks or (presumably) turkeys would still be possible, though young trees might require some protection using treeshelters. Integration of geese or pigs would require careful manipulation of the factors described above to eliminate damage. If artificial protection is needed (and only if), then standard treeshelters would be appropriate for young trees and geese. For young trees and pigs, the large stake and shelter designs used in ruminant agroforestry trials would be required. This might not guarantee protection from rooting and may even invite damage from exploratory behaviour. Integration of pigs and young trees may be impossible without deviating substantially from standard pig management regimes, particularly in terms of rotation lengths and stocking rates.

Protection of older trees against geese and pigs would demand either individual fencing or the use of chemical repellents, as discussed in Chapter 4. The value of chemical repellents in protecting against these animals has, however, not been tested.

Soil management

The two main issues in soil management arise from the nutrients supplied via animal dung and from soil compaction. Figure 6.1 gives the average fertiliser content of various manures at common stocking rates. Equivalent local, mineral application rates will depend on dunging patterns. These will reflect the location of the animals through time in relation to the distribution of the trees. Pigs, for example, given adequate space, will use specific defecation sites away from resting areas. On the basis of experience with sheep in other systems and the proposed value of trees for shade, shelter and security, congregation around trees is also likely to occur. A large amount of manure will also be removed in poultry housing litter.

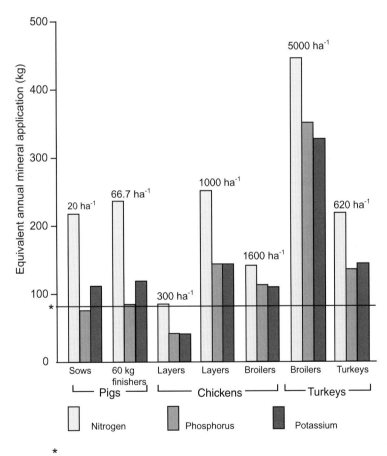

*
N limit advocated for young plantations (Moffat and Bird, 1989)

Figure 6.1 Fertiliser content of fresh chicken, turkey and domestic pig manures under several representative management regimes (adapted from Archer and Nicholson, 1992; MAFF, 1978; 1993; Westerman *et al.*, 1985). (Chicken figure refers to phosphate rather than phosphorus and potash rather than potassium. Turkey figure includes a contribution from wood shavings. Sow figure assumes the mineral proportions in the manure are identical to those in the manure of 60 kg finishers. Pig occupation is for 33% of the time and poultry occupation for 50%.)

The levels in Figure 6.1 suggest that there is a risk that conventional outdoor stocking regimes could result in excessive nutrient application. Traditional free-range egg units are a clear exception. Other poultry enterprises are likely to be acceptable given sufficient manure removal with housing litter. For pig manure levels to be beneficial, rather than detrimental, stocking rates would have to be reduced and/or rest periods extended. Such practices would also help to prevent soil compaction. This is particularly important for soil around tree bases, which is rendered vulnerable by increases in soil water following stem run-off.

Even where net nutrient inputs are safe/beneficial, there might be uneven tree responses across a range and the possibility of damage to individual trees. Additionally, recommended limits are based on infrequent applications of large quantities of nitrogen. These levels could be higher for nitrogen applied frequently in small amounts, as would occur in agroforestry systems.

The manipulation of the ratio between animal numbers, tree numbers and land area is vital in determining relative manuring levels per tree and the amount of mechanical pressure on soils. This in turn determines the resulting pattern of benefits.

In summary, systems involving poultry would carry little risk of deleterious soil interactions. On the contrary, beneficial manure inputs could be expected. Soils under pigs run considerable risk of nutrient overload and structural damage, with implications for tree growth and pollution. A neutral or positive outcome would depend on careful design and management, appropriate to the prevailing conditions.

Plant and animal populations

The vegetation understorey in forest systems occupied by pigs or poultry will be affected by soil changes (particularly nutrient enrichment), direct consumption and incidental damage from foraging. During pig occupation, there will be a net reduction in surface plant cover, with a loss of species diversity and changes in botanical composition. On commercial, pasture-based domestic pig enterprises, it is not unusual to see a complete absence of vegetation. After pig removal, soil nutrient enrichment may cause a growth flush

and effect further floristic change.

The effect of poultry is likely to be much less given the absence of incidental damage from foraging or consumption of subterranean material. However, some botanical changes will occur. At the least, changes in herbaceous biomass, species composition and diversity and plant recruitment will occur due to manuring effects and a reduction in seed survival (although soil seedbanks will be undisturbed).

Animal stocking rates and paddock rotations must be manipulated according to the desirability or otherwise of these changes. For example, pigs can cause extensive and possibly undesirable changes to ground flora. Alternatively, pigs can be used for rejuvenation of derelict woodland and, if used repeatedly, for weeding plantations.

Tree planting will, of course, affect pasture growth on grassland, and the appropriate lessons of agroforestry research with grazing animals (see Chapter 5) should be applied to geese husbandry. Other non-grazing species will be largely unaffected by pasture loss, although soil exposure reduces the animal-carrying capacity and leads to dirtier housing conditions.

Changes in animal populations can also be expected in these systems, through predation, disturbance, soil and vegetation changes and feed wastage. The net effect depends on the proportion of the total habitat type occupied, the density and duration of occupation, and the capacity of surrounding habitats to absorb any immigration and act as refuges/reservoirs. The long-term ecological impacts depend on this and on the relative values of existing, replacement and recovery populations.

Faunal changes are likely to be more extreme with pigs than with poultry, because of both enterprise sizes and greater ecological disturbance. Again, ecologically sensitive sites should be avoided, while both pigs and poultry could be incorporated within integrated pest management schemes. If existing woodland is used, resident game populations (e.g. of pheasants) will be eliminated within the enterprise area; the importance of this depends on the remoteness of refuges for displaced animals. Sporting values may be decreased but, if refuge is nearby, waste feed could provide supplementary fodder and may actually result in higher game populations!

Technical management

With poultry, unrestricted access to the trees for forestry activities is possible as poultry housing is normally designed to allow temporary isolation from the range. A similar approach with pigs would require more time and effort since accommodation, with the exception of finishing kennels, is not normally designed for confinement. Where housing is not provided or isolation is logistically impossible, manipulation of the timing of integration and the rotation of the enterprise in order to match forest work schedules would be required. Alternatively, low animal stocking rates would ensure that sufficient land exists for animals to evade disturbance by forestry activities.

Potential weed flushes following occupation may need treatment. Should biocides be required as part of forest management, allowing animals access to range during or immediately after application may not be possible. The risk of poisoning would be particularly strong following insecticide use, when consumption of dead insects would allow the toxin to become concentrated in the domestic animal.

In turkey and chicken enterprises, the removal of the lower branches of trees on range may be necessary to prevent overnight perching and roosting. Trees near fences may also need pruning to prevent their use as an access route by predators and as an escape route for the birds.

Net impacts on the management of a poultry enterprise depend on the proportion and design of tree cover. Increased vegetation cover can provoke outdoor laying and a reluctance to return to housing at night. These potential problems could be solved by feeding indoors in the evening and by preventing access to range in the early morning, the peak egg-laying period. The presence of trees, and possibly of undergrowth, can interfere with observation and catching of birds. This might delay identification of health problems. Movement of mobile housing might also be impeded by tree cover.

The impact on the management of an outdoor pig enterprise also depends on the location and type of tree cover. As well as the consequences for disease management, any difficulties in inspecting stock would affect the accuracy of record keeping. An inability to match individual pig performance to aspects of management would reduce the efficiency of culling programmes and the possibility of identifying targeted management improvements. Difficulties in stock collection could delay weaning.

The risk of compaction and waterlogging is increased around feeding and watering points. These may have to be moved regularly or be converted to semi-permanent concrete sites. Ground feeding should be avoided, and feed and feed hoppers should be designed to reduce scavenging.

In a pre-existing forest, trees will have to be removed to provide sites and access for housing and equipment, water supplies and electric fencing. New woodland also needs to be designed to account for these issues.

Recommended practices: pigs

Table 6.2 lists promising designs for pig–tree enterprises.

Pre-existing woodland

The complete merger of an unmodified commercial pig enterprise at stocking rates used on pasture with an unmodified forestry enterprise is unlikely to function successfully. Exceptions are where soil conditions or tree damage are not important, such as in timber plantations at rotation end or in unproductive natural woodland. Even so, complete spatial integration would still place significant technical burdens on the pig enterprise, which might not be compensated for by cheaper rents or sales premium benefits.

Extensification of a pig enterprise, by radically reducing stocking rates, would facilitate greater compatibility with all forms of forestry. This is not possible for normal domestic pig enterprises, where the marginal financial environment restricts the degree to which management control can be reduced and output allowed to drop. Such an approach could work for small herds with a high value, such as rare breeds or those aimed at a local or specialist market.

Extensification is more appropriate for wild boar–tree enterprises. The animals have a much greater unit value and can thus sustain a low input–low output system. They are also less responsive to intensified management, so the opportunity cost of extensification is small. Their nutritional and climatic demands are lower than those of domestic pigs and are more easily met by forest resources such as shelter and natural fodder. However, electric fencing alone is insufficient to contain wild boar and this limits the potential for occupation of large areas, due to the high cost of semi-permanent fencing.

More promising alternatives are those where one of the two components acts in a supporting role for a conventional pig or forest enterprise. A heterogeneous climatic and behavioural environment for the animals can be achieved by locating pig paddocks with partial access to mature tree cover such as at forest margins or in woodland clearings (Plate 18). This arrangement would demand little change to conventional pig management regimes. A promising role for domestic pigs is as a silvicultural management tool with incidental agricultural production. On land where there is an

anticipated delay before planting, replanting or natural regeneration, a temporary pig enterprise could be established or admitted to prepare the ground and earn revenue or rent. Vegetation clearance, aeration of surface soil layers, nutrient enrichment and break-up of debris would be expected.

Pig herds could be used also for weeding of young plantations or cleaning of mature woodlands. Small finishing herds, contained by electric netting, would be more manageable, less likely to damage the trees and would demand less specialist skills than a breeding herd. Rapid rotation and regular return times would improve tree survival and prevent deleterious consequences arising from weed-flushes. A similar approach could be taken for controlling outbreaks of appropriate pests (i.e. those which spend part of their life cycle in the upper soil layers or on the soil surface).

Domestic pigs in these proposed roles could not be expected to replace conventional, silvicultural practices and the concept would demand convincing practical evidence of its validity before wide application could occur. These techniques might be favoured where conventional methods are inappropriate, such as on poor terrain or in chemically sensitive areas, or when combined with more conventional techniques. In all cases,

Table 6.2 Promising enterprises featuring the integration of pigs and trees. Lowest numbers indicate highest rankings.

Design	Main conditions	Ranking
A Forest margins or glades with conventional pig enterprise	Unutilised woodland or commercial forest stands at rotation end	1
B Open forest ground immediately prior to planting or regeneration and conventional pig enterprise	None	2
C Domestic pigs used for weeding, cleaning and pest control	Depends on success of technique and management	3
D Wild boar used for weeding, cleaning and pest control	Small herds only and depends on success of technique and management	4
E As G but with an extensive domestic pig enterprise	Small herds with high value stock or high premiums	5
F As G but with an extensive wild boar enterprise	Small herds	6
G 100% spatial integration of conventional pig enterprise and pre-existing mature mature woodland	High premiums or low rent for pig enterprise, unutilised woodland or commercial forest stands at rotation end	7

skilled management would be required to produce successful outcomes. Wild boar or the older, more robust domestic breeds might be more successful in these roles, given their greater environmental resilience and reduced dependency on management inputs such as shelter and health care. However, rapid rotation of wild boar would, again, probably involve prohibitive fencing costs.

New tree plantings
The only promising systems using pigs and new tree plantings would be those where the animals are employed in a silvicultural role as described above. Otherwise, new tree plantings could be considered only as a precursor to developing the appropriate forest design for pig-tree systems incorporating pre-existing woodland.

Economic projections
Spreadsheet modelling has provided theoretical estimates of the likely financial performance of some of these enterprises. One model evaluated the financial performance of a finishing pig enterprise in unutilised woodland (item A in Table 6.2). The net margins produced for the pig herd were consistently in excess of those for an equivalent pasture-based enterprise, the forest enterprise remaining unvalued. In the optimal design, this advantage was relatively independent of any reasonable variation in the assumptions used regarding the interactions between the animal and tree components. In particular, given no decrease in feed efficiency and a minimum sales premium of £0.02 kg^{-1} (dead weight), margins were still 8.8% higher, even when all other interactions (labour use, stocking rates, rents, etc.) were assumed to be at their most disadvantageous. Provided the labour demand of the enterprise was not at the limits of the available labour of one full-time employee, the model showed that the three interactions with the greatest ability to influence pig enterprise performance were sales premia, rent differences and microclimatic changes affecting feed conversion efficiency. In appropriate circumstances, all three should lead to net incremental improvements in the agroforestry system compared to the pasture-based default system.

Another model evaluated the incremental financial performance of a commercial Corsican pine plantation which used a finishing pig herd to replace/supplement conventional silvicultural methods of ground preparation, weeding and cleaning (items B and C in Table 6.2). This system was less successful, although the results did not account for any non-market implications, such as reduced pesticide use. The potential benefits to the forest enterprise in terms of cost savings were highly sensitive to any induced tree mortality during weeding. Even at relatively low mortalities, the benefits were offset by future revenue reductions. A net benefit depended on the assumption that pigs can successfully replace conventional silvicultural treatments without causing any additional mortality in the tree crop. This assumption has yet to be adequately tested. It was also clear from the model that cost savings are dwarfed by the potential variability in pig performance. If only a few pigs are needed for silvicultural purposes, then 'forest-owned' pig herds should not be used. Instead, animals should be transferred from a larger herd, in order to avoid debilitating fixed costs. Therefore, most promise would be where a farmer's pasture-based herd can temporarily utilise forest sites and benefit from low rents and higher sales premiums, while providing silvicultural benefits to the forest owner. This delineation of responsibilities might also remove a potential skills barrier to implementation.

Recommended practices: chickens and turkeys

Promising designs for enterprises integrating forestry with chickens or turkeys have also been identified and are listed in Table 6.3.

Pre-existing natural woodland
As with pigs, complete integration with pre-existing natural woodland is not recommended. This is primarily due to the likely technical problems for management and for the erection of housing and fencing. Large-scale poultry housing could not be used without considerable site preparation costs. Such integration might be feasible if small, mobile

houses are used, which could take advantage of open spaces and reduce the need for site preparation, or if financial benefits from premia or lower rent provide sufficient compensation. However, woodland edges or clearings are preferable as locations, providing a greater range of climatic and behavioural benefits. The mixture of open space and tree cover should be more intimate than for pigs and provide access to cover at any point on the range rather than in one area. Again, such areas might be more easily exploited using mobile housing.

Pre-existing plantations

Similar conclusions can be applied to plantation forests where canopy cover is complete (Plate19). Various immature stages in forest development show more promise, providing benefits equivalent to the mixture of open and covered spaces described above. In a conventional timber plantation, integration would be most timely during the pre-thicket stage or immediately after thinning. Wide-spaced plantations, such as poplars or fruit orchards, are particularly suitable. Again, mobile or temporary housing would be more appropriate, allowing the poultry enterprise to exploit suitable sites as they became available in a commercial forest.

There is also some potential to use chickens and turkeys in a silvicultural role. This would be limited to controlling suitable pests within small, afforested areas, particularly orchards. In comparison with pigs, the reduced potential to damage tree growth confers even greater promise on this concept, although the potential benefits are both qualitatively and quantitatively smaller. Again, practical evidence would be needed to support the validity of these suggestions.

New plantings

Establishment of new woodlands specifically for integration is promising for both fixed and temporary enterprises. Wide-spacing or zonal planting can be incorporated within the tree layout to ensure the suitability of the site throughout the forest rotation.

Economic projections

Financial analysis of a broiler chicken unit integrated with new farm woodland (item A in Table 6.3) has been undertaken. From this analysis it was clear that changes to tree yield or cover were considerably less important than the loss of the prevailing farm woodland premium grant. However, additional sales premia had the potential to compensate for this loss. The net incremental

Table 6.3 Promising enterprises featuring the integration of poultry and trees . Lowest numbers indicate highest rankings.

Design	Main conditions	Ranking
Conventional chicken and turkey enterprise		
A New woodland planting	Tree guards or shelters may be necessary	1
B Wide-spaced plantation or orchard	None	2
C Commercial timber plantation	Pre-thicket, immediately post-thinning	3
D Forest margins or glades	Intimate mixture of tree cover and open areas	4
E Chickens and turkeys used in pest control	Depends on success of technique and management	5
F 100% spatial integration with pre-existing natural woodland	High premiums or low rent for poultry enterprise, mobile housing	6
Conventional duck and geese enterprise		
A New woodland planting	Very wide spaced with individual tree protection	1
B Young plantations or orchards	Individual tree protection	2
C Forest margins or glades	Timber trees immediately prior to felling or unutilised woodland	3
D Geese used for weeding	Individual tree protection, depends on success of technique and management	4

change that could be attributed to interactions between animal and tree was then more or less dependent on the direction of any induced change in feed efficiency. The desirability of this agroforestry system would depend on its net performance compared with a woodland-only enterprise, a pasture-based broiler enterprise and any other agricultural enterprise displaced by tree planting. If free-range broilers prove viable in their own right, then there are further benefits to be obtained from the appropriate use of a wooded range. These benefits could plausibly outweigh any associated loss of grant. Indeed, if feed efficiency benefits can be appropriated, then free-range broiler production might become viable even where they are not an attractive option for pasture.

Recommended practices: ducks and geese

Promising designs for enterprises integrating forestry with ducks or geese are included in Table 6.3. The risk of bark stripping and/or the undesirability of significant canopy structures from behavioural and (for geese) grass yield perspectives precludes intimate spatial integration of these birds with conventionally spaced trees. Integration with conventional forest systems could only be at the margins of non-timber producing woodland or of plantations immediately prior to felling. Complete integration would be possible with very young plantations or in orchards, provided treeshelters or other forms of individual tree protection were employed. New plantings are equally as appropriate as for chickens and turkeys, provided net tree densities are low. This would prevent both canopy encroachment and pasture deterioration and reduce tree protection costs. Geese might prove suitable for weeding young plantations, provided that due attention is paid to rotation and return times to ensure continued weed suppression.

Conclusions

In specific situations, non-ruminant livestock can be integrated with trees. Management of such systems is not always as straightforward as for ruminants, but there are potential benefits, notably in terms of marketable animal products, financial returns, improved animal welfare and benefits to the environment.

References

ARCHER, J.R. and NICHOLSON, R.J. (1992). Liquid waste from farm animal enterprises. In: *Farm animals and the environment*, ed. C. Phillips and D. Piggins. CAB International, Wallingford, 325-343.

BROOM, D.M. (1988). The scientific assessment of animal welfare. *Applied Animal Behaviour Science* **20**, 5-19.

BROWNLOW, M.J.C. (1992). Acorns and swine; historical lessons for modern agroforestry. *Quarterly Journal of Forestry* **86**(3), 181-190.

BROWNLOW, M.J.C. (1994). Towards a framework of understanding for the integration of forestry with domestic pig (*Sus scrofa domestica*) and wild boar (*Sus scrofa scrofa*) husbandry in the UK. *Forestry* **67**(3), 189-218.

CLOSE, W.H. (1987). The influence of the thermal environment on the productivity of pigs. In: *Pig housing and the environment*, ed. A.T. Smith and T.L.J. Lawrence. BSAP Occasional Publication No. 11. BSAP, Edinburgh, 9-24.

GRAVES, H.B. (1984). Behaviour and ecology of wild and feral swine (*Sus scrofa*). *Journal of Animal Sciences* **58**(2), 482-492.

GREER, E.B. (1983). Heat stress and reproduction in pigs: its role in seasonal infertility. In: *Recent advances in animal nutrition in Australia: 1983*, ed. D.J. Farrell and P. Vohra. University of New England Publishing Unit, Armidale, 216-230.

MAFF (1978). *Poultry manure as a fertiliser.* Advisory Leaflet 320, Ministry of Agriculture, Fisheries and Food, Middlesex.

MAFF (1993). *Solving the nitrate problem: progress in research and development.* Ministry of Agriculture, Fisheries and Food, London.

MOFFAT, A.J. and BIRD, D. (1989). The potential for using sewage sludge in forestry in England and Wales. *Forestry* **62** (1), 1–17.

STOLBA, A. and WOOD-GUSH, D.G.M. (1989). The behaviour of pigs in a semi-natural environment. *Animal Production* **48**, 419-425.

WESTERMAN, P.W., SAFLEY, L.M., BARKER, J.C. and CHESGEIR, G.M. (1985). Available nutrients in livestock waste. In: *Agricultural waste utilization and management.* Proceedings of the 5th International Symposium on Agricultural Wastes, 16-17 December 1985, Chicago. ASAE, Michigan, 295-307.

Chapter 7

Arable crops in agroforestry systems

Lynton Incoll and Steven Newman

Introduction

Since the late 1980s, research into silvoarable systems in the UK has been concerned with developing and testing a design for what is essentially a temperate form of tropical alley cropping, a design which would optimise the yield of trees and crops and the management of the complex system. Silvicultural aspects of such a design, including the spacing of trees within rows and their tree row understorey, are described in detail in Chapter 4. Here we are concerned with the design of temperate silvoarable systems which are compatible with good crop husbandry, and with the special requirements for management. As there are presently few commercial silvoarable systems in the UK, the discussion that follows is based on research results which are described later in the chapter.

Design of temperate silvoarable systems

Choice of type of tree

The rationale for the choice of species is described in Chapter 4. When choosing trees to go with arable intercrops, those with the deciduous habit are preferred in the northern European environment. This allows a temporal separation of the use of resources of light and water during the growing seasons of both tree and crop components. For winter crops, sown in early autumn, there is no competition for water until bud break in spring (Figure 7.1) and little competition for light by the dormant leafless tree. This is especially the case with late leafing species such as walnut (Newman *et al.*, 1991a). In a winter cereal/poplar system, for example, the winter cereal will have carried out a

large proportion of its photosynthesis before the poplar comes into leaf. When crops are harvested in mid to late summer, leaves of trees can continue to assimilate carbon into dry mass and transpire water until leaf fall without competition from crops (Figure 7.1). On the other hand, there is very little time available for tree management, i.e. pruning and thinning, between harvesting and ploughing. The advantages of temporal separation of the use of resources are much less for spring-sown arable crops, such as threshing peas, which may be used as a break crop in a cereal rotation. Spring sowing gives more time for silvicultural operations in autumn and winter but crop yields will be lower and may be affected more by the presence of the trees in leaf. For example, in spring crops, growth stages which are particularly sensitive to shading, may occur when trees have a fuller canopy.

Spatial arrangement of arable alleys and rows of trees

Planting trees within fields has to be done so that the mechanised management of the crops is not impeded (see Plate 22). Many arable farmers manage crops with 'tramlines' 12, 18 or 24 m apart and have 12, 18 or 24 m spray or fertiliser spreader booms. Ploughs, drills and harvesters are also adapted to this system covering submultiples of 12, 18 and 24 m. Consequently in silvoarable systems, if the tree rows are 2 m wide (see Chapter 4), trees should be planted in rows at least 14, 20 or 26 m apart. These different alley widths will produce different final outcomes as the system approaches maturity, the narrower widths allowing canopy closure over the alleys so that they would have to be converted into silvopastoral management whereas the wider alleys should be able to continue as arable right up

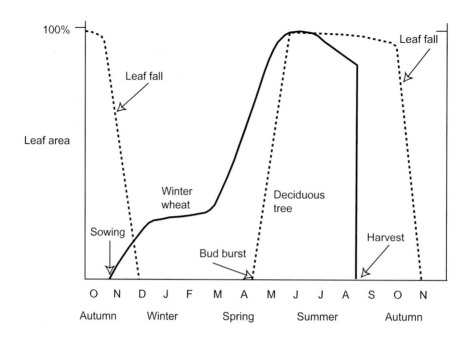

Figure 7.1 A year in the life of a temperate silvoarable system showing how an arable crop, winter wheat, can use light and nutrients when the deciduous trees are dormant, and the trees can remain active after the crop is harvested. Leaf area of deciduous tree ---- and winter wheat crop ——, each as a proportion of their maximum area.

to tree harvest, though with perhaps less than the full width being cultivated.

The within-row spacing of trees, discussed in detail in Chapter 4, will depend on the final product required, being small if large numbers of small diameter trees are required in short rotations and large for large diameter timber after longer rotations. Information on the optimum within-row distance is not available from traditional forestry sources. There are as yet no good yield models for the asymmetric planting characteristic of silvoarable systems. The densities of trees are lower in silvoarable systems with tree rows 14 to 26 m apart, than in the conventional square plantings of farm woodland or plantation forests (Table 7.1). The density of 184 trees ha⁻¹, used by Bryant and May Ltd to obtain veneer logs for match splints, was in an 8 m equilateral triangle planting giving rows about 7 m apart (see Chapter 4). This density would be obtained in rows 14 m apart if trees were planted about 3.9 m apart in the rows.

As tree rows should be orientated north-south to reduce shading of the crop (see Chapter 4), alleys will also consequently be orientated north-south, or as close to north-south as field boundaries allow without cutting off unmanageable odd-shaped areas of crop (Plate 20). Where the field boundary to be followed is not straight but without sharp angles it will be more practical, and aesthetically more pleasing, for the tree rows to follow this line, i.e. curved but still parallel with each other. In arable cropping, headlands have to be wide enough for agricultural machinery to turn, therefore tree rows have to end at the inner edge of the headland rather than at the field boundary.

Choice of crop

Some crops in normal arable rotations are not suitable for temperate alley cropping, including:

• those harvestable with high machinery that might damage the adjacent tree canopy, for example row crop harvesters such as maize harvesters;

Table 7.1 Spacing of trees within and between rows in conventional square planting and asymmetric agroforestry designs and the resulting densities of trees per hectare.

Spacing in row Y (m)	Density (ha⁻¹)			
	Square planting Y (m) x Y (m)	Agroforestry Y (m) x 14 (m)	Agroforestry Y (m) x 20 (m)	Agroforestry Y (m) x 26 (m)
1	10 000	714	500	384
2	2 500	357	250	192
3	1 111	238	167	128
4	625	179	125	96
5	400	143	100	77
6	278	119	83	64
7	204	102	71	55
8	156	89	63	48

- those harvestable with specialised machinery with sideways projections, for example stone removing machinery for potatoes, potato harvesters and sugar beet lifters.

Crops harvestable by a combine harvester are suitable and include those of normal arable rotations in the UK, e.g. wheat, barley, oilseed rape, linseed, threshing peas and field beans.

In all other respects, the husbandry of the arable crops is entirely conventional in that it does not differ from that of a monoculture of the same crop.

Special requirements for management

These silvoarable systems have been deliberately designed to allow normal management of arable crops. The only potential problem is the application of herbicides for the control of weeds in the crop or in the tree row edge. This has to be done with care so as to prevent drift onto the trees when they are in leaf. This can be achieved by applying at the minimum boom height in still weather and by fitting the very young trees with 60 cm high treeshelters. If possible, herbicide should be applied when trees are leafless. Once trees have clean trunks above the height of the spray boom there still remains a risk from herbicide falling on epicormic shoots or root suckers. The former should be removed as they

emerge and the latter at least annually, or before any herbicide is applied if the trees are in leaf.

As it is only possible to cultivate along the alleys in silvoarable agroforestry systems, it is essential to turn the plough layer in opposite directions across the arable alley from year to year to counter the repeated movement of soil away from one tree row and towards the one on the other side of the alley. A similar movement of soil can be seen along hedges on field boundaries.

Early silvoarable research

During the 1960s and 1970s Bryant and May (Forestry) Limited examined the effects of alley cropping on the growth of commercial poplars. Trials on estates in Herefordshire on soils derived from old red sandstone, and in Suffolk on deep fen peat, were designed to compare the growth of poplars where:

1. Both adjacent alleys were cropped to the full width each year.

2. Only the central strip of both adjacent alleys was cropped annually and the margin between crop and tree row was kept fallow by rotation.

3. Both adjacent alleys were permanently kept fallow.

In both trials the clone was 'Robusta', a hybrid black poplar known to be intolerant of competition. Weed growth within the tree rows was restricted as far as possible but was not controlled in treatment 1 above and is believed to have contributed to competition within the rooting zone of the poplars during the first years of establishment. The trials lasted for approximately ten years and showed the following results on the Herefordshire site, compared with growth under fallow conditions:

- Tree growth was severely reduced in the first two or three years by cropping in both adjacent alleys.

- Tree growth was reduced less severely when only the centre of each alley was cropped.

Results from the Suffolk trial showed no significant differences between treatments.

It was believed that competition for moisture and some nutrients, particularly nitrogen, were at times limiting in mineral soils reliant on rainfall only for water, whereas water and nitrogen were freely available in the Suffolk peat. In the 1970s the alternate fallow/cropping system was adopted as standard practice on the Western Estates in Herefordshire, having several advantages over an earlier system (Beaton, 1987). These trials were only designed to examine the effect of alley cropping on tree growth and although cereal yields were estimated, no detailed measurements of the alley crop were made.

Recent silvoarable research

Silvoarable research in the UK in the early 1980s concentrated on fruit and nut trees with crops (Newman, 1986; Dupraz and Newman, 1997). A number of experiments have been established since the late 1980s (see Chapter 2) which have given additional insights into the potential of silvoarable systems in Britain. The results of these experiments will be considered in two parts: the effects of trees on crop yield and the effects of crops on tree growth.

Effects of trees on crop yield
Old Wolverton experiment
This Open University silvoarable agroforestry experiment was established in 1988 (see Table 2.1)

at Old Wolverton near Milton Keynes with tree rows 1.5 m wide and 14 m apart and orientated north–south, with the arable alley (the cultivated strip) 12.5 m wide. Two Belgian hybrid poplar varieties, 'Beaupré' and 'Boelare', were planted through a black plastic mulch strip at 1 m apart in the tree row (Plates 10 and 11). At 1 m spacing, in a biomass experiment, the trees effectively formed a dense hedge in the second year (Newman et al., 1988; Newman and Wainwright, 1989; Newman et al., 1991b). At the end of the biomass experiment, the trees were thinned to 2 m and 3 m spacings in 1991 (Plate 21) and the 2 m spacing was thinned to 4 m in 1994. Trees reached about 14 m height in 1993 around five years after planting. The yield of the crops was not seriously affected until 1993 when the closely spaced trees that formed a solid hedge reached a height equivalent to the alley width of approximately 14 m (Table 7.2). Yields were calculated per total area (of crop plus tree row) so that a relative yield of 0.89 means that there has been no reduction in yield per unit area of crop but only a reduction in total yield of 11% due to the area taken out of production by the tree rows. In 1994, crop yield in the arable alleys was reduced to 8% of the yield of the adjacent sole crop. For timber trees, varieties 'Scott Pauley' and 'Fritzi Pauley', spaced at 6 m within the rows there was still no significant effect on crop yield seven years after planting.

Leeds furniture-timber tree experiment
This field experiment, which was planted in 1989 (see Table 2.1), consists of silvoarable, arable control (sole crop) and forestry control treatments replicated four times. The alleys are 14 m wide containing a 12 m wide strip of arable crop. The trees (ash, cherry, sycamore and walnut) are 4 m apart in the 2 m wide tree rows which have an understorey dominated by red fescue or timothy grasses. The forestry control consists of trees planted on a 2 m x 2 m grid (Incoll et al., 1997b).

In early years, yield in the arable alleys exceeded that of the arable control by as much as 23% (Table 7.3). From 1994 on, the establishment of a grass understorey in the tree rows provided overwintering sites for slugs which reduced the yield in 1994-1996. This reduction in yield was in the first 1.5 m

Table 7.2 Relative yield (RY) of crops in alleys between tree rows with various within-row tree spacings at Old Wolverton.

Trial	Date and year(s) from planting						
	1988 Year 1	1989 Year 2	1990 Year 3	1991 Year 4	1992 Year 5	1993 Year 6	1994 Year 7
Closely spaced trees							
RY	0.89	0.89	0.89	0.89[a]	0.89	0.54[a]	0.08
Spacing/m	1	1	1	1	2 and 3	2 and 3	2 and 3
Widely spaced trees							
RY	0.89	0.89	0.89	0.89	0.89	0.89	0.89[a]
Spacing/m	6	6	6	6	6	6	6

RY = alley crop yield (t ha^{-1})/sole crop yield (t ha^{-1}). Sole crop yield was measured in an area without tree rows but with identical crop husbandry. Yields in most years were measured at a weighbridge.

[a]Yields measured by quadrat sampling (1991) or plot combine (1993, 1994).

strip closest to the tree row so that any effect that trees may have had on yield was confounded by the effect of slug predation of seedlings (Figure 7.2) (Griffiths *et al.*, 1998). Mild winters have also led to increased populations of rabbits in the UK and the low relative yield in 1996 (78.1%) reflects greater damage by rabbits in one replicate agroforestry plot. The reduction due to slugs could be prevented by application of molluscicides or by different management of the tree-row understorey.

These yields are all per unit cropped area and take no account of the loss of land in the tree rows to cultivation which is 14% in this case, i.e. yields in the remaining cultivated area would have to be 14% greater to compensate. (The corresponding figures for alleys 20 or 26 m wide are 10% and 7.7% respectively.)

MAFF-sponsored trial with poplar
The three replicates of this trial which were planted at Leeds, Cirencester and Silsoe in 1992 (see Table 2.1) have tree rows 2 m wide with four varieties of poplar, 'Beaupré', 'Gibecq', 'Robusta' and 'Trichobel', with trees 6.4 m apart in the rows. The rows are 10 m apart with an 8 m arable alley (Plate 22). The tree rows are orientated approximately north–south and the poplar sets were planted through a black plastic mulch strip.

The arable alleys contain three arable treatments: continuous cropping with combinable crops on both sides of a tree row; alternate cropping with crop one side of a tree row and fallow on the other, the cropped alley alternating from one side of a row to the other from year to year; and continuous fallow on both sides of a tree row. There are three replicates of each treatment and an arable control treatment at each site (Incoll *et al.*, 1997a).

If trees significantly affect the alley crop by competing for water, nutrients and light, then the ranking of crop yields might be predicted to be:

control crop (sole crop or monoculture) > alternately cropped treatment > continuously cropped treatment.

At each site, the actual yields in the alternately cropped areas were greater than those in the continuously cropped areas for four of the six crops in 1994/5 and 1995/6 beside 3- and 4-year-old trees respectively. These data must be treated with caution, however, because the alternately cropped yield was significantly greater than the control yield (Silsoe 1994/95 and 1995/96 and Leeds 1994/95) or significantly less than the control yield (Leeds 1995/96 and Cirencester 1994/95 and 1995/96) (Table 7.4). In 1994/95, the control yields for winter wheat of 7.8–8.2 t ha^{-1} at

Leeds and Silsoe were above the typical national average (Nix, 1995), and the yield of 2.8 t ha⁻¹ for winter beans at Cirencester, although below average, was still acceptable.

No consistent effect of a particular poplar clone on crop yields has been established. The greater growth of 'Beaupré' compared to the less vigorous clones has not, as yet, resulted in a measurable effect on crop yields. However, there appears to be an effect of distance from the tree row on the yield of the crop (e.g. in 1995/96, Figure 7.3) but this has only been consistently so (five out of six crops) at the driest site, Leeds. Yields close to the tree rows could be reduced by competition with the trees for water, nutrients and/or light.

In conclusion, these results are representative of the first five years of cropping. They show that consistent evidence of an effect of trees in reducing yield has not yet been obtained.

Effects of crops on tree growth

Old Wolverton experiment

The effect of crops on tree growth cannot be assessed in this experiment because it does not include either woodland-density planting of poplar or poplars in tree rows where there is no competition from crops.

Leeds furniture-timber tree experiment

After the first three years, the growth of the trees between the arable alleys of this experiment remained around 15% less than that in a

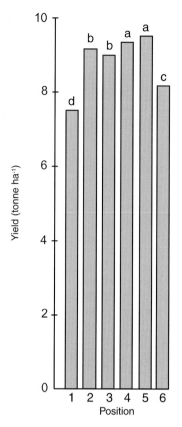

Figure 7.2 The distribution of yield of winter wheat (t ha⁻¹) in 1.5 m strips across a 12 m alley in the Leeds furniture-timber tree experiment in 1995. Positions 1 and 6 are in the arable alley next to tree rows. The tramline is between positions 3 and 4. Values with the same letter are not significantly different.

Table 7.3 Mean yields (t ha⁻¹) of arable crops in the arable control areas, and the arable alleys of the Leeds furniture-timber tree experiment since 1990, expressed per unit cropped area not total area.

Year	Crop	Treatment	
		Arable control	Arable alley
1990	Threshing peas	5.9	5.3 (90.8)
1990/91	Winter wheat	7.6	8.3 (108.4)
1991/92	Winter wheat	6.6	6.8 (103.4)
1992/93	Winter barley	5.1	6.3 (122.7)
1994	Threshing peas	4.5	4.2 (94.2)
1994/95	Winter wheat	9.3	8.8 (95.0)
1995/96	Winter wheat	10.4	8.1 (78.1)
1996/97	Winter barley	5.7	5.6 (98.2)

Figures in parentheses are yields as a percentage of the arable control.

Table 7.4 Mean yields (t ha⁻¹) of the arable crops in the control area, and the continuous and alternately cropped areas in the silvoarable system at each site for 1994/95 and 1995/96, expressed in terms of the cropped area.

Year	Crop	Treatment		
		Control (t ha⁻¹)	Alternately cropped (t ha⁻¹)	Continuously cropped (t ha⁻¹)
Cirencester				
1994/95	Winter beans	2.8^a	2.0^b	2.0^b
			(71)	(71)
1995/96	Winter wheat	10.1^a	8.6^b	7.9^c
			(85)	(78)
Leeds				
1994/95	Winter wheat	8.2^b	8.8^a	7.8^b
			(108)	(95)
1995/96	Winter barley	7.7^a	7.0^b	6.9^b
			(91)	(90)
Silsoe				
1994/95	Winter wheat	7.8^c	8.6^a	8.1^b
			(110)	(104)
1995/96	Winter wheat	7.5^b	9.1^a	7.3^b
			(121)	(98)

Values in parentheses express the yield as a percentage of the control. Values with the same letter ($^{a, b, c}$) within each site are not significantly different at $p=0.05$.

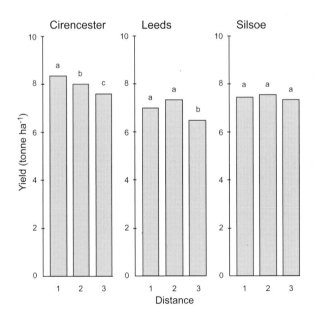

Figure 7.3 Effect of distance from a row of trees on yield of winter barley at Leeds and winter wheat at Cirencester and Silsoe in 1995/96 in the continuously cropped treatment. Yields were measured in strips parallel to row of trees, strip 3 being closest and strip 1 being furthest from the row of trees. Values with the same letter (within each site) are not significantly different at $p=0.05$.

77

Table 7.5 The mean height[a] (m) of trees in the Leeds furniture-timber tree experiment in agroforestry tree rows and in forestry-density planting (forestry control plots) since the winter of 1990/91.

Year	Treatment	
	Forestry control	Agroforestry tree rows
1990/91	2.8	2.6 (93.0)
1991/92	3.4	3.0 (89.1)
1992/93	3.9	3.3 (85.5)
1993/94	4.4	3.7 (82.3)
1994/95	4.8	4.0 (83.0)
1995/96	5.1	4.3 (84.2)
1996/97	5.6	4.7 (85.3)

Figures in parentheses are heights as a percentage of the forestry control. [a] Mean of three species: ash, cherry and sycamore (walnut is not planted at forestry density).

forestry-density planting (forestry control) at 2 m spacing (Table 7.5). The lower height cannot be ascribed solely to an effect of competition for resources by the crop because the widely-spaced agroforestry trees are more exposed to wind than forestry control trees.

MAFF-sponsored trial with poplar
If crops affect tree growth, continuous cropping would be expected to depress tree growth most and continuous fallow least, with alternate cropping intermediate in effect. Up until 1996/97, an effect of cropping treatment on tree growth has only been consistently demonstrated at the Cirencester site where trees in the continuously cropped treatment have always been smaller than those in the other treatments (Figure 7.4). At Leeds, significant effects of arable treatment on tree height first appeared in the winter of 1995/96 with significant differences in 1996/97 between all treatments with a rank order as predicted.

The significant effects of cropping on poplar growth observed in 1996 were the clearest observed so far in this experiment. In the initial years, the plastic mulch created an environment around the newly developing root system of trees that was free of weed and crop competition. By 1995 however, the tree roots at Silsoe had extended to at least a distance of 3.5 m (Burgess *et al.*, 1996, 1997) indicating the potential for competition between tree and crop roots for water and nutrients. The competition for resources is likely to become more critical as the poplars continue to grow.

The cropping treatments have no value in deciding on the best crop husbandry because it is unlikely that a fallow or partial fallow system of cropping would be economically viable. However they demonstrate that intercropping will affect tree growth, so far by 3% per year so that the duration of the tree rotation might have to be extended. Despite this effect the cultivar 'Beaupré' has grown consistently well on all three trial sites, achieving a mean height overall of 6.5 m in 4 years, 30% greater than the mean of the other three varieties.

Various lessons have been learnt relating to practical management from this most recent trial: these include the importance of careful planting, the feasibility of using a plastic mulch for weed control, the choice of an alley width that is compatible with field machinery, and the desirability of finding appropriate methods for controlling weeds between the plastic mulch and cropped area (Plate 23). The feasibility of the system is no longer in doubt; an economic evaluation is presented in Chapter 11.

Conclusions and current recommendations

These experiments, which are still only in the first half of the potential tree rotation, show that from the point of view of establishment and subsequent silvicultural and agricultural management, silvoarable agroforestry is a possible land-use system in northern maritime Europe.

A current recommendation for a system is shown in Box 7.1. The environmental, social and economic impacts of such a system are considered in Chapters 8, 10 and 11.

As the trees grow there will be competition between trees and crop. In the narrower alleys this may eventually lead to the conversion to silvopastoral management. In wider alleys where canopies will never meet across the alley, e.g. 26 m

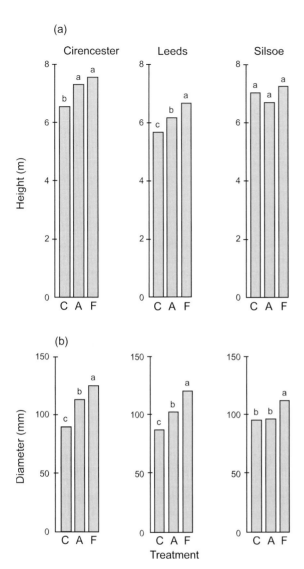

(a)

Cirencester   Leeds   Silsoe

Height (m)

C A F   C A F   C A F

(b)

Diameter (mm)

C A F   C A F   C A F

Treatment

Figure 7.4 Effect of cropping treatment on (a) the mean height and (b) the mean diameter at breast height (1.3 m) of all trees at each of the three sites at the end of 1996. Values with the same letter (within each site) are not significantly different at $p=0.05$. C: continuously cropped; A: alternately cropped; F: fallow.

between tree rows, arable cropping may always be possible, with competition only close to the trees. To date, no experiments have been set up to test this proposition.

Arable farmers adopting such a land-use system will not need advice about the arable cropping. They will, however, need advice about silviculture

Box 7.1 Current recommendations for a silvo-arable agroforestry system

- Tree material: hybrid poplar sets.
- Planted into continuous black plastic strip mulch with narrow, herbicide-treated strips between mulch and crop or circular plastic mulch disks with planted herbaceous understorey containing nectar-producing species.
- Trees initially protected from animal damage by plastic tubes.
- Trees 6 m apart in the tree row.
- Tree row 2 m wide.
- Alley 14, 20 or 26 m wide.
- Arable crop 12, 18 or 24 m wide within alley.
- Combinable crop with standard commercial husbandry, autumn-sown crops preferable.
- Duration of tree rotation 20–25 years.
- Tree pruned to 2 or 3 whorls and maintaining a canopy depth of approximately 50% of tree height, crown correction if necessary to maintain a dominant leader (Plate 24).
- Epicormic shoots and tree suckers removed.

which is currently regarded as the province of foresters. The present standard of management of farm woodland leaves much to be desired and there is a need for much better education of farmers of the need to actually care for trees if reasonable returns are expected at maturity.

Acknowledgements
The research at the Open University would not have been possible without the help of Dr R.M. Morris and Sir Ralph Verney KBE Bt. Funding is gratefully acknowledged from The Open University, the Ministry of Agriculture, Fisheries and Food, The European Commission and the Department for International Development. The research at Leeds would not be possible without the support of D.T. Corry, C. Wright and D. Hardy of the Field Research Unit of the School of Biology and numerous summer assistants. Funding is gratefully acknowledged from the Ministry of Agriculture, Fisheries and Food, the Yorkshire Agricultural Society, the British Ecological Society and the Leeds Literary and Philosophical Society.

REFERENCES

BEATON, A. (1987). Poplars and agroforestry. *Quarterly Journal of Forestry* **81**(4), 225–233.

BURGESS, P.J., NKOMAULA, J.C. and MEDEIROS-RAMOS, A.L. (1997). Root distribution and water use in a four-year old silvoarable system. *Agroforestry Forum* **8**(3), 15–18.

BURGESS, P.J., STEPHENS, W., ANDERSON, G. and DURSTON, J. (1996). Water use by a poplar-wheat agroforestry system. *Aspects of Applied Biology* **44**, 129–136.

DUPRAZ, C. and NEWMAN, S.M. (1997). Temperate agroforestry: the European way. In: *Temperate agroforestry*, ed. A.M. Gordon and S.M. Newman. CAB International, Wallingford, 181–230.

GRIFFITHS, J., PHILLIPS, D.S., COMPTON, S.G., WRIGHT, C. and INCOLL, L.D. (1998). Slug number and slug damage in a silvoarable agroforestry landscape. *Journal of Applied Ecology* **35,** 252–260.

INCOLL, L.D., BURGESS, P.J., EVANS, R.J., CORRY D.T. and BEATON, A. (1997a). Temperate silvoarable agroforestry with poplar - Annual Report 1996. *Agroforestry Forum* **8**(3), 12–15.

INCOLL, L.D., CORRY, D.T., WRIGHT, C. and COMPTON, S.G. (1997b). Temperate silvoarable agroforestry with quality hardwood timber species - Annual Report 1996. *Agroforestry Forum* **8** (3), 9–11.

NEWMAN, S.M. (1986). A pear and vegetable interculture system: land equivalent ratio, light use efficiency and dry matter productivity. *Experimental Agriculture* **22,** 383–392.

NEWMAN, S.M., LAWSON, G.J., CALLAGHAN, T.V., WAINWRIGHT, J. and SCOTT, R. (1988). Biomass production from agroforestry. In: *Proceedings of bioenergy* 1988, Naples.

NEWMAN, S.M. and WAINWRIGHT, J. (1989). An economic analysis of energy from biomass: poplar silvoarable systems compared to poplar monoculture. In: *Euroforum new energies*, vol.3, Proceedings of International Congress at Saarbrucken, 1988. Stephens, Bedfordshire, 456–458.

NEWMAN, S.M., WAINWRIGHT, J., OLIVER, P. and ACWORTH, J.M. (1991a). Walnut agroforestry in the UK: Research (1900-1991) assessed in relation to experience in other countries. In: *Proceedings of the 2nd North American conference on agroforestry.* Missouri, USA, 74–94.

NEWMAN, S.M., PARK, J., WAINWRIGHT, J., OLIVER, P., ACWORTH, J.M. and HUTTON, N. (1991b). Tree productivity, economics and light use efficiency of poplar silvoarable systems for energy. In: *Proceedings of the 6th European conference on biomass energy industry and environment*, Athens, April 1991. Applied Science, London, 151–158.

NIX, J.(1995). *Farm management pocketbook.* Wye College, University of London.

FURTHER READING

BEATON, A., INCOLL, L.D. and BURGESS, P.J. (1999). Silvoarable agroforestry. *Scottish Forestry* **53** (1), 28–32.

GORDON. A.M. and NEWMAN, S.M. (1997). *Temperate agroforestry.* CAB International, Wallingford.

Environmental and Landscape Impacts

Chapter 8

Environmental impacts

Jim McAdam

Introduction

This chapter reviews the likely impact of silvoarable and silvopastoral agroforestry systems on wildlife conservation in the UK. The two systems will be dealt with separately because they have different strategies for their introduction, land disturbances and management.

Agroforestry systems have complex interactions between the individual components and research has primarily concentrated on quantifying physical and economic outputs with less investigation of any ecological interactions. Hence there are only tentative conclusions at this stage for most aspects of the effect on conservation and biodiversity. However, some groups of organisms have already shown a response to the introduction of agroforestry systems and have made an impact on the landscape. Grazing will not be dealt with in this chapter.

Wildlife and biodiversity in silvoarable systems

Effects on invertebrates

At the small number of sites in the UK (Chapter 7) where silvoarable systems are under scientific investigation, the arable crop is managed conventionally although the presence of the trees may restrict herbicide use. Opportunities for enhancing biodiversity within these systems relate mainly to the strip of ground in which the trees are planted. Although this strip is usually covered in black plastic for the first years after tree establishment to suppress competing vegetation, the subsequent establishment of vegetation beneath the trees may harbour pest species, natural enemies, beneficial insects, pollinating bees and other wildlife which will affect the crop.

Ground beetles, normally good indicators of environmental change, have given inconclusive results (Philips et al., 1994). Trees increased populations of some species of carabid beetles, other species favoured the arable controls. Trees did not affect five species of rove beetles (in the genus *Tachyporus*) in summer populations, but silvoarable areas had more carabids than arable areas in winter (Philips et al., 1994). There were lower aphid populations in crops adjacent to tree rows than in purely arable systems (Naeem et al., 1995). High levels of aphid parasitoids were encouraged by the trees and aphids moved into the grass strip in summer. With slugs, the reverse was true (Griffiths et al., 1994). There was greater slug diversity in silvoarable systems than in arable controls but the numbers of slugs moving from the grass strip refugia into the cereal crop could pose a potential pest problem which would almost certainly reduce arable crop yields. There is, however, clear evidence from shelter belts planted on arable land that the trees enhance wildlife generally (Dix et al., 1995).

Effects of management on non-crop flora

In a silvoarable system opportunities to enhance flora biodiversity exist either through management of the tree strip or by reducing herbicide use in the cereal crop (McAdam, 1996). There is little evidence to date of any benefits in floral diversity accruing from silvoarable systems. However, this could be changed if consensus decisions were taken to introduce less invasive vegetation. Corry (personal communication) has proposed that the trees might be planted into strips sown with a species like white clover which encourages beneficial insects such as parasitoid wasps and predators, enriches the soil, enhances floral diversity and looks more attractive than plastic. Although clover can be an aggressive species it has been demonstrated to be far less competitive to establishing trees than grass species and in addition clover contributes nitrogen which has enhanced tree growth in arable land. If at all possible a wildflower mixture of stable species composition should be established.

Key effects of silvoarable systems on wildlife and biodiversity

Silvoarable systems

- have higher populations of small mammals, flying arthropods and hoverflies than arable systems

- encourage beneficial insects which enrich the soil and enhance floral diversity when strips are sown with white clover or wildflower mixture.

Wildlife and biodiversity in silvopastoral systems

Silvopastoral systems can be created in two ways (Sibbald and Sinclair, 1990). The first approach uses stands of mature trees which have been thinned and pasture established within the respaced stand or individual mature spaced trees growing in a grazed pasture situation. In the second approach trees are planted into pasture and grazing continues as the primary land use.

Both systems will affect wildlife in different ways and the effects on flora, invertebrates and birds will be reviewed. This information comes largely from studies by Crowe (1993) using mature poplar and from the National Network Silvopastoral Experiment (NNE) (Hoppé *et al.*, 1996a).

Effects on invertebrates

All collections are based on ground trapping using pitfall traps placed either randomly or in relation to trees in each plot. Ground beetles and spiders have been shown to be good biological indicators

of disturbance or habitat change (Stork, 1990) and these have been investigated at all the UK Network sites. In a comparison of the spiders collected on the sycamore plots at the north-east Scotland (MLURI Glensaugh) site and the Northern Ireland (DARD Loughgall) site (Dennis *et al.*, 1996; Johnston, 1996) more spider individuals were collected from the agroforest than woodland or pasture and more species were collected from the woodland than any other agroforest or pasture at both sites.

At the Northern Ireland site spider communities and spider richness was greater in the agroforestry treatment where trees had been planted at the closer 5 m x 5 m spacing, than at the wider 10 m x 10 m spacing. Greater numbers of spiders (but not greater species richness) were found in sycamore than in the ash. Species richness was greatest near the trees and abundance of individuals greatest far from the trees.

Carabid beetles were trapped at the same two sites (Dennis *et al.*, 1996; Cuthbertson and McAdam, 1996). Although 43 species were trapped on the MLURI site in 1995, there were no obvious differences in the numbers of species associated with each treatment. A nearby mature coniferous shelterbelt had fewer species recorded than the agroforest or open pasture. Approximately twice as many individual beetles were trapped from the agroforest than the woodland, with the open pasture approximately intermediate between the two, although ground beetles are sensitive to aspect as well as the shade cast by trees (P. Dennis, personal communication). Twenty-three species were collected from the Northern Ireland site. Over half of the individuals trapped were from two species: *Pterostichus melanarius* and *P. niger* (Plate 25 (a)). There were significantly more species and individuals in the woodland (2 m x 2 m, 2500 stems ha^{-1}) than the agroforest or the open pasture and tree species did not affect the presence of beetles at this stage in the NNE. Pitfall traps located near the trees collected a greater species diversity and richness than traps in the open pasture.

Invertebrates seem to be encouraged to grassland sites by the presence of trees. This in turn will provide more food for birds. Spiders seem to respond more rapidly than other groups to the introduction of trees. There are distinct groups of beetles which colonise woodlands, a group of open grassland species and a more intermediate grouping found associated with the high density agroforest. Spiders and staphylinid (rove) beetles appear to respond more rapidly to the introduction of silvopastoral systems than do carabid (ground) beetles (Dennis *et al.*, 1996).

Effects on birds

The above-mentioned invertebrates form an important food supply for birds. The effects of increasing the amount and diversity of food and providing structural diversity to the grassland habitat enhances cover and increases bird numbers and species diversity, in addition to providing roosting and nesting sites. Birds have been regularly recorded on the NNE sites by observing them alighting on the plot at three times in the day during spring/summer and autumn/winter (Jones and Eason, 1995). Surrounding land-use practices and habitat diversity clearly affect birds. For example at the North Wales site (established in 1989) only small numbers of bird species (2–4) were attracted to the newly established silvopasture whereas 20–30 species were recorded from surrounding woodland. On a more mature silvopastoral site such as the MLURI Glensaugh site, 15 bird species were recorded. Fieldfares (*Turdus pilaris*, 57%, Plate 25(b)) and carrion crows (*Corvus corone*, 35%) were by far the most common species. Carrion crows occurred equally in both seasons. Flocking fieldfares were predominant in autumn/winter and as many as 150 individuals were recorded on a single plot. Carrion crows decreased with decreasing tree density. Fieldfares used the woodland for perching and open pasture for feeding. The same number of species were recorded on the agroforest and the open pasture. Significantly more species were observed on the woodland plots than on pasture and agroforest (Agnew and Sibbald, 1996).

In Northern Ireland, overall, 35 and 27 species were recorded over the 6-year period (1992–1996) at the Loughgall (lowland) and Broughshane (upland) NNE sites respectively (Toal and

McAdam, 1995). At Loughgall, although there was considerable year to year variation, consistently more birds were recorded on the agroforest in summer and winter than either the open pasture or the woodland. At Broughshane, in both winter and summer, more birds were attracted to the higher density agroforest than any other treatment. Numbers in the woodland were very low. Species diversity was greater in the lowlands (Loughgall) than the uplands (Broughshane) and a greater diversity of birds (though lesser numbers) was found on the open pasture and woodland at Loughgall in both summer and winter. The same trend was not found at Broughshane.

At the lowland IGER sites in Southern England, 11 and 18 species were observed from the agroforest and woodland areas respectively and a further five species hunted at low level over the areas as a whole. The presence of trees significantly increased bird species diversity over a range of sites (Jones and Eason, 1995). A summary of the birds likely to benefit most from agroforestry is presented in Table 8.1.

At Glensaugh, the presence of trees (in an agroforest) appeared to reduce the numbers of carrion crows which are important predators of upland sheep over a range of sites (Table 8.2). Trends at the other site were not consistent, suggesting that the influence of the surrounding landscape on birds must be taken into consideration.

Overall, the results show that even at this early stage agroforestry systems can have an impact on birds. They appear to encourage birds which would normally be associated with hedgerows and woodlands, while sustaining grassland birds, so creating an assemblage of species which may prove unique to agroforestry systems but one which will probably change with time.

Effects on flora

In establishing stands

The six sites of the NNE (Sibbald and Sinclair, 1990) represent a range of pasture from 20-year-old swards (the MLURI site) to those sown the year prior to the trials commencing (the DARD Loughgall site). In the NNE, pasture composition has not been affected by the tree canopy in the

Table 8.1 Birds attracted to agroforestry plots in grassland areas in upland and lowland sites in the UK (after: Toal and McAdam, 1995; Agnew and Sibbald, 1996; Jones and Eason, 1995).

Upland	Lowland
mistle thrush[a], skylark,	mistle thrush[a], song thrush,
redwing, curlew[a], woodcock[a],	blackbird, redwing,
fieldfare, wood pigeon,	fieldfare, wood pigeon,
starling, magpie[a], jackdaw,	magpie[a], woodcock[a],
rook, hooded crow[a], raven,	jackdaw, rook, hooded crow[a],
tits, finches,	robin, wren, dunnock,
meadow pipit, robin, wren,	chaffinch[a], goldfinch[a],
sparrow hawk, kestrel, merlin, hen harrier	finches, tits, swallows and
	sand martins (aerial feeding above trees),
	sparrow hawk

[a] Found nesting.

Table 8.2 Density of carrion crows (numbers during a 20 min observation period) in grassland, woodland and three agroforests (100, 200 and 400 stems ha-1). Data from the Silvopastoral National Network experiment.

	Grassland	Agroforestry			Woodland
		100 trees ha-1	200 trees ha-1	400 trees ha-1	
North Wales (winter) 1994	4	1	-	1	0
North Wales (spring) 1995	1	4	-	1	1
North-east Scotland 1995	7	4	2	1	0
Lowland, Northern Ireland 1992-1996	5	19	-	24	0
Upland, Northern Ireland 1992-1996	22	31	-	49	1
Upland, South Wales 1994	-	13	13	13	0

first 5–7 years of the silvopastoral system, even at 5 m x 5 m spacing with mean tree heights over 3 m (McAdam, 1996; McAdam and Hoppé, 1996).

During a 3-year tree establishment phase at each site, a 1 m circular area was kept vegetation free with herbicide at the base of each tree in the agroforest. At the Loughgall, lowland site (reseeded 1 year before the trial commenced) this sprayed area has been recolonised by *Lolium perenne* with a small proportion of *Poa annua*, and is now not significantly different in botanical composition from the rest of the sward away from the influence of the trees. This contrasts with previous experience of plant colonisation of bare ground areas in pasture. At Glensaugh where the sward was old, permanent pasture (though *Lolium* dominated), the area around the trees has been colonised by a grass or broadleaved species flora which is completely different from the rest of the plot. It can be concluded that as pastures mature they build up a bank of seeds and a soil structure which results in pasture diversity when bare ground is created.

In agroforestry, animal behaviour is modified, animals spend more time trampling and lying around the trees and defecating and urinating away from the trees (Nwaigbo *et al.*, 1995). Behavioural patterns such as these will initiate the sort of pasture changes recorded by Crowe and McAdam (1992b) in a more mature stand.

Some trees (e.g. sycamore) have thick, heavy leaves which shade pasture, whereas others such as larch buffer sward temperatures and initiate change (Eason, 1988). As the trees mature, leaf litter becomes more important as an ecological factor. Stock readily consume leaves of species such as ash, and grazing should be carried on into autumn to reduce the effect of leaf litter on pasture composition. The effect of pruning the lower branches of the tree will affect pasture composition. Woodland will be more species diverse than agroforest, for example within the woodland plots of the Loughgall site, 17 higher plant species were found within the woodland as opposed to six within the agroforest.

In silvopastoral systems the understorey vegetation can be managed either directly through sward and livestock management or indirectly through tree species selection and canopy manipulation. Guidelines exist on grassland management for nature conservation (e.g. Haggar and Peel, 1994) and these can be adapted to suit silvopastoral systems though the imposition of a tree canopy will create conditions which will further influence sward management decisions. There is scope to create biophysical models of tree growth which will predict changes in microclimate and canopy and enable decisions on biodiversity enhancement to be made.

In mature stands
Crowe (1993) used a 35-year-old, mature poplar stand planted at 8 m x 8 m diagonal spacings into grazed, permanent pasture to investigate the effect of the tree canopy on microclimate, botanical composition and herbage yield in swards maintained at a range of herbage mass levels (Crowe and McAdam, 1992a). A comparison with an adjacent, non-planted area with the same management history was possible. Pasture species composition was significantly different

under the tree canopy compared with the open sward. Species such as *Lolium perenne*, *Poa trivialis*, *Trifolium repens* and *Cirsium arvense* favoured the open pasture whereas *Agrostis capillaris*, *Holcus lanatus* and *Poa annua* performed better under the tree canopy. Of particular interest was the finding that the seasonal pattern of growth and production of these grass species was altered under the trees with the balance of production between the species altering throughout the season. This 'compensation' and adaptation resulted in seasonal levels of production being maintained at a relatively high level (increased production before and after tree leaf canopy appearance and fall) although the pattern of production was altered.

This work shows that over the life history of any silvopastoral system, significant changes in ground vegetation will occur but the underlying ecological factors which will determine this succession and the likely effect of these vegetation changes on fauna are not known.

Key benefits of silvopastoral systems for biodiversity

Silvopastoral systems
- attract a variety of spiders and woodland insects

- encourage birds normally associated with hedgerows and woodlands while sustaining grassland birds

- build up a bank of seeds and soil structure during establishment which results in pasture diversity

- bring about significant changes in ground vegetation during the life history of the stand but underlying ecological factors and effects on fauna are not known.

The physical environment

Nutrient leaching

A current source of concern is the leaching of nitrate from agricultural land into aquifers and watercourses, with implications both for human health and for aquatic life. Research on a silvorable system with poplars in Sweden (Browaldh, 1995) and with cherry (*Prunus avium*) on a silvopastoral system (Campbell and Mackie-Dawson, 1991) has shown that the trees retrieve leached nitrate and significantly reduce the amount getting into the groundwater. Phosphate leached below the grass-root zone has been shown to be taken up by the tree root network at a lower depth in the soil profile (Lehmann *et al.*, 1997).

High solar radiation

Where availability of moisture (rather than lack of photosynthetically active radiation) is the limiting factor in plant growth – and this is regularly the case over large areas of eastern England, which habitually have soil moisture deficits in excess of 100 mm – direct sunlight can contribute to water stress rather than to the production of dry matter. This is a well-known phenomenon in Hungary, and anecdotal evidence from the Plain of York during the dry summer of 1996, where a potato crop was observed to yield considerably better under large oak trees than out in the open field, is supported by experimental data from arid and semi-arid Africa (Belsky *et al.*, 1993). In addition, sunlight can overheat and damage leaves directly. With climate change holding out the prospect of hotter summers and more frequent droughts, shade from trees could well be an asset in arable crop production. Shade will also benefit the welfare of animals grazing in agroforests (Sibbald *et al.*, 1995).

Wind speed

It has been demonstrated that the effect of windbreaks at frequent intervals in the landscape – as opposed to single windbreaks – is to decrease wind speeds over the landscape as a whole (Jensen, 1949). An agroforestry system is effectively a series of windbreaks within a short distance of each other and can therefore be expected to be an efficient means of reducing wind speeds. Apart from the consequent increase in comfort, this can also be expected to reduce the energy needed to heat buildings to leeward of such plantings (Meyer, 1990) and to reduce wind damage of all kinds. In a district where a number of agroforestry systems had been established this effect could be expected to extend to a whole landscape. In a silvopasture, Hoppé *et al.* (1996b) found that sycamore and ash planted at 400 stems ha[-1] significantly reduced wind speeds in the canopy region but ash had a much greater effect than sycamore. This reduction was not found at ground level.

Key effects of silvoarable and silvopastoral systems on the physical environment

Silvoarable and silvopastoral systems modify the physical environment through the effect of trees on:

- nutrient cycling
- shade
- reduction in wind speed.

These changes create the types of conditions which favour wildlife.

Conclusions

Even in relatively recently established agroforestry systems, where the tree canopy is not having a significant effect on ground vegetation or output, the presence of trees attracts small mammals, some invertebrate groups and slugs and enhances the diversity of the ground flora. Silvopastoral systems encourage birds, either through the spatial habitat diversity created or the increased levels of invertebrates which act as a feed source.

A generalised summary of the effects of agroforestry systems in the UK on a range of organisms, based on current and completed research programmes and observation, is presented in Table 8.3.

Table 8.3 Summary of evidence for the predicted impact of agroforestry systems on biodiversity (numbers and species) in the UK.

Groups	System	
	Silvoarable	Silvopastoral
Small mammals	↑[1]	0
Birds	0	↑[2,3]
Carabid beetles	|[4]	↔[5,6]
Staphylinid beetles	↔S ↑W[4]	↔[7]
Spiders	0	↑[7]
Flying arthropods	↑[8]	0
Aphids	↓[9]	0
Hoverflies	↑[4]	0
Slugs	↑[10]	0
Flora	↑[11]	↑[12,13]

↑ = Consistent increase over agricultural systems.
↓ = Consistent decrease over agricultural systems.
↔ = No effect found.
| = Conflicting effects from sites or species.
0 = No information available; S = summer effect;
W = winter effect.

Sources: 1. Wright, 1994. 2. Toal and McAdam, 1995. 3. Jones and Eason, 1995. 4. Philips *et al.*, 1994. 5. Cuthbertson and McAdam, 1996. 6. Dennis *et al.*, 1996. 7. Johnston, 1996. 8. Peng *et al.*, 1993. 9. Naeem *et al.*, 1995. 10. Griffiths *et al.*, 1994. 11. Corry, personal communication. 12. McAdam, 1996. 13. McAdam and Hoppé, 1996.

> While this list reveals the dearth of experimental evidence available, it does indicate broad trends which show that there is potential for agroforestry to enhance biodiversity in agricultural systems in the UK. Agroforestry systems also improve the physical environment through more efficient nutrient capture and their modification of the microclimate.

REFERENCES

AGNEW, R.D.M. and SIBBALD, A. (1996). The avifauna of the Glensaugh silvopastoral site. *Agroforestry Forum* **7** (3), 20–21.

BELSKY, A.J., MWONGA, S.M., AMUNDSON, R.G., DUXBURY, J.M. and ALI, A.R. (1993). Comparative effects of isolated trees on their undercanopy environments in high-rainfall and low-rainfall savannas. *Journal of Applied Ecology* **30** (1), 143–155.

BROWALDH, M. (1995). The influence of trees on nitrogen dynamics in an agrisilvicultural system in Sweden. *Agroforestry Systems* **30**(3), 301–313.

CAMPBELL, C.D. and MACKIE-DAWSON, L.A. (1991). Below-ground competition between trees and grass in a silvopastoral system. *Agroforestry in the UK* **2**(3), 39–40.

CROWE, S.R. (1993). The response of *Lolium perenne* and *Holcus lanatus* to shading in relation to a silvopastoral agroforestry system. PhD Thesis, Queen's University of Belfast.

CROWE, S.R. and MCADAM, J.H. (1992a). Some effects of grazing management on a mixed species sward poplar–sheep agroforestry system. Proceedings of 14th General Meeting of the European Grassland Federation Lahti, Finland, 655–656.

CROWE, S.R. and MCADAM, J.H. (1992b). Sward dynamics in a mature poplar agroforestry system grazed by sheep. In: *Vegetation management in forestry, amenity and conservation areas. Aspects of Applied Biology* **29**, 413–418.

CUTHBERTSON, A. and MCADAM, J.H. (1996). The effect of tree density and species on carabid beetles in a range of pasture–tree agroforestry systems on a lowland site. *Agroforestry Forum* **7**(3), 17–20.

DENNIS, P., SHELLARD, J.F. and AGNEW, R.D.M. (1996). Shifts in arthropod assemblages in upland silvopasture. *Agroforestry Forum* **7**(3), 14–17.

DIX, M.E., JOHNSON, R.J., HAMELL, M.O., CASE, R.M., WRIGHT, R.J., HODGES, L., BRANDLE, R.J.E., SCHOENBERGER, M.M., SUNDERMANN, N.J., FITZMAURICE, R.L., YOUNG, L.J. and HUBBARD, K.G. (1995). Influence of trees on abundance of natural enemies of insect pests: a review. *Agroforestry Systems* **29**, 303–311.

EASON, W.R. (1988). Effect of tree litter on sward botanical composition and growth. In: *Proceedings of a research meeting held at the Welsh Agricultural College, Aberystwyth 13–15 September 1988*. British Grassland Society, Hurley, UK.

GRIFFITHS, J.G., PHILLIPS, D.S., WRIGHT, C., COMPTON, S.G. and INCOLL, L.D. (1994).

Problems with slugs in a silvoarable agroforestry system. *Agroforestry Forum* **5**(2), 24–26.

HAGGAR, R.J. and PEEL, S., eds (1994). *Grassland management and nature conservation.* Proceedings of a joint meeting between the British Ecological Society and the British Grassland Society, Leeds. Occasional Symposium No. 28. British Grassland Society, Hurley, UK.

HOPPÉ, G.M., SIBBALD, A.R., MCADAM, J.H., EASON, W.R., HISLOP, M. and TEKLEHAIMANOT, Z. (1996a). The UK National Network Silvopastoral Experiment: a coordinated approach to research. In: *Proceedings of the European Society for Agronomy, 4th Congress*, vol. 2, ed. M.K. van Ittersum, G.E.G.T. Venner, S.C. van de Geijn and T.H. Jetten. Veldhoven, The Netherlands, 630–631.

HOPPÉ, G.M., DUNBAR, P. and MCADAM, J.H. (1996b). Modification of wind profiles in developing silvopastoral systems. *Agroforestry Forum* **8**(1), 20–22.

JENSEN, M. (1949). Investigations in the shelter effect of landscape. From a publication by *Hedeselskabet*, Denmark.

JOHNSTON, R. (1996). The effect of tree density and species on spiders in a range of lowland pasture–tree agroforestry systems. Unpublished BSc Thesis, Queen's University of Belfast.

JONES, D. and EASON, W.R. (1995). The influence of a developing agroforestry system on bird population dynamics. *Quarterly Journal of Forestry* **89**(2), 120–125.

LEHMANN, J., WULF, S. and ZECH, W. (1997). Can trees recover nutrients under high leaching conditions. In: *Agroforestry for sustainable land use*, Montpellier, France, 23–29 June 1997, 155–158.

MCADAM, J.H. (1996). Vegetation change and management in temperate agroforestry systems. *Aspects of Applied Biology* **44**, 95–100.

MCADAM, J.H. and HOPPÉ, G.M. (1996). The effect of tree spacing on pasture composition in a silvopastoral system. *Agroforestry Forum* **7**(3), 22–26.

MEYER, R.L. (1990). Shelterbelt benefit to home heating cost. *Transactions of the Agricultural Society of England* **33**, 2003–2010.

NAEEM, M., COMPTON, S.G., PHILLIPS, D.S. and INCOLL, L.D. (1995). Factors influencing aphids and their parasitoids in a silvoarable agroforestry system. *Agroforestry Forum* **6**(2), 20–23.

NWAIGBO, L.C., SIBBALD, A.R. and HUDSON, G. (1995). Tree-scale trends in available soil nutrient and cone penetration resistance in a grazed hybrid larch (*Larix eurolepis*) silvopastoral system. *Agroforestry Forum* **6**(2), 48–50.

PENG, R.K., INCOLL, L.D., SUTTON, S.L., WRIGHT, C. and CHADWICK, A. (1993). Diversity of air-borne arthropods in a silvoarable agroforestry system. *Journal of Applied Ecology* **30**, 551–562.

PHILIPS, D.S., GRIFFITHS, J., NAEEM, M., COMPTON, S.G. and INCOLL, L.D. (1994). Responses of crop pests and their natural enemies to an agroforestry environment. *Agroforestry Forum* **5**(2), 14–20.

SIBBALD, A.R and SINCLAIR, F.L. (1990). A review of agroforestry research in progress in the UK. *Agroforestry Abstracts* **3**, 149–164.

SIBBALD, A.R., DICK, J. and JASON, G.R. (1995). The effects of the presence of widely-spaced trees on the behaviour of sheep. *Agroforestry Forum* **6**(2), 22–25.

STORK, N. (1990). *The role of ground beetles in ecological and environmental studies.* Intercept, Andover, Hampshire.

TOAL, L. and MCADAM, J.H. (1995). Avifauna in establishing silvopastoral systems in Northern Ireland. *Agroforestry Forum* **6**(2), 25–30.

WRIGHT, C. (1994). The distribution and abundance of small mammals in a silvoarable agroforestry system. *Agroforestry Forum* **5**(2), 26–28.

Chapter 9

Agroforestry in the landscape

Simon Bell

Introduction

The landscape of Britain which we see today has emerged as the result of many factors: the long continuity of traditional land-use patterns is overlaid with more recent industrial and urban influences, infrastructure and development. The landscape has changed and will continue to change. One of the most significant agents of change in the countryside has been agriculture itself: the extent to which certain crops are grown or forms of husbandry practised and the landscape these create. Except in places where climate or terrain limit the degree to which modern agriculture can flourish and eradicate earlier patterns, it is now no longer the case that economically based husbandry necessarily produces landscapes which people find aesthetically appealing (Bell, 1995).

The countryside is highly valued by an increasingly urbanised population who see it as a refuge and contrast from their daily life. The balance between humans and nature and the variation from tame, enclosed landscapes to wild remote places over relatively short distances gives a richness and diversity which makes Britain's landscape almost unique.

The introduction of new forms of agriculture or forestry into well-loved landscapes should be undertaken with some care (Bell, 1998). These can bring about sudden changes which may cause anxiety to residents and visitors who are used to seeing a particular landscape in a particular way. The patterns produced by such crops or plantations can seem out of keeping with the historical landscape, and to have few references or predecessors to help them blend into the continuity of the rural scene.

Agroforestry is one such potential land use which, if practised on any degree of scale and laid out in an insensitive fashion, is likely to provoke an adverse reaction and be seen by many people as another negative change. It will be important, therefore, to consider the character of the landscape where agroforestry is to be carried out and the layout of the trees themselves with a view to fitting it into the landscape. In certain places agroforestry may not be appropriate at all, or the economic consequences of making the changes necessary to the layout or scale may remove its viability in that place. Most of the time, however, it should be possible to combine practicalities, cost and any environmental requirements into an acceptable design. The following suggestions should be considered in order to comply with the requirements of the *Lowland landscape design guidelines* and the *Forest landscape design guidelines* (Forestry Authority, 1992, 1994).

Characteristics of agroforestry in the landscape

Agroforestry, whether silvopastoral or silvoarable, is a new component in many ways, depending on the tree species, spacing and location. It could be argued that many earlier, now traditional forms of silviculture were actually varieties of agroforestry. Wood pasture, where pollarded or fully-crowned trees were grown at wide spacing while animals grazed beneath, produces very fine landscapes often highly valued in visual, nature conservation and heritage terms. Orchards of apples, pears, plums and cherries comprise widely spaced trees with grass growing beneath which was frequently grazed by sheep or cut for hay. These, too, are valued as traditional components of the landscape. More recently, poplars planted for matchwood, widely spaced and high pruned, allow grazing beneath or sometimes arable crops, at least when the trees were young.

Orchards and poplar plantations have tended to be located in particular places such as low lying or frost draining areas in richer soils in intensively managed, small scale landscapes. Their layout, rows of evenly spaced trees of clonal origin, that are all similar if not identical in appearance, leads to a pattern of regularity and geometry. This is only at home in small scale landscapes where there is a strong structure of hedgerows and hedgerow trees.

Modern agroforestry is not yet a common sight in the landscape, but examples from other countries suggest that it can look very artificial, geometric and rigid when laid out in straight rows, equally spaced, with trees high pruned to standard heights, of one species and in visually prominent locations. The practicalities of agroforestry will to some extent dictate the constraints under which it can be practised.

It is best to divide design considerations between the two types, silvopastoral and silvoarable. These are looked at in the next two sections.

Design of silvopastoral systems

This type of system is likely to be the more flexible in terms of layout but also more prominent because of the more hilly landscapes in which it might be expected to be found. If most landscapes are more rural or upland, then a reduction in the degree of formality and geometry will be important in order to fit in with landscape character. The features it will be possible to vary to achieve this are the shape of the area planted, the straightness of the rows of trees, the spacing between and within rows and the species or variety of trees. As grazing will presumably preclude the use of shrubs and leave a clean floor beneath the trees, then blending edges into the surrounding landscape may be difficult.

Different landforms will require different approaches as follows:

1. *Flat landscapes seen from level views*

(a) Where hedgerows and trees remain strong (Figure 9.1 (a) and (b)). In this case, the plan shape of the area is not so critical. With some degree of variation of the row direction and tree spacing quite a relaxed, informal wooded appearance could result. The tree crowns will coalesce with one another and give the appearance of fairly dense woodland. If there are to be large expanses of planting, open fields should be retained amongst the areas in order to break down the scale, interlock the tree masses and open space and unify the landscape while maintaining some views into and through the landscape. This is especially important along public roads and rights of way or near settlements. Hedges and hedgerow trees will help to break up the profile and tie the area into the surrounding pattern.

(b) Where hedgerows and trees are absent (Figure 9.2 (a) and (b)). The same principles apply as above except that the planted area may tend to 'float' or seem unconnected with the landscape. Siting the planting near to other features, perhaps so that it can coalesce in the view with other woodlands, or next to farmsteads, is likely to help. The plan shape may be more important in shorter views as straight edges show up as vertical walls, even where the tree spacing is irregular. Some shape variation, however small, will relieve this.

2. *Undulating or rolling landforms with views of knolls and higher points*

(a) Strong field patterns (Figure 9.3). In this landscape type whole fields can be planted as long as they are not accumulated into areas which are too large for the intimate scale of such landscapes. Where the landform is stronger then some edges may be better shaped to follow it. If knolls are prominent then it is appropriate to clothe the whole feature, not a portion of it. The irregular row and spacing layout of trees is increasingly important. Coalescing canopies are particularly critical on skylines.

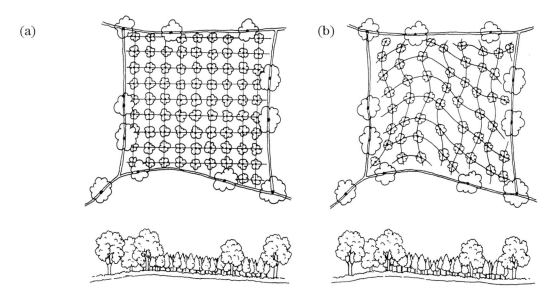

Figure 9.1 Design of silvopastoral systems on flat landscapes with a strong hedgerow pattern. (a) The straight rows give canopy coalescence but the ranks are strongly evident and inadequate space is provided near mature hedgerow trees. (b) This better solution achieves a varied spacing by setting out the planting in wavy instead of straight lines with irregular spacing along the rows. This breaks up the geometry, crowns coalesce to provide a woodland effect and open space is provided around existing hedgerow trees.

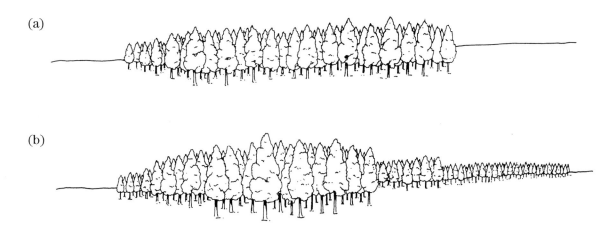

Figure 9.2 Design of silvopastoral systems in flat, open landscapes with no hedgerow pattern. (a) In this perspective view a rectangular layout appears to float in the open landscape. (b) A more varied layout of curving edges relieves the geometry. Tying the planting visually to another feature such as an existing woodland helps to unify it into the landscape.

(b) Open, unenclosed (Figure 9.4). In the absence of field patterns the planted areas must respond much more to the landform for example in the way that edges run across ridges or hollows. Generally they should extend down ridges and rise up into hollows. This way they look more compatible. Smaller areas may float unless positioned closer to one another or coalescing in the view. Locating planting in hollows or on complete knolls is to be preferred if conditions allow.

3. *Long even slopes or areas seen from elevated views* (Figure 9.5 (a) and (b))

In these areas the plan shape becomes more important. Geometric shapes are inappropriate even in enclosed landscapes as the colour and texture of the planted area is more visually dominant. Planted areas should therefore follow landform. Scale considerations mean that small scale areas relatively high on slopes look very awkward. An irregular layout of rows and spacing is particularly important in this landscape type.

Design of silvoarable systems

The principal difference between silvopastoral and silvoarable systems is the need to manoeuvre machinery between the rows of trees, and to turn at the ends, without damaging the trees or the soil. Since silvoarable systems are only contemplated on good sites where access for machinery is not a problem and where crop yields achieved between the trees are adequate, the type of landscapes where this is likely to be found is limited to better quality, lowland areas. This is fortunate since the restrictions on row direction and tree spacing would otherwise severely limit how well such plantings can be fitted into the landscape.

The main design considerations are the same as for silvopastoral systems in terms of plan shape and interval of trees within the rows (see Figure 9.6 (a) and (b) and Plate 26). Headlands for turning may mean wider spaces between trees and hedges or fences but irregular outlines within regular fields should present no problem. One means to tie such areas into the landscape is to combine the silvoarable planting with areas of more traditional farm woodland either physically or visually.

Species choice

If species choice can be varied, then the selection should be in favour of mixture rather than monoculture. Mixtures could be of appropriate species, either broadleaves or conifers, chosen to

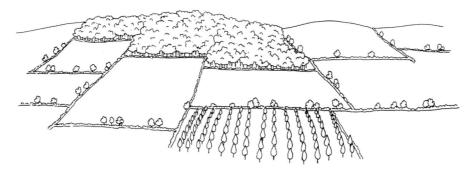

Figure 9.3 Design of silvopastoral systems on rolling topography with a strong field pattern where views of knolls and higher points are obtained.

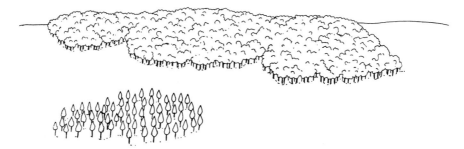

Figure 9.4 Design of silvopastoral systems on rolling, unenclosed topography requires consideration of landform and the use of techniques to avoid small floating blocks.

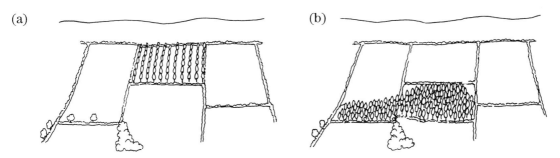

Figure 9.5 Design of silvopastoral systems on long, even slopes or areas seen from elevated views. (a) Small rectangular shapes perched high on a slope and laid out in straight rows looks very awkward. (b) Better scaled irregular shapes following landform and tied into other landscapes features, with varied spacing, looks far more comfortable.

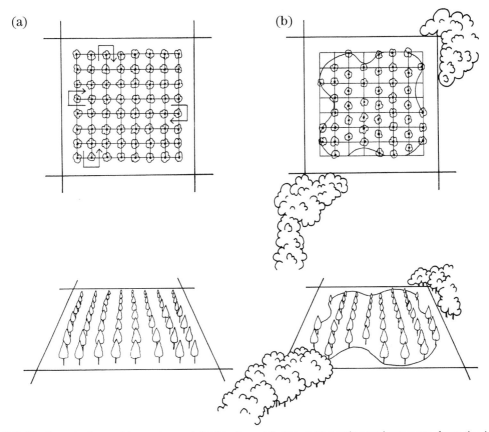

Figure 9.6 Design of silvoarable systems. (a) This layout is too rectangular and separate from the landscape. (b) This layout is varied in shape and spacing of trees in rows. It is also tied into the surrounding landscape either using existing woodlands or by planting woods to create links.

fit into the landscape. Mixtures can be intimate or arranged into irregularly shaped blocks (Figure 9.7 (b) and (c)). Avoid alternate rows (Figure 9.7 (a)), checkerboard or other systematic ways of planting mixtures. If one species is preferred then it could be possible to add small variations in an irregular way around the perimeter (Figure 9.7 (d)). If clones are grown, say of poplar, then some variation would help to reduce the artificial appearance such plantings can display.

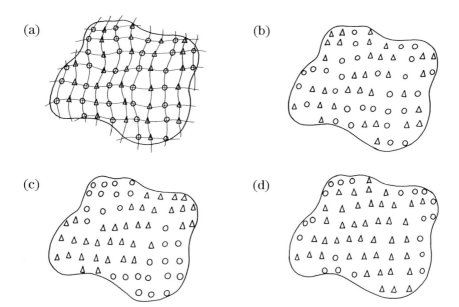

Figure 9.7 Layout of species mixtures in silvoarable systems. (a) A good design of wavy rows but species are planted in alternate rows leading to a striped appearance. (b) A more random mix of species is informal and more natural. (c) Two species planted in irregularly sized and shaped areas are easier to lay out and manage. (d) Groups of one species are placed at intervals around the perimeter of a main species.

Other means of achieving variety

Variety and therefore further reduction in formality can be increased by planting over a period to obtain a more varied canopy height within an area, or by adding new areas over time (Figure 9.8). Such additions need to be interlocked into the shape of the earlier block in order to achieve unity.

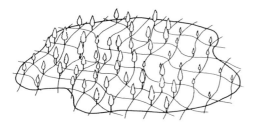

Figure 9.8 Variety can be achieved by planting areas of different ages next to each other.

Practicalities and costs of design

Any design, if it is to be achieved, must balance the aesthetic result with practicality and cost. Each of the solutions suggested above has been developed with practicality very much in mind.

However, each site and proposal for planting requires its own, unique solution. Costs might be increased in terms of layout, especially of wavy lines and intimate species mixtures. Other than that, if fencing, machinery use and other operations can be carried out with few added complications, then the options should be pursued. This will help ensure that such systems of husbandry can take a place in the countryside to its enhancement and certainly not its detriment.

REFERENCES

FORESTRY AUTHORITY (1992). *Lowland landscape design guidelines*. HMSO, London.

FORESTRY AUTHORITY (1994). *Forest landscape design guidelines*. HMSO, London.

BELL, S. (1995). New woodlands in the landscape. In: R. Ferris-Kaan, ed. *The ecology of woodland creation*. Wiley, Chichester.

BELL, S. (1998). *The landscape value of farm woodlands*. Forestry Commission Information Note 13. Forestry Commission, Edinburgh.

Section Four

Social and Economic Impacts

Chapter 10

The social implications of agroforestry

Chris Doyle and Terry Thomas

Social and economic context

Over the next decade farming systems will face continued pressures for change as they adjust to reduced public financial support for food production and a gradual convergence of farm prices to world market levels (Buckwell, 1995; 1996). Therefore, the 15% decline in agricultural employment observed over the last 15 years (Ministry of Agriculture, Fisheries and Food, annual) may be expected to continue, with the movement of farm workers to jobs in factories, slaughterhouses and local authorities (Strak and Mackel, 1991; O'Cinneide *et al.*, 1997). The common feature of many of these off-farm jobs is that they require a fairly basic level of manual skills and little or no retraining. However, in the 1990s the opportunities for manual employment in rural areas declined as economic pressures increased and industries became increasingly capitalised (Strak and Mackel, 1991; O'Cinneide *et al.*,1997). In this economic environment, Grundy *et al.* (1989) have stressed that forestry might provide the right type of jobs to absorb future displaced agricultural labour, as the work is not amenable to mechanisation. However, whether forestry in general or agroforestry in particular will play a significant role in future rural employment will depend on three factors:

- the willingness of farmers to plant trees;

- the willingness of the government to subsidise farm forestry;

- public attitudes to forestry in general and agroforestry in particular.

The second of these factors is likely to depend on the perceived wider local and regional economic benefits arising from increased farm forestry and agroforestry, while the third will partly reflect society's view of the non-market benefits of agroforestry connected with amenity, habitat, landscape and animal welfare. Accordingly, this chapter looks at three interrelated issues, namely:

- the attitude of farmers to forestry in general and agroforestry specifically;

- the wider employment impacts of agroforestry;

- the non-market benefits of farm woodlands.

Farmer attitudes to forestry and agroforestry

There have been a number of studies undertaken in recent years to examine the attitudes of farmers to establishing farm woodlands (Scambler, 1989; Sidwell, 1989; Appleton, 1990; Bishop, 1990; Gasson and Hill, 1990; Johnson, 1992; Dibden and Uzzell, 1992; Williams *et al.*, 1994; Thomas and Willis, 1997). These have tended to suggest that the majority of farmers regard forestry as an 'inappropriate' use of productive land and as 'irrelevant' as an alternative source of income. Consequently, where farmers do consider converting part of their land area to trees, they tend to select the worst land as the most suitable (Crabtree and MacMillan, 1989; Ni Dhubháin and Gardiner, 1994; Williams *et al.*, 1994). However, this attitude relates only to conventional forestry, where planting incentives are seen as inadequate to take land totally out of farm production, especially as the shift into trees is perceived as being an irreversible land-use change. In contrast, in so far as it involves the diversification of existing grassland and arable systems rather than the total displacement of agriculture, agroforestry should encounter less resistance from farmers. However, the problem is that the vast majority of farmers are unaware that agroforestry implies fewer trees and greater flexibility of land use, coupled with the ability to retain agricultural output for a considerable period of the rotation.

Nevertheless, it is difficult to substantiate these views about the relative attractiveness of agroforestry to farmers. Because of the novel nature of the system, there is a relative paucity of information on farmer attitudes. However, recent studies in Wales and Northern Ireland, reported by Thomas and Willis (1997) and McAdam *et al.* (1997) respectively, have confirmed that farmers know little about agroforestry. In addition, even where they are aware of the potential of such land-use systems, the existing public financial support for agroforestry is seen as weak, inflexible and unpredictable. That lack of knowledge may be a key factor in constraining investment in agroforestry has been shown by the results from a programme initiated by the Department of Agriculture for Northern Ireland, in the autumn of 1996, and designed to raise the awareness of farmers about agroforestry (Thomas and Willis, 1997). This demonstrated that if farmers were shown agroforestry systems, they showed a high level of interest. In the study only 17% of farmers surveyed stated that they were not interested in agroforestry at all, while at the other end of the spectrum 15% declared that they were highly interested. This impression was reinforced by a survey of farmers attending an open day, which was part of the project. Indications were that only 25% of the participants saw no role for agroforestry on their farm after visiting the demonstration project, while 50% said that they were very likely to establish agroforestry. For those reacting positively, the potential benefits of agroforestry were seen to be (1) that it was a more flexible system than conventional forestry and (2) that it offered a stable land use against a background of an uncertain future for the agricultural industry. Furthermore, there was evidence to indicate that it was considered to be an environmentally friendly system, as well as having positive implications for animal welfare in

certain cases (McAdam *et al.*, 1997).

On the other hand, the Welsh studies revealed that, even where farmers were aware of the potential benefits of agroforestry, the existing system of grants was seen as militating against the adoption of agroforestry compared to conventional forestry (Willis *et al.*, 1993; Bullock *et al.*, 1994). In general, rates of grant for agroforestry schemes are merely determined on a pro rata basis, relative to conventional forestry payments, depending on number of trees per hectare. However, Thomas and Willis (1997) note that this fails to recognise the true costs of production of agroforestry systems. Only in Northern Ireland has a different approach to public funding been adopted. Since 1995, farmers investing in agroforestry have been entitled to 50% of the grant eligible for conventional forestry under the Woodland Grant Scheme, subject to a minimum planting of 400 trees ha^{-1}, though not under the Farm Woodland Premium Scheme. As a consequence McAdam *et al.* (1997) reported that farmers in Northern Ireland felt that grants for agroforestry were adequate.

Concentrating on the financial subsidies ignores the fact that the reasons why farmers plant trees are many and varied (Thomas and Willis, 1997). In particular, a study by Appleton and Crabtree (1991) of Scottish farmers participating in the Farm Woodland Scheme showed considerations relating to landscape, wildlife conservation, game and shelter were all much more important than increasing farm income, when deciding whether to plant trees. Thus, the farmers participating in the survey were asked to give each of their stated objectives for planting trees a score from 1 (low priority) to 3 (high priority). The objectives with the highest scores are presented in Figure 10.1.

Looking at Figure 10.1, it is evident that non-market benefits, such as amenity and conservation, were ranked more highly than economic considerations. Critically, studies by McAdam *et al.* (1997) of the motives of farmers in Northern Ireland for specifically considering agroforestry underlined that environmental, recreational and animal welfare benefits may be key determinants, especially as the revenue from

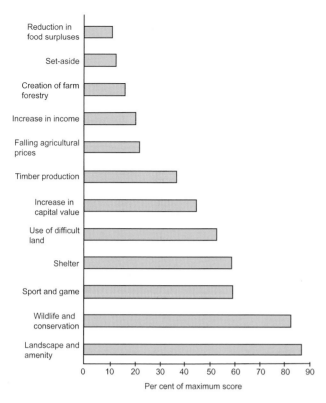

Figure 10.1 Principal motives for planting trees. Source: Appleton and Crabtree (1991).

timber may be a very minor component of this land-use system.

Wider employment impacts of agroforestry

The willingness of the government to increase the financial incentives for agroforestry may not be independent of the perceived socio-economic benefits in terms of rural employment. Any expansion of agroforestry might be expected to have wider social and economic impacts in terms of incomes and employment beyond the farm gate, especially in the more remote rural areas of Wales, Scotland and northern England. However, estimating these socio-economic benefits is not easy, because of the complex nature of the land-use system and the absence of actual studies.

On the one hand, agroforestry may strictly be regarded as an agricultural system, based predominantly though not exclusively on grassland farming, with timber as a 'minor' component. A measure of the wider social and economic benefits may then be gauged from the employment directly and indirectly supported by a grass-based, livestock system. Typically, every 60 to 100 ha of grassland devoted to lowland sheep and cattle systems in the UK will support around 1 man in farming (Scottish Agricultural College, 1997). In turn, regional studies in Wales (Midmore, 1987), Scotland and southern Ireland (O'Cinneide et al., 1997) have shown that for every man directly employed in livestock farming another 0.5-1.3 are employed in the industries that both supply inputs and process the output. It is a reasonable assumption that agroforestry systems would have similar employment impacts.

However, whether the implied total (gross) employment effects of 2 to 4 jobs per 100 ha of agroforestry can be regarded as a measure of the net benefits to society is open to debate. If, in the absence of agroforestry, the land were to have no alternative productive use, then the gross employment effects would be a correct measure of the wider socio-economic gains. However, if the use of land for agroforestry is primarily seen as a partial displacement of traditional grass-based livestock farming rather than a productive use for 'surplus' land, the net social gains from introduction of agroforestry will largely be linked to the 'added' forestry component of the system.

A very approximate estimate of the socio-economic gains that may be realised from the 'forestry' component of agroforestry systems can be obtained by reviewing the work done on conventional forestry systems. These show that, in the UK, 1 man is directly employed in managing timber production for every 100 to 250 ha of woodland (Scottish Agricultural College, 1990; Strak and Mackel, 1991; Central Statistical Office, 1997). However, McNicol et al. (1991), the Scottish Industry Department (1994) and Slee and Snowdon (1996) have shown that in areas like Scotland and Wales, every job in forestry creates 0.2 to 0.5 additional jobs outside. Thus, for every 100 ha of forestry, the implication of these studies is that 0.5 to 1.5 jobs in totality are created in the rural economy. This is only 25 to 40% of the estimated gross employment impacts of livestock farming.

However, the relatively small observed employment impacts associated with forestry may underestimate the potential gains. In particular, McNicol *et al.* (1991) noted that the wider employment impacts of forestry depended to a considerable extent on whether or not the output of timber led to the creation of timber processing and timber-using industries in the region. Where it does, they estimated that an additional 3 to 4 jobs were created for every job in forestry. More recently Slee and Snowdon (1996) put the figure at 1 to 2 additional jobs per man employed in forestry, but they also showed that, where employment creation was a specific objective of the forestry programme, then figures of 3 to 4 jobs per person in forestry were achievable. Based on these observations the potential employment impacts of forestry may be nearer 2 to 4 jobs per 100 ha.

The implications of this analysis of potential direct and indirect employment impacts of forestry for agroforestry are that even where agroforestry involves displacing a traditional, grass-based, livestock system, there are unlikely to be negative socio-economic impacts on employment in the region. The reason for this is that any employment losses arising from a reduction in livestock output may confidently be expected to be compensated for by the job gains arising from the added 'forestry' component of the system.

However, regardless of whether agroforestry leads to the direct creation of new jobs on farms, in so far as it increases the incomes of farm households, it should still have an economic effect on the wider local economy. Through consumption expenditures of farm households, the enhanced incomes may be expected to increase the purchases of goods and services. Studies of rural areas in Scotland (Doyle and Mitchell, 1994) and Wales (Midmore, 1987) have indicated that an increase of £1 in farm incomes may increase overall incomes in the local economy by between £1.50 and £1.75. A similar study

conducted in the west of Ireland (O'Cinneide *et al.*, 1997) suggested that for every £1 increase in farm incomes from forestry, incomes in the wider local economy grew by £1.36. Finally, McNicol *et al.* (1991) estimated that for the UK as a whole the figure might be nearer £2 for every £1 increase in the income of the forestry owner, but could be as high as £5. Equally, the adoption of agroforestry systems could add value to existing grassland systems by either increasing agricultural output or increasing the returns per unit of output. Thus, especially in hill areas, the presence of agroforestry may increase the shelter provided for animals with benefits in terms of output.

Against this, given the very limited commercial experience with agroforestry systems, some caution is needed in projecting the socio-economic benefits, until the actual evidence becomes available. In the first place, the scale of planting is likely to be modest. Statistics provided by the Ministry of Agriculture, Fisheries and Food (annual) indicate that the scale of tree planting under two other farmland diversification schemes, namely the Farm Woodland Scheme and the Farm Woodland Premium Scheme, has been comparatively small. Over the 4-year period 1992-96, 5360 applications were approved for converting 34 000 ha to woodland, representing 6.3 ha per application. At least in the short run, areas planted under agroforestry are unlikely to be significantly larger. Second, the potential socio-economic gains from agroforestry may not be easily realised. This is indicated by recent experiences of the Farm Woodland Scheme. Despite confident expectations that the Scheme would prove economically attractive to farmers, surveys of those who had applied to plant trees under the Scheme in England (Gasson and Hill, 1990; Hill, 1994) and in Scotland (Appleton and Crabtree, 1991) have indicated that few expect woodland planting to boost significantly the total farm income or to create on-farm jobs. Similarly, projections by Thomas (1990) and Thomas and Willis (see Chapter 11) suggest that, while agroforestry may represent a viable alternative to traditional agricultural land uses, the *gain* in income may only be slightly larger than those from traditional activities.

Non-market benefits

All this underlines that the benefits to society of agroforestry may be linked as much to non-market benefits, associated with landscape, habitat creation, wildlife conservation and recreation, as to any market benefits, such as employment. Although the House of Commons Environment Committee (1993) questioned whether there were unequivocal environmental gains from farm forestry, the evidence is growing that it can generate environmental and amenity benefits (see Chapter 8). In particular, Swain (1987) has stressed that much agroforestry takes place on poorer quality and unimproved grassland. Because another tier is added to the vegetation and the ground vegetation is not shaded out completely, the wildlife implications are not as severe as with conventional forestry. Given a mosaic of open pastures and trees, agroforestry will benefit some wildlife and lead to species diversification. At the same time, the planting of small blocks of trees in agroforestry systems will improve the visual appearance of the landscape by compartmentalising the land area and reducing the sensation of openness. Additional environmental benefits can be expected to come through reductions in nitrogen use and a lower stocking intensity that are generally consequences of switching from all livestock to agroforestry systems (Doyle *et al.*, 1986; Lloyd, 1990). This underlines the point made earlier that many farmers see the primary benefits of agroforestry as environmental.

The significance of the non-market benefits for forestry in general in the UK was recognised by Slee and Snowdon (1996). They specifically attempted to quantify the benefits arising from recreation provision, increased wildlife diversity and landscape enhancement. Using estimates by Willis and Benson (1989), Garrod and Willis (1992), Hanley and Spash (1993) and Spash and Hanley (1994), they estimated the recreational, conservation and landscape benefits of afforestation. In addition, the benefits of increased woodland planting through acting as a sink for carbon and counteracting the continued rise in atmospheric carbon dioxide concentrations was also considered, using values provided by Pearce (1991). The exercise showed that the social value of forestry could be significantly improved when these non-market benefits were included. Thus, the discounted benefits, assessed at a discount rate of 8% over a 30-year rotation, in respect of recreation and wildlife conservation for a conventional woodland in Scotland, were put at between £150 and £650 per ha. The benefits of carbon sequestration were worth another £180 to £225 per ha. In contrast, the discounted net benefits of the timber production on its own were negative and worth between minus £1000 and minus £1700 per ha. Thus, the non-market benefits represented an important and significant social justification for any public funding for forestry. There is every reason to believe that the same is true of agroforestry systems, although no economic evaluation of the non-market benefits of such systems has been carried out.

Pointers to the future

This review of farmer attitudes, the wider employment consequences and the non-market benefits of agroforestry underlines three key factors:

• Agroforestry may be a more attractive proposition to farmers than conventional forestry, in that it involves a 'diversification' of grassland and arable land uses rather than a total displacement of farming. Moreover, the survey by the Department of Agriculture for Northern Ireland (Thomas and Willis, 1997) indicated that, against a background of considerable uncertainty regarding the future of the agricultural sector, agroforestry was seen as a land-use system offering 'flexibility'. However, two factors holding back the widespread adoption of such systems of farm forestry are (1) ignorance and (2) lack of financial incentives. As the Northern Ireland initiative clearly demonstrated, there is a real need to raise farmer awareness of agroforestry and its benefits. At the same time, the financial grants for agroforestry need to be reviewed, since they are generally perceived to be inadequate. Only in Northern Ireland, where more attractive financial incentives apply, was this reported not to be the case.

- For government the appeal of agroforestry is that it may be a way of absorbing agricultural labour, which would be otherwise displaced by the continued rationalisation of farming. As a land-use system, it is relatively easily integrated into farming, as it requires little or no retraining. Through linkages with industries that supply inputs and process the outputs, it is also capable of stimulating off-farm employment. However, whether these jobs will be created locally will depend on a coordinated and integrated approach to farm forestry in rural areas. Without this coordination, the likelihood is that few of the jobs generated in the forestry-related industries will be in peripheral rural areas.

- The non-market benefits of agroforestry, connected with recreation, amenity and conservation, may be as important as the income and employment effects. As surveys have revealed, considerations relating to animal welfare, landscape and wildlife conservation are a primary determinant in many decisions to plant trees on farms. Furthermore, the willingness of the general public to fund grants for agroforestry will be strongly related to the non-market services delivered by increased farm forestry.

However, while the wider socio-economic implication of agroforestry appear positive, the extensive adoption of such systems in the UK will depend on whether farmers perceive agroforestry as a relatively profitable and flexible use of land. Chapter 11 explores this issue.

REFERENCES

APPLETON, Z. (1990). The impact of the Farm Woodland Scheme in Scotland. *Scottish Agricultural Economic Review* **5**, 145–157.

APPLETON, Z. and CRABTREE, J.R. (1991). *The Farm Woodland Scheme in Scotland: An economic appraisal*. Scottish Agricultural College Economic Report No. 27. SAC, Aberdeen.

BISHOP, K.D. (1990). Multi-purpose woodlands in the countryside around towns. PhD Thesis, University of Reading.

BUCKWELL, A. (1995). UK attitude to development of the CAP. *SAC Outlook Conference, Edinburgh, 8 November 1995*. Scottish Agricultural College, Edinburgh.

BUCKWELL, A. (1996). Agricultural economics in a brave liberal world. *European Association of Agricultural Economics, Edinburgh 3–7 September 1996*, Plenary Papers, 1–8.

BULLOCK, C.H., MACMILLAN, D.C. and CRABTREE, J.R. (1994). New perspectives on agroforestry in lowland Britain. *Land Use Policy* **11**, 222–233.

CRABTREE, J.R. and MACMILLAN, D.C. (1989). UK fiscal changes and forestry planting. *Journal of Agricultural Economics* **40**, 314–322.

CENTRAL STATISTICAL OFFICE (1997). *Annual abstract of statistics 1996*. HMSO, London.

DIBDEN, C. and UZZELL, D. (1992). *Access and the woodland manager: a study of woodland managers perceptions of and attitudes towards access in Oxfordshire*. Department of Psychology, University of Surrey.

DOYLE, C.J., EVANS, J. and ROSSITER, J. (1986). Agroforestry: an economic appraisal of the benefits of inter-cropping trees with grassland in lowland Britain. *Agricultural Systems* **21**, 1–32.

DOYLE, C.J. AND MITCHELL, M. (1994). *Effectiveness of farm policies on social and economic development in rural areas in Scotland*. Report prepared for the Scottish Agriculture and Fisheries Department. Management Division, Scottish Agricultural College, Auchincruive.

GARROD, G.D. and WILLIS, K.G. (1992). The amenity value of woodland in Great Britain. *Environmental and Resource Economics* **2**, 415–434.

GASSON, R. and HILL, P. (1990). *An economic evaluation of the farm woodland scheme*. Wye College Occasional Paper No. 17. Wye College, University of London.

GRUNDY, D.S., HATFIELD, G.R. and THOMPSON, J. (1989). *The contribution of forestry to rural employment*. HMSO, London.

HANLEY, N. and SPASH, C. (1993). *Cost-benefit analysis and the environment*. Edward Elgar, Cheltenham.

HILL, P. (1994). Farm woodland revisited. *Farm Management* **8,** 423–431.

House of Commons Environment Committee (1993). *Forestry and the environment*, vol 1. HMSO, London.

JOHNSON, J.A. (1992). A harvest of discontent: some perceptions of the impacts on lowland forest management of the fiscal changes of 1988. *Quarterly Journal of Forestry* **86,** 150–162.

LLOYD, C.J. (1990). Ecological and environmental consequences: are they a limitation or an incentive to agroforestry? In: *Agriculture: marginal agricultural land and efficient afforestation*, ed. L. Bock and J. Rondeux. Office of Official Publications of the European Communities, Luxembourg, 3–10.

MCADAM, J.H., GAZEAU, S. and PONT, F. (1997). An assessment of farmer attitudes to agroforestry on sheep and cereal farms in Northern Ireland. *Agroforestry Forum* **8** (3), 5–8.

MCNICOL, I., MCGREGOR, P. and MUTCH, W. (1991). *Forestry expansion – a study of technical, economic and ecological factors: development of the British wood processing industries*. Occasional Paper 38. Forestry Commission, Edinburgh.

MIDMORE, P. (1987). *The impact of farm prosperity on the rest of the Welsh economy*. Discussion Paper, Department of Agricultural Economics, The University College of Wales, Aberystwyth.

MINISTRY of AGRICULTURE, FISHERIES and FOOD (annual). *Agriculture in the United Kingdom*. HMSO, London.

NI DHUBHÁIN, A. and GARDINER, J.J. (1994). *Farm forestry in the rural economy*. Conference of Agricultural Economics Society, Exeter, April 1994.

O'CINNEIDE, B., DOYLE, C.J., SERRÃO, A. and CUDDY, M. (1997). *The impact of CAP reforms on peripheral regions of the community*. Report to the European Commission. Scottish Agricultural College, Auchincruive.

PEARCE, D. (1991). *Forestry expansion – a study of technical, economic and ecological factors: assessing the returns to the economy and society from investments in forestry*. Occasional Paper 47. Forestry Commission, Edinburgh.

SCAMBLER, A. (1989). Farmers' attitudes towards forestry. *Scottish Geographical Magazine* **105**, 47–49.

SCOTTISH AGRICULTURAL COLLEGE (1990). *Agriculture, forestry and fisheries in Ayrshire*. A report prepared for Enterprise Ayrshire. Management Division, Scottish Agricultural College, Auchincruive.

SCOTTISH AGRICULTURAL COLLEGE/CHADWICK, L., ed. (1997). *The farm management handbook 1997/98*. Scottish Agricultural College, Edinburgh.

SCOTTISH INDUSTRY DEPARTMENT (1994). *Scottish input–output tables for 1989*, vol. 1. HMSO, Edinburgh.

SIDWELL, C.M. (1989). Farm woodlands in Scotland – some results of a survey. *Scottish Agricultural Economics Review* **4**, 103–108.

SLEE, B. and SNOWDON, P. (1996). An economic appraisal of rural development forestry in Scotland. *Scottish Agricultural Economics Review* **9**, 9–19.

SPASH, C. and HANLEY, N. (1994). *Preferences, information and biodiversity preservation*. Discussion Papers in Ecological Economics, No. 94/1, University of Stirling.

STRAK, J. and MACKEL, C. (1991). *Forestry expansion – a study of technical, economic and ecological factors: forestry in the rural economy*. Occasional Paper 45. Forestry Commission, Edinburgh.

SWAIN, P.J. (1987). *Farm forestry: a study of aspects of farm forestry in New Zealand, Denmark, Sweden, Finland and California*. ADAS/WOAD, Aberystwyth.

THOMAS, T.H. (1990). Evaluating the economics of temperate agroforestry using sensitivity analysis: a case study of poplar, cereals and livestock in the lowlands of the Welsh Borders. In:

*Agriculture: marginal agricultural land and efficient afforestation,*ed. L. Bock and J. Rondeux. Office of Official Publications of the European Communities, Luxembourg, 103–122.

THOMAS T.H. and WILLIS, R.W. (1997). *Agroforestry research and development in the United Kingdom. Progress, perceptions and attitudes: a review.* Report to the Ministry of Agriculture, Fisheries and Food. School of Agriculture and Forest Sciences, University of Wales, Bangor.

WILLIAMS, D., LLOYD, T. and WATKINS, C. (1994). *Farmers not foresters: constraints on the planting of new farm woodland.* Department of Geography Working Paper No. 27. University of Nottingham, Nottingham.

WILLIS, K.G. and BENSON, J.F. (1989). Recreational values of forests. *Forestry* **62**, 331–346.

WILLIS, R.W., THOMAS, T.H. AND VAN SLYCKEN, J. (1993). Poplar agroforestry: a re-evaluation of its economic potential on arable land in the United Kingdom. *Forest Ecology and Management* **57**, 85–97.

Chapter 11

The economics of agroforestry in the UK

Terry Thomas and Rob Willis

Background

A variety of woodland planting and management schemes have been introduced to bring about policy objectives concerned primarily with agricultural diversification, habitat creation and an increase in biodiversity. Among the arguments used to support these objectives is the economic case that extra revenue can be generated directly from the adoption of farm woodland and indirectly via valued activities occurring beyond the farm, in both downstream and upstream sectors.

Woodland activity will provide replacement incomes for farmers as they move out of some of their existing forms of production, and it will enhance the prosperity of the rural economy, while also meeting a range of environmental goals. The overall thrust of policy is to reduce stock levels, increase tree cover and in the process contribute to a range of environmental benefits and landscape enhancements.

Agroforestry technology

Agroforestry is one option available under these woodland planting schemes. It entails the mixing of trees with either crops and/or livestock on the same area of land and contrasts with more traditional forms of woodland establishment and management where trees are separated from the agricultural enterprise as in farm woodland.

Much of the resurgence of interest in agroforestry in Europe has stemmed from political, economic and environmental issues associated with agricultural development (Thomas and Alcock, 1987). The emergence of food surpluses and their social costs coupled with negative environmental and socio-economic impacts associated with specialisation and intensification has led to a re-evaluation of both agricultural and forestry production.

> There is now an emphasis on the development and support for land-use systems capable of satisfying multiple objectives. In this context agroforestry is seen as being capable of functioning in a great many ways. These include: reduction of agricultural production; improving animal welfare; increased production of high quality timber; sustaining employment in rural areas by broadening the skills base; maintaining rural infrastructure; providing amenity; fire protection; soil erosion control.

Current UK support arrangements for agroforestry

Grant aid specifically for agroforestry was introduced in 1991 and became available under two schemes. The Woodland Grant Scheme provides assistance to cover the establishment of forestry on all land types. In addition, the 'Better Land Supplement' provides an additional incentive for planting on cereal or temporary grassland. Table 11.1 illustrates the size of payments available under both schemes for conventional forestry and agroforestry in Great Britain. The lower levels of establishment grant for agroforestry are explained by the fact that payments are made on the relative number of trees compared to the maximum grant for conventional forestry. These arrangements are

Table 11.1 Planting grants for trees on farm land (agroforestry)1998[a].

Size of area planted	Species	
	Conifer	Broadleaved
Under 10 ha	700 £ ha^{-1} [b]	1350 £ ha^{-1}
Over 10 ha	700 £ ha^{-1}	1050 £ ha^{-1}

[a]These payments assume a minimum planting density of 2250 stems ha^{-1}. For agroforestry, the full rate remains payable subject to a minimum planting density of 1100 stems ha^{-1}. Where planting density is less than this reduced amounts of grants and supplements are payable on a pro rata basis.

[b]For broadleaves and conifers 70 % of payments are made immediately after planting and 30 % after 5 years subject to satisfactory stand establishment and management.

different in Northern Ireland (see Chapter 10). However, the productivity of swards in agroforestry using ash and sycamore is likely to remain unaffected until year 12 of the rotation (McAdam and Hoppé, 1997). Similarly, unlike conventionally planted farm forestry, the forage area in an agroforest continues to qualify as a part of the forage area of the farm for IACS (Integrated Agricultural Control System) purposes. Overall stocking rate, sheep premia and extensification payments are also therefore unaffected.

Economic analysis of system performance is now being undertaken on a continuing basis. A spreadsheet modelling system has been developed to interface with a biophysical model of a silvopastoral system (Thomas and Willis, 1996; Thomas and Willis, 1997a; 1997b; Auclair, 1997). This enables economic evaluations to be undertaken rapidly in order to examine the significance of new technical information, policy developments and changes in prices and costs applying to each of the various elements within the systems.

The next section presents the results of a comparative analysis of the economic performance of broadleaved agroforestry under sample lowland and upland conditions in the UK. The biophysical datasets used to illustrate the system have been supplied from upland and lowland silvopastoral sites within the UK National Agroforestry Network (Hoppé *et al.*, 1996). The

information is a combination of recorded measurements of tree and sward productivity over a 10-year period encompassing the early growth of the trees, actual simulations and heuristic evaluations. It has been necessary to adapt existing forest yield models to the wider spacings used in agroforestry and some of the assumptions will require further testing. In addition, the process model component of the bioeconomic modelling system is still not fully developed, calibrated and validated. Whereas the tree component appears to work satisfactorily under an appropriate range of climatic and topographic conditions, the model still fails to adequately represent the impact of tree growth on pasture productivity (Sibbald, personal communication). However, it does represent the best knowledge and understanding available relating to the physical productivity of tree and understorey components under these conditions. In all economic calculations the value of harvested timber has been derived from Forestry Commission price-size curves (Whiteman *et al.*, 1991).

Evaluating the economics of agroforestry

A lowland broadleaved silvopastoral system

The lowland agroforestry site at Loughgall in Northern Ireland is typical grade 3 undulating lowland land capable of supporting a range of grass-based livestock systems. The agroforestry system being evaluated here comprises ryegrass-based pastures with ash *(Fraxinus excelsior)* planted at 400 stems per hectare, growing at an estimated General Yield Class 12. The various materials, quantities and costs of establishment are shown in Appendix 1, Table A1.1.

It is assumed that 5 % of the stand will be thinned in year 21, and a further 21 % in year 26, leaving 300 trees per hectare to grow to rotation age. These trees will be felled at 40 years of age with an estimated volume of 1 m^3 per tree. Volume removed in thinnings is estimated to be around 50 m^3 per hectare based upon extrapolation from conventional yield tables (Edwards and Christie, 1981). Pruning of the trees commences in Year 4 and ceases in Year 26, at which time a pruned height of 3 m will have been attained. Sheep are initially stocked at 12 ewes per hectare. As yet no decline in stocking rate has proved necessary in order to maintain sheep performance despite a 20 % shading of the grass under the trees (Hoppé and McAdam, 1997). Future gradual reductions in sward productivity are likely as the tree canopy develops further. A projection technique (Thomas, 1991), has been used to schedule grazing productivity from its current level through the remainder of the rotation to reflect two grazing productivity scenarios. They assume an overall reduction in agricultural productivity of 10% and 25 % over a 30 year rotation, reflecting the best and worst possible outcomes of the capacity of the site to retain grazing activity later into the rotation. The results from this site show no decline up to 9 years after planting (McAdam *et al.*, 1998). Figure 11.1 illustrates the decline in sheep stocking rate which can be expected under both grazing productivity scenarios.

Table 11.2 illustrates data in the analysis, which have been used relating to the materials, quantities, costs and revenues associated with the animal management component of the system. An economic evaluation of the lowland site planted at 400 stems per hectare is presented in Tables 11.3 and 11.4. Since the land was previously farmed as a

grazing system, equivalent data on the financial performance for the agriculture as a sheep grazing enterprise are also provided.

Before discussing the results, it is important to understand how they were calculated. Comparing returns from an agroforestry system with those from an agriculture system is not straightforward. Whereas agricultural costs are incurred and revenues gained within a single production period, agroforestry returns will occur over many production periods; moreover costs, for example those associated with tree planting, have to be set against future revenues from trees many years hence. These can be addressed using Discounted Cash Flow Analysis to reduce all the *future* costs and revenues to a single equivalent *present* value, taking due account of the fact that time places a value on money since it can earn money through time. In this way, returns from each system become directly comparable and, by subtracting one from the other, a 'net benefit' can be calculated. This can be expressed as a single 'lump sum' or as an equivalent annual value, in much the same way as an annuity is calculated. In all of the results that follow, the net benefit is calculated by subtracting the present value of net returns of the agriculture system from those of the agroforestry system. The net benefits themselves are expressed not as 'lump sums' but as what they would mean as an equivalent to an annual payment. The discount rate used in all three examples illustrated here is 5 %. In all cases,

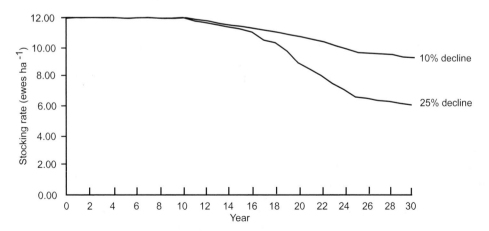

Figure 11.1 Projected changes in stocking capacity under ash trees in a lowland silvopastoral system at Loughgall, Northern Ireland. Two different scenarios are assumed: a 10% and 25% decline in agricultural productivity averaged over the whole rotation.

Table 11.2 Gross and net margins, lowland sheep, Loughgall, Northern Ireland, 1997.

Animal management: lowland sheep[a]	Price per unit	Yield	Value (£ ha^{-1})
Revenues			
Lamb sales	£1 kg^{-1}	880 kg ha^{-1}	880
Cull ewe	£29 ewe^{-1}	0.2 ewe yr^{-1}	70
Wool	£2.50 fleece^{-1}	1 fleece ewe^{-1}	30
HLCA payment			
Ewe premium	£14.75 ewe^{-1}	1 payment ewe^{-1}	177
Total revenue			**1157**
Variable costs			
Ewe replacement	£70 ewe^{-1}	0.2 ewe yr^{-1}	168
Concentrates	£140 t^{-1}	0.35 t ha^{-1}	49
Bulk feed (silage)	£6.12 ewe^{-1}		73
Other	£3.6 ewe^{-1}		43
Veterinary	£5.20 ewe^{-1}		62
Forage variable cost:			
Fertiliser	£125 t^{-1}	0.16 t ha^{-1}	20
Total variable costs			**416**
Gross margin			**741**
Fixed costs			
Labour[b]	£3.5 h^{-1}	1 h ewe^{-1}	42
Net margin			**699**

[a]Assumes an initial stocking rate of 12 ewes ha^{-1}.
[b]Labour costs are based on local shepherd rates in 1997.
Abbreviations: h: hour; ha: hectare; kg: kilogram; t: tonne; yr: year.

a higher discount rate would reduce the viability of both the agriculture and agroforestry systems, but would also improve the net benefit in favour of agriculture. A lower discount rate would increase the viability of both systems but improve the net benefit in favour of agroforestry.

Table 11.3 illustrates the net advantage (or disadvantage) from agroforestry on lowland grassland in comparison with orthodox grazing. Each grazing productivity scenario was evaluated to determine the impact of grants and subsidies and their removal at year 10. Labour costs for all tree management operations such as pruning and thinning are based on local rates for agricultural workers in 1997 or assumed to be undertaken by family labour in winter at no cost.

The competitive position of agroforestry is influenced by the value of the grazing returns under all three policy scenarios. This is because grazing returns that accrue in the early part of the rotation have a greater present value than those that accrue later. The longer the level of the initial grazing plateau is maintained therefore, the greater the positive impact on the discounted present value of future returns for the system as a whole. As a corollary to this, the economic uncertainty associated with not knowing precisely how stocking rates will actually change later in the rotation itself diminishes, since at *any* given level of grazing productivity, the positive impact on the present value of future returns declines the later in the rotation it occurs.

Table 11.3 The financial advantage from lowland agroforestry compared with agriculture under various technical scenarios.

Possible reduction in grazing capacity as a result of the trees	Annual net benefit to lowland silvopastoral agroforestry in excess of returns from agriculture		
	Under current support arrangements (£ ha⁻¹)	With no grants and subsidies (£ ha⁻¹)	With subsidies removed in year 10 (£ ha⁻¹)
25 %	-36.50 (-14.87)	-47.57 (-8.37)	-13.82 (7.81)
10 %	14.75 (36.38)	-8.37 (13.26)	25.38 (47.01)

Figures in parentheses relate to result when labour costs for tree management are excluded.
All values have been discounted at 5 % per annum.
Timber values have been derived from Forestry Commission Price-Size Curves (Whiteman *et al.*, 1991).

Table 11.4 The impact of product price changes on the financial advantage from lowland agroforestry compared with agriculture under various technical scenarios.

Possible reduction in grazing capacity resulting from trees	The net benefit to lowland silvopastoral agroforestry in excess of returns from agriculture (£ ha⁻¹)			
	Food prices constant Timber prices +1 %	Food prices constant Timber prices +2 %	Food prices –1 % Timber prices +1 %	Food prices –2 % Timber prices +2 %
25 %	12.47 (34.10)	83.27 (104.9)	42.78 (64.41)	136.41 (158.04)
10 %	63.72 (85.35)	134.52 (156.15)	77.75 (99.38)	159.14 (180.77)

Figures in parentheses relate to result when labour costs for tree management are excluded.
All values have been discounted at 5 % per annum.
Timber values have been derived from Forestry Commission Price-Size Curves (Whiteman *et al.*, 1991).

These results suggest that on the basis of existing prices and support arrangements, differences in profitability between grazing and lowland agroforestry systems are very small. Changing assumptions with respect to the impact of reductions in grazing productivity, policy scenarios and labour costs do have an impact which is largely favourable to agroforestry but again, differences are not large.

Table 11.4 illustrates the effect of price changes on the 'status quo' position presented in Table 11.3. Two types of price trend scenarios are created. Firstly, agricultural prices are held constant and forestry prices allowed to rise on an annual basis by up to 2 % throughout the rotation. Secondly, a divergent price scenario is created where agricultural prices are assumed to decline and forestry prices assumed to rise, again by up to 2 % per annum throughout the rotation.

It is evident that even very small increases in timber prices relative to meat prices make agroforestry capable of securing higher financial returns than can be obtained from monoculture grazing. If prices were to diverge, then for all scenarios, agroforestry appears an especially attractive option. The current uncertainty in meat markets coupled with the EU policy toward the extensification in livestock production and increased biodiversity in pastoral systems further enhances the attractiveness of agroforestry.

An upland broadleaved silvopastoral system

The site at Glensaugh in north-east Scotland is typical of an upland farming situation. Since the site was established to the same protocol as that at Loughgall the quantities of materials, factor prices and therefore establishment costs have been assumed as identical in both cases. Subsequent management costs differ in two respects. Firstly, two management systems are evaluated: one is a non-thin regime, the other undertakes a single thinning in year 30. Secondly, unlike the lowland situation, pruning begins in year 4 and is repeated every 5th year until year 36, at which time a pruned height of 5.75 m is achieved. Pruning above 3 m is carried out on a selective basis to favour the final crop trees. The intention of this pruning regime is to realise clean boles of high value timber acceptable to the veneer and furniture markets (Kerr and Evans, 1993). This same pruning regime is also applied to the non-thin system. Establishment and management costs are illustrated in Appendix 1, Table A1.2.

Tree growth data have, in this case, been generated by the tree modelling component of the ALWAYS model (Bergez and Msika, 1996; Auclair, 1997) using an assumed Yield Class of 8. The tree component in this particular silvopastoral system is sycamore *(Acer pseudoplatanus)*, spaced at 400 stems per hectare. Two systems are evaluated. The first is a thinned system where 200 trees are extracted at year 30 with an estimated volume of 0.013 m³ per tree and the remainder at year 60

with an estimated volume of 0.896 m³ per tree. The second is a non-thinned system with felling again taking place at year 60 with an estimated volume of 0.335 m³ per tree. The pasture is grazed with sheep at an initial stocking rate of 13.35 ewes per ha. The impact of tree growth and pasture production in the Scottish uplands has been previously observed to be directly related to tree height, crown length and crown diameter (Sibbald *et al.*, 1994). This relationship was used to predict pasture productivity and associated sheep stocking rates for the rotation. The resultant grazing profile (Figure 11.2) predicts that a gradual decline can be expected from year 16 onwards.

Table 11.5 illustrates the quantities, costs and returns relating to the upland sheep system being evaluated. Returns are illustrated in both gross and net margin per hectare. These will of course reduce as the stocking capacity of the site declines. Table 11.6 shows an economic evaluation of the upland site. The same three policy scenarios are presented although in this case only one grazing profile is assumed, that which is modified by a thinning of the trees and shown as the upper curve in Figure 11.2. Results for the *status quo* show that agroforestry is less competitive with agriculture though the deficit is approximately halved if a thinning is included. There is a marginal improvement in the relative position of agroforestry if tree management costs are excluded.

However, as with the lowland system, these

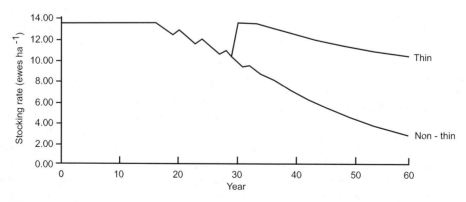

Figure 11.2 Simulated changes in stocking capacity under sycamore trees in an upland silvopastoral system at Glensaugh, Scotland.

112

Table 11.5 Gross and net margins, upland sheep, Glensaugh, Scotland, 1997.

Animal management: upland sheep[a]	Price per unit	Yield	Value (£ ha^{-1})
Revenues			
Lamb sales	£1 kg^{-1}	731.51 kg ha^{-1}	731.51
cull ewe	£29 ewe^{-1}	0.25 ewes yr^{-1}	94.25
Wool	£2.50 fleece^{-1}	1 fleece ewe^{-1}	32.5
HLCA payment	£6.75 ewe^{-1}	1 payment ewe^{-1}	87.75
Ewe premium	£19.70 ewe^{-1}	1 payment ewe^{-1}	256.1
Total revenue			**1202.11**
Variable costs			
Ewe replacement	£70 ewe^{-1}	0.25 ewe yr^{-1}	227.5
Concentrates	£125 t^{-1}	0.643 t ha^{-1}	80.38
Vet and med.	£5.29 ewe^{-1}		68.77
Other	£3.34 ewe^{-1}		43.42
Forage variable cost:			
Fertiliser	£145 t^{-1}	0.15 t ha^{-1}	21.75
Total variable costs			**441.82**
Gross margin			**760.30**
Fixed costs			
Labour[b]	£4.80 h^{-1}	4 h ewe^{-1}	249.6
Net margin			**510.70**

[a]Assumes an initial stocking rate of 13 ewes ha^{-1}.

[b]Labour costs are based on local shepherd rates in 1997.

Abbreviations: h: hour; ha: hectare; kg: kilogram; t: tonne; yr: year.

results are sensitive to very small changes in future price levels for timber and meat. Table 11.7 shows, for example, that if a thinning is introduced and the *status quo* is assumed as a benchmark, a 1 % rise in the price of timber has the effect of reducing the deficit of £67.13 per ha to £51.88 and this effect is exponential for further price rises. If labour costs are removed and a 2 % price divergent scenario is assumed, agroforestry is currently capable of generating a marginally higher return than agriculture in this situation.

These are typical examples of disadvantaged or severely disadvantaged areas of the United Kingdom as designated under the Less Favoured Area directives of the European Union. If government policy is to increase tree planting on farm land in these types of areas for whatever reason (environmental, amenity or diversification), yet retain a working population in agriculture, agroforestry systems are the only mechanisms that are likely to be capable of delivering a solution. This is because they allow existing farming activities to be continued, albeit at a reduced level of productivity while meeting the stated policy objectives.

Although this analysis has been conducted without consideration of non-market benefits, measurements within agroforestry systems in the UK indicate that significant environmental benefits can accrue within these systems (see Chapters 8 and 10). As these systems mature, amenity will also become an increasingly important product, both in terms of access to parkland environments and landscape diversity.

Table 11.6 The financial advantage from upland agroforestry compared with agriculture under various technical scenarios

Thinning regime	Annual net benefit to upland silvopastoral agroforestry in excess of returns from agriculture		
	Under current support arrangements (£ ha^{-1})	With no grants and subsidies (£ ha^{-1})	With subsidies removed in year 10 (£ ha^{-1})
Non-thin	−123.14 (−108.23)	−114.83 (−99.92)	−81.08 (−66.17)
Thin	−67.13 (−52.84)	−86.07 (−71.78)	−52.32 (−38.03)

Figures in parentheses relate to result when labour costs for tree management are excluded.
All values have been discounted at 5 % per annum.
Timber values have been derived from Forestry Commission Price-Size Curves (Whiteman *et al.*, 1991).

Table 11.7 The impact of product price changes on the financial advantage from upland agroforestry compared with agriculture under various technical scenarios

Thinning regime	Annual net benefit to upland silvopastoral agroforestry in excess of returns from agriculture (£ ha^{-1})			
	Food prices constant Timber prices +1 %	Food prices constant Timber prices +2 %	Food prices −1 % Timber prices +1 %	Food prices −2 % Timber prices +2 %
Non-thin	−115.85 (−100.94)	−102.80 (−87.88)	−81.87 (−66.95)	−48.39 (−33.47)
Thin	−51.88 (−37.59)	−24.54 (−10.24)	−41.47 (−27.18)	−8.97 (5.32)

Figures in parentheses relate to result when labour costs for tree management are excluded.
All values have been discounted at 5 % per annum.
Timber values have been derived from Forestry Commission Price-Size Curves (Whiteman *et al.*, 1991).

Where a small cost is incurred by adopting agroforestry in terms of income foregone, the Northern Ireland situation suggests that farmers who adopt agroforestry would appear to regard the non-market benefits as outweighing the financial costs to them as individuals. In the upland situation, however, the differences in financial performance between the two types of systems are greater when considered in proportion to the existing level of agricultural returns. In this situation, it is unlikely that farmers will regard the non-market benefit to themselves as being sufficient to outweigh these proportionally higher amounts of income forgone.

These evaluation results suggest that in an upland situation:

- Silvopastoral agroforestry is less competitive with agriculture than in the lowlands.

- There is a high level of sensitivity to potential future changes in level and type of support available for agriculture and forestry and future changes in relative prices for meat and timber.

- Small increases in the relative price of timber to food can bring about a substantial change, moreover environmental benefits will still accrue.

- The final evaluation will depend on society's valuation of the non-market costs and benefits of the system and whether it actually wishes to pay for them.

A lowland broadleaved silvoarable system

Silvoarable agroforestry was last practised on a commercial scale in the early 1970s on good farming land in lowland Britain. The system combined the production of timber from poplar (*Populus* spp.) on a 25-year rotation with a range of cereal and pulse crops grown as an understorey. After about seven years, cereal yields would have typically fallen to some 40 % of the open field levels, to be replaced by a grass ley and animals grazed for the remainder of the rotation (A. Beaton, personal communication). The system was financially attractive under the economic conditions of the time, but became unviable when the demand for poplar timber for matches collapsed. A variety of clones were used which were planted at a triangular spacing of 7.9 m and, on a site of average quality, were capable of achieving Yield Class 12.

Since that time, fundamental changes have taken place both in the design of farm machinery and in the use of herbicides and pesticides, and margins in arable production have declined in real terms. The system was re-evaluated in the late 1980s and was seen to be still profitable on marginal arable land (Thomas, 1990). Subsequently, there have been remarkable increases in potential productivity possible from the tree component (Gossens *et al.*, 1988; Meirsonne and Van Slycken, 1996). Fast-growing poplars, initially bred in Belgium, have been planted in a series of trials at various spacings throughout the UK in 1988. Provisional yield tables relevant to UK conditions are now available (Christie, 1994). Observed poplar growth using these clones suggests that yield classes per hectare of between 18 and 26 are capable of being achieved on a wide range of sites across the UK.

The economic impact arising from using the improved genetic material was re-evaluated with the BEAM model POPMOD (Willis *et al.*, 1993), assuming relatively modest productivity levels of Yield Class 18 to 22. Results indicated that with the adoption of net margin accounting for agriculture, the introduction of appropriate grant structures and the prospect of significant real reductions in agricultural prices, poplar-based agroforestry was becoming a viable land-use option on good arable land. Alternatively, under conditions of neutral support, only a relatively small decrease in agricultural prices of 2 % per annum would be required to make the system clearly the most profitable option under a wide range of site conditions (Willis *et al.*, 1993).

This latest re-evaluation is based on data supplied by the University of Leeds and relates to its experimental silvoarable site at Headley Hall farm near Leeds. Analysis using POPMOD provides an updated evaluation of the comparative performance against lowland monoculture cereal production. Whereas this site is typical of much of grade 2 agricultural land and capable of supporting a wide range of cropping activities, its exposed aspect and the calcareous nature of the soil does not make it a site particularly suited to poplar. Current assessments of actual poplar growth suggest a Yield Class of between 16 and 18 is likely to be achieved. Therefore, in order to represent the potential of the system across a range of sites the analysis presented below presents potential returns assuming a range of Yield Classes from 14 to 22.

The agricultural enterprises suggested for this analysis together with associated yield levels, prices, variable and fixed costs, gross margins, net margins and current subsidies are presented in Appendix 2, Tables A2.1, A2.2, A2.3. (In the absence of more specific information regarding the relationship between yield class of poplar and initial site productivity for cereals, these have been assumed to be an average achievable across all yield classes.) A traditional 'four course' rotation is assumed which extends over a fixed rotation length of 25 years following the sequence: winter wheat, winter wheat, winter barley and threshing peas. In the economic analysis, agricultural gross margins are adjusted to a Net Margin basis by including as far as possible labour and machinery costs. These are typically included as variable costs in tree establishment and management operations, thus a more effective measure of the comparative economic performance of the two systems is obtained (Willis *et al.*, 1993).

The trees in this example are poplar (*Populus euroamericana*, Ghoy). They are spaced at 6.4 m within and 20 m between the rows, giving an overall density of 78 trees per hectare. This design has been selected for evaluation on the basis of compatibility with modern farming machinery. A 20 m spacing will create an 18 m alley after having allowed for a 1 m wide strip of black polythene into which the trees are planted. The polythene is required to maintain a weed-free area immediately around the tree. An additional 0.5 m on either side of the edge of the plastic is kept crop and weed free in order to prevent damage to the polythene by farm machinery. These weed-free strips also serve to prevent the ingress of pernicious weeds into the arable alley. Spray booms of 18 m length are most typical on large arable farms in lowland England. Materials, quantities and costs for establishing and managing the tree component of the system are shown in Appendix 1, Table A1.3.

By establishing the trees, there is an immediate loss of 10 % of the cropping area. Subsequently cereal yield can be expected to decline further as the trees grow, reflecting both underground competition for water and nutrients and above ground competition for light. As with the silvopastoral systems already considered, in order to provide an economic analysis of the potential returns from the system over the course of a whole rotation, it is important to be able to provide a realistic representation of this change in agricultural production. The only approach which has been effectively validated over the course of a whole rotation is an empirical one developed under radiata pine (*Pinus radiata*) in New Zealand (Percival and Knowles, 1988). This describes understorey dry matter production as a function of simple tree canopy measurements, namely the length and density of green crowns per unit area of land. The same basic approach has also been found to be highly reliable in predicting dry matter production under Sitka spruce (*Picea sitchensis* (Bong.) Carr.), using the following equation (Sibbald *et al.*, 1994):

$$AY = 8.98 \times (1 - (2.18 \times 10^{-4} \times GCL))$$

Where:

AY = total annual herbage yield in tonnes per hectare

8.98 = initial or 'base' herbage yield in tonnes per hectare

GCL = green crown length in metres per hectare.

In adapting this equation for the current application, the absolute level of initial open field cereal production in tonnes per hectare has been substituted for initial herbage yield. Similarly, values for green crown length of poplar have been substituted. Cereal yields per hectare per annum are then expressed as a percentage of initial production for each year of the rotation.

This may overstate the actual yield reduction to some extent since the equation is based on conifer species. Nevertheless, the crowns of these fast growing clones are undoubtedly dense and cast heavy shade. In the absence of any other information relating to UK conditions this is the only course open at the present time in order to represent the likely effect of trees on crop yields at this tree spacing. The results of this exercise are shown in Figure 11.3.

In Figure 11.3, the rate of crown development is itself directly related to yield class, and inversely related to agricultural productivity at any point in time. Separate 'agricultural decay' functions are therefore shown for each yield class at an inter-row spacing of 20 m. Since projected green crown area is a function of both the size of individual crowns and their density per unit area, the effect on agricultural production of a 10 m inter-row spacing (156 stems per hectare), assuming Yield Class 18, is also shown. The only validation of these functions currently possible is to compare predicted with actual cereal production on sites at an appropriate yield class. In Leeds, for example, assuming Yield Class 18, a yield reduction of some 13.8 % is being currently observed (year 5). This compares with a predicted 14 % from Figure 11.3. These functions appear to be reasonable representations of what is likely to happen to cereal yields later in the rotation.

Table 11.8 provides a comparison of the profitability of a poplar-based silvoarable system. Column 1 illustrates the profitability with all existing subsidies removed from both systems. The results indicate negative net benefits to agroforestry ranging from minus £117.70 to minus £16.38 per hectare when compared with arable monoculture under a range of scenarios. The degree of competition under 'free market conditions' is strongly influenced by the

116

quality of the site in terms of poplar growth. Differences in negative net benefit reflect the opportunity cost to the land in terms of revenue forgone as a result of planting the trees, their differential productivity on different sites and their consequential longer term impact on crop productivity at 20 m spacings. Column 2 of Table 11.8 presents the same information on the basis of including the existing support arrangements for tree and agricultural components. Whereas the data in columns 1 and 2 look very similar, it is important to appreciate these are *differences* in returns between the systems. The effect of removing subsidies from the monoculture is to reduce overall returns to the system by 42 %. For the polyculture, this reduction varies depending on the compensating contribution of the value of the poplar wood. These results in effect illustrate the minimum financial incentives necessary to create a 'level playing field' in order to encourage farmers to introduce fast growing poplars into their fields.

Future scenarios

A further complication with the results in Table 11.8 arises since the whole system of land-use support in the European Union is currently under review. The liberalisation of trade on a global scale and concomitant negotiations under GATT have already given rise to a major restructuring of existing price differentials which, in the case of the European Union, will imply a 20 % cut in current levels of prices for the main cereal products into the medium term. The internal response of the Community has now emerged in the form of the Fischler proposals outlined in Agenda 2000 (Darke, 1997). These currently suggest that whereas the overall level of support is unlikely to be reduced significantly, its mechanism of delivery will be re-orientated in the form of enhanced area payments designed to give rise to agricultural extensification, greater biodiversity, amenity and access in the countryside. Whereas farmers will be exposed to price reductions per unit of output of the order of 20 % for cereals, the negative impact of this on returns will be cushioned by an increase of 22 % in the area payment per hectare which is invariant with yield.

The revised mechanisms recognise an agenda which reflects an increasing unwillingness on the part of the non-farming taxpayer to accept the rural *status quo*. They consider that the provision of continuing support for arable agricultural practices has tended to create costly agricultural surpluses and negative impacts on a range of desirable, though non-tradable, environmental goods.

These developments have important implications for the future viability of silvoarable systems. Under the new arrangements, farmers' returns will be made up of a variable proportion of crop revenues subject to a substantial reduction in price and a fixed payment per unit area. For those choosing to practise agroforestry, the proportion of their income arising from agricultural returns and therefore attracting reduced free market prices will be much less than their monoculture

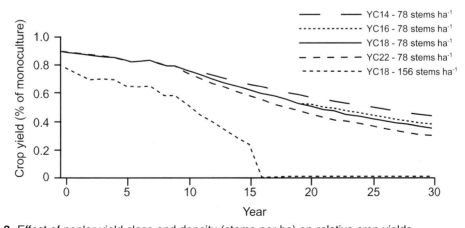

Figure 11.3 Effect of poplar yield class and density (stems per ha) on relative crop yields.

Table 11.8 A comparison of the profitability of a lowland poplar based silvoarable system planted at an inter-row spacing of 20 m with an existing arable monoculture in the UK under different subsidy scenarios.

Poplar yield class	1 Discounted annuitised net benefit with no subsidy[a] (£ ha⁻¹)	2 Discounted annuitised net benefit with subsidy[b] (£ ha⁻¹)	3 Discounted annuitised net benefit with subsidy[c] (£ ha⁻¹)	4 Reduction in agricultural production per hectare (%)
14	−117.70	−115.26	−73.27	25.83
16	−89.25	−86.81	−43.34	25.54
18	−68.79	−66.35	−22.16	26.30
22	−16.38	−13.94	32.61	28.77

[a]All tree planting grants have been removed which, at 78 trees ha⁻¹, amounts to £95.94. Similarly, all area payments for the crop rotational elements in both systems described in Appendix 2, Tables A2.1–2.3 have been removed.
[b]The type and level of subsidies here are those explained in Table 11.1 for the trees and Appendix 2, Tables A2.1–A2.3.
[c]In this simulation, cereal intervention is cut by 20 % to a 'safety net' level of 95.35 ECU per tonne. An increase of 22 % in the non-crop specific area payment is introduced. An increase of 6.5 ECUs per tonne is assumed for protein crops (in this case threshing peas).

counterparts. They will however continue to attract the same area payments and secure additional returns from the timber market. This prospect is illustrated in column 3 of Table 11.8 which compares the likely performance of the two systems under the proposed Agenda 2000 regime. On the best poplar sites, the silvoarable system can now be expected to outperform the monoculture. Even on the less productive sites, the negative net benefits required to be financed in order to produce a level playing field are now substantially reduced. Column 4 illustrates the crop reduction that can be expected over a whole rotation as a result of the presence of the trees.

Key points in relation to future viability

The analysis brings out the following:

- Wide spaced poplar trees as an integral part of cropping systems are likely to have a useful and important part to play in securing emerging agri-environmental objectives in lowland Britain.

- The differences in profitability between the silvoarable system and the monoculture are very small. Where negative values are indicated, they could be perceived as minimum payments from the taxpayer necessary to secure a range of environmental products within the context of the commercially orientated lowland arable farm business.

- Agroforestry technology is certainly capable of delivering such products in a more flexible manner and at substantially reduced social costs than other less sustainable policy instruments which have preceded it in the past 20 years.

REFERENCES

AUCLAIR, D. (1997). *The ALWAYS project*. Final Report, EU, DG XII.

BERGEZ, J.E. and MSIKA, B. (1996). A silvopastoral model for the EU. In: *Western European silvopastoral systems*, ed. M. Etienne. Science Update, INRA, Paris, 207–220.

CHRISTIE, J.M. (1994). *Provisional yield tables for poplars in Britain*. Technical Paper 6. Forestry Commission, Edinburgh.

DARKE, M., ed. (1997). *Farm law no. 26*. Moniter Press, 7–13.

EDWARDS, P. N. and CHRISTIE, J.M. (1981). *Yield models for forest management*. Forestry Commission Booklet 48. Forestry Commission, Edinburgh.

GOOSENS, R., STEENACKERS, V. and VAN SLYKEN, J. (1988). *Provisional yield levels of the Unal poplar clones: 'Primo', 'Ghoy', and 'Beaupre'*. Proceedings: 18th Session International Poplar Commission, Beijing, China, 174–187.

KERR, G. and EVANS, J. (1993). *Growing broadleaves for timber*. Forestry Commission Handbook 9. HMSO, London.

MEIRESONNE, L. and VAN SLYCKEN, J. (1996). *Revised yield tables of 'beaupré' and 'ghoy'*. Proceedings: 20th Session of the International Poplar Commission, October 1996, Budapest, Hungary. Report No. IBW Bb R. 96.005, Ministry of the Flemish Community, Institute for Forestry and Game Management.

PERCIVAL, N. S. and KNOWLES, R. L. (1988). Relationships between radiata pine and understorey pasture production. In: *Agroforestry symposium proceedings*, ed. P. Maclaren. Forest Research Institute Bulletin No. 139. Rotorua, New Zealand, 152–164.

SIBBALD, A. R., GRIFFITHS, J. H. and ELSTON, D. A. (1994). Herbage yield in agroforestry systems as a function of easily measured attributes of the tree canopy. *Journal of Forest Ecology and Management* **65**, 195–200.

THOMAS, T.H. and ALCOCK, M.B. (1987). Agroforestry – with particular reference to silvopastoral systems and their potential role in the UK. *Agricultural Progress* **62**, 54–64.

THOMAS T.H., PENELOZA, R. and KELLAS, J.F. (1990). Temperate agroforestry developments in Australia, New Zealand and Chile. In: *Marginal agricultural land and efficient afforestation*, ed. L. Bock and R.J. Rondeaux. CEC Journal of Agriculture. EUR 10841 EN. European Commission, Brussels, 81–102.

THOMAS, T.H. (1990). Evaluating the economics of temperate agroforestry using sensitivity analysis: a case study of poplar, cereals and livestock in the lowlands of the Welsh Borders. In: *Marginal agricultural land and efficient afforestation*, ed. L. Bock and R.J. Rondeaux. CEC Journal of Agriculture. EUR 10841 EN. European Commission, Brussels, 103–122.

THOMAS, T.H. (1991). A spreadsheet approach to the evaluation of the economics of temperate agroforestry. *Journal of Forest Ecology and Management: Special issue on agroforestry* **45**, 1–4.

THOMAS, T.H. and WILLIS, R.W. (1996). *Putting the economics into biophysical agroforestry models*. Annual Report Agroforestry Modelling and Research Co-ordination, ed. G. J. Lawson. ODA Forestry Research Programme PN R5652. Institute of Terrestrial Ecology, Edinburgh, 139–158.

THOMAS, T.H. and WILLIS, R.W. (1997a). Linking bioeconomics to biophysical agroforestry models. Interfacing biophysical and financial models of agroforestry systems. *Agroforestry Forum* **8** (2), 40–42.

THOMAS, T.H. and WILLIS, R.W. (1997b). Creating analytical structures for the bioeconomic evaluation of agroforestry systems. In: *Agroforestry for sustainable land use; fundamental research and modelling, temperate and tropical applications*. Proceedings of an International Workshop, Montpellier, France. CIRAD, Montpellier, 239–245.

WHITEMAN, A., INSLEY, H. and WATT, G. (1991). *Price–size curves for broadleaves*. Forestry Commission Occasional Paper 32. Forestry Commission, Edinburgh.

WILLIS, R.W., THOMAS, T.H. and VAN SLYCKEN, J. (1993). Poplar agroforestry: a re-evaluation of its economic potential on arable land in the United Kingdom. *Forest Ecology and Management* **57**, 85–97.

Appendix 1

Economic evaluation of silvopastoral systems: materials and cost of establishment

Table A1.1 Establishment and management costs for an ash-based silvopastoral system, planted at an inter-row spacing of 5 m (400 trees ha^{-1}). All costs are in £97/98.

Activity	Unit costs (£)	Requirement ha^{-1}	Total (£)
Establishment			
Ground preparation[a]	0.04 m^{-2}	400 m^2	16
Plants	0.40	400 plants	160
1 split post (2 m)	1.20	400 posts	180
1 anchor peg	0.25	400 pegs	100
1 tree guard	1	400 guards	400
Labour: planting and protecting[bc]	3.5 h^{-1}	60 h	210
Subsequent activities			
Beating up: year 2			
Materials	1 plant^{-1}	40 plants	40
Labour[c]	3.50 h^{-1}	6 h	21
Weeding: years 1–3			
Materials	0.04 m^{-2}	400 m^2	16
Labour[cd]	3.50 h^{-1}		
Pruning:[cd]			
No. 1, year 3			37.87
No. 2, year 7			130
No. 3, year 9			130
No. 4, year 15			416
No. 5, year 20			74.10
No. 6, year 25			58.50
Annual maintenance labour[c]	3.50 h^{-1}	3 h	10.50

[a] Ground preparation costs are assumed to be a preliminary 'spot weeding' with herbicide prior to planting.

[b] Labour requirements for installation of tree protection and support are assumed at 0.16 h per tree. This can be expected to vary depending on site conditions.

[c] Labour costs are based on casual labour rates in 1997.

[d] Labour requirements per ha for pruning depend on the height to which the trees are pruned, the length of stem that is actually pruned and the numbers of trees per ha. Labour for formative pruning is assumed at 0.05 h m^{-1}. For tree heights of 2.5, 5 and 10 m, labour requirements per metre pruned have been estimated as 0.1 h m^{-1} pruned for the first lift and 0.2 h m^{-1} pruned for all subsequent lifts. Differences in pruning costs per ha for each of the five lifts reflect differences in tree numbers pruned and differences in pruned length in more mature trees.

Table A1.2 Establishment and management costs for an upland sycamore-based silvopastoral system, planted at an inter-row spacing of 5 m (400 trees ha⁻¹). All costs are in £97/98.

Activity	Unit costs (£)	Requirement ha⁻¹	Management system	
			Thin total cost (£ ha⁻¹)	Non-thin total cost (£ ha⁻¹)
Establishment				
Ground preparation [a]	0.04 m⁻²	400 m²	16	16
Plants	0.40	400 plants	160	160
1 split post (2 m)	1.20	400 posts	480	480
1 anchor peg	0.25	400 pegs	100	100
1 tree guard	1	400 guards	400	400
Labour [bc]	3.50 h⁻¹	60 h	210	210
Subsequent activities				
Beating up: year 2				
Materials	1 plant⁻¹	40 plants	40	40
Labour [c]	3.50 h⁻¹	6 h	21	21
Weeding: years 1–3				
Materials	0.04 m⁻²	400 m²	16	16
Labour [cd]	3.50 h⁻¹			
Pruning: [cd]				
No.1, year 4			117.71	117.71
No.2, year 8			33.09	33.09
No.3, year 12			41.63	41.63
No.4, year 16			175.92	175.92
No.5, year 20			187.50	187.50
No.6, year 24			181.85	181.85
No.7, year 28			140.29	140.29
No.8, year 32			97.01	159.58
No.9, year 33			14.55	50.94
No.10, year 37			0	18.37
No.11, year 41			0	4.48
No.12, year 45			0	3.11
No.13, year 49			0	2.05
No.14, year 53			0	1.06
Annual maintenance labour [c]	3.50 h⁻¹	3 h	10.50	10.50

[a] Ground preparation costs are assumed to be a preliminary 'spot weeding' with herbicide prior to planting.

[b] Labour requirements for installation of tree protection and support are assumed at 0.16 h per tree. This can be expected to vary depending on site conditions.

[c] Labour costs are based on casual labour rates in 1997.

[d] Labour requirements per ha for pruning depend on the height to which the trees are pruned, the length of stem that is actually pruned and the numbers of trees per ha. Labour for formative pruning is assumed at 0.05 h m⁻¹. For tree heights of 2.5, 5 and 10 m, labour requirements per metre pruned have been estimated as 0.1 h m⁻¹ pruned for the first lift and 0.2 h m⁻¹ pruned for all subsequent lifts. Differences in pruning costs per ha for each the 14 lifts reflect differences in tree numbers pruned at each lift and differences in pruned length in the more mature trees. Resources for thinning are accounted for in the 'road side' value of the harvested crop which is 'net' of extraction costs.

Table A1.3 Establishment and management costs for a poplar-based silvoarable system, planted at an inter-row spacing of 20 m and intra-row spacing of 6.4 m (78 trees ha^{-1}). All costs are in £97/98.

Activity	Unit costs (£)	Requirement ha^{-1}	Total (£)
Establishment			
Ground preparation[a]	–	–	–
Plants	1	78 plants	78
Plastic mulch	0.1 m^{-2}	500 m	50
Labour: planting[b]	7 h^{-1}	2 h	14
Mulch laying	0.20 m^{-2}	500 m	100
Subsequent activities			
Beating up: year 2			
Materials	1 plant^{-1}	8 plants	8
Labour[b]	7 h^{-1}	0.5 h	3.50
Weeding: years 1–5			
Materials			1
Labour[b]	7 h^{-1}	8	56
Pruning:			
No. 1, year 3	7 h^{-1}	5.2 h[c]	36.40
No. 2, year 4	7 h^{-1}	5.2 h	36.40
No. 3, year 6	7 h^{-1}	9.1 h	63.70
No. 4, year 7	7 h^{-1}	13.0 h	91.00
No. 5, year 9	7 h^{-1}	15.6 h	109.20
Annual maintenance	7 h^{-1}	3 h	21

[a] Ground preparation costs are assumed to be part of the normal field preparation activities prior to planting the arable crop.
[b] Labour costs are based on agricultural workers rates in East Anglia in 1997.
[c] Total time for pruning 78 trees.

Appendix 2

Agricultural enterprises used in the POPMOD analysis

Table A2.1 Rotational budgets for the cropping elements in the lowland silvoarable system: crop 1/2.

		Crop 1/2: winter wheat	
	Price per unit	**Yields**	**Value (£ ha^{-1})**
Revenues			
Crop revenue	£100 t^{-1}	8.5 t ha^{-1}	850
By-product 'A'	£20 t^{-1}	2.5 t ha^{-1}	50
By-product 'B'	£0 t^{-1}	0 t ha^{-1}	0
Total revenue winter wheat			900
Area payment	£257 ha^{-1}		257
Variable costs			
Seed	£310 t^{-1}	0.18 t ha^{-1}	55.8
Fertiliser	£120 t^{-1}	0.47 t ha^{-1}	56.4
Sprays	£12.27 l^{-1}	4.6 t ha^{-1}	56.4
Other	£2.5 t^{-1}	1 t ha^{-1}	2.5
Total variable costs			171.1
Gross margin			**985.9**
Fixed costs			
Fuel and repairs			87
Labour[a]	£7 h^{-1}	19 h ha^{-1}	133
Total fixed costs			**220**
Net margin			**765.9**

[a] Labour costs are based on agricultural workers rates in East Anglia in 1997.

Table A2.2 Rotational budgets for the cropping elements in the lowland silvoarable system: crop 3.

	Price per unit	Crop 3: winter barley Yields	Value (£ ha^{-1})
Revenues			
Crop revenue	£75 t^{-1}	7.5 t ha^{-1}	562.5
By-product 'A'	£20 t^{-1}	2 t ha^{-1}	40
By-product 'B'	£0 t^{-1}	0 t ha^{-1}	0
Total revenue winter barley			602.5
Area payment	£257 ha^{-1}		257
Variable costs			
Seed	£270 t^{-1}	0.16 t ha^{-1}	43.2
Fertiliser	£120 t^{-1}	0.5 t ha^{-1}	60
Sprays	£22 l^{-1}	1.75 l ha^{-1}	38.5
Other	£2.5 t^{-1}	1 t ha^{-1}	2.5
Total variable costs			144.2
Gross margin			**715.3**
Fixed costs			
Fuel and repairs			87
Labour[a]	£7 h^{-1}	18 h ha^{-1}	126
Other 1			1
Other 2			2
Total fixed costs			**216**
Net margin			**499.3**

[a] Labour costs are based on agricultural workers rates in East Anglia in 1997.

Table A2.3 Rotational budgets for the cropping elements in the lowland silvoarable system: crop 4.

	Price per unit	Crop 4: threshing peas Yields	Value (£ ha^{-1})
Revenues			
Crop revenue	£100 t^{-1}	5 t ha^{-1}	500
By-product 'A'	£3 t^{-1}	0 t ha^{-1}	0
By-product 'B'	£0 t^{-1}	0 t ha^{-1}	0
Total revenue threshing peas			371
Area payment	£371 ha^{-1}		
Variable costs			
Seed	£360 t^{-1}	0.2 t ha^{-1}	72
Fertiliser	£0 t^{-1}	0 t ha^{-1}	0
Sprays	£10.17 l^{-1}	6 l ha^{-1}	61.02
Other	£7 t^{-1}	3 t ha^{-1}	21
Total variable costs			154.02
Gross margin			**716.98**
Fixed costs			
Fuel and repairs			50
Labour[a]	£7 h^{-1}	10.5 h ha^{-1}	73.5
Total fixed costs			**123.5**
Net margin			**593.5**

[a] Labour costs are based on agricultural workers rates in East Anglia in 1997.

Glossary

Agroforestry Land-use practices where trees are combined with crops and/or animals on the same unit of land.

Alley The area between rows of trees where crops are grown in a silvoarable system.

Apical dominance Growth concentrated on the leader, which tends to produce a straight stem and a conical crown.

Bare-rooted stock Plants lifted from the nursery soil and despatched to the planting site with their roots bare of soil.

Clone A genetically identical group of plants originating from a single plant by vegetative reproduction.

Contact herbicide A herbicide that kills the parts of a plant with which it comes into contact.

Crown length The distance from the uppermost shoot of a tree to the lowest part of the leafy canopy.

Cultivation The tilling of soil and its vegetation or brash cover with implements to provide a favourable environment for efficient establishment and early uniform growth of plants; to adjust water relations; and to improve root anchorage.

Final crop spacing The density of trees which exists prior to the felling of the trees for timber.

Formative pruning Pruning a young plant to achieve a desired shape or form.

Mulch A suitable material, e.g. black polythene, bark, applied to the soil surface to conserve moisture, reduce soil temperature fluctuations and suppress weed growth around a young tree.

Pannage The right to pasturage of pigs in a forest or wood.

Provenance The place in which any stand of trees, whether indigenous or non-indigenous, is growing. Seed collected from such stands.

Residual herbicide A herbicide which remains active in the soil for a period after it has been applied, and affects weeds growing into treated soil.

Rotational grazing A system for managing grazing livestock through regular movement of the animals to fresh pasture.

Sawlog Log usually of at least 14 cm top diameter, which is intended for conversion at a sawmill.

Senescence The process of growing old before death.

Sets Whole woody shoots (usually longer than 1 m) that will root easily when inserted into the soil.

Silvopastoral system Where trees are grown in grazed pasture.

Silvoarable system Where crops are grown between rows of trees and/or shrubs.

Soil compaction A reduction of soil porosity usually caused by surface loading which can lead to poor root penetration and reduced water holding capacity and aeration.

Stolon An above ground horizontal stem.

Systemic herbicide A herbicide that enters and is moved within the plant and can affect parts of the plant remote from the point of application.

Veneer log High quality timber that is to be sliced or peeled for veneer production. Usually this means that the log must be above a minimum diameter and branch and knot free.

Yield Class A classification of rate of growth in terms of the potential maximum mean annual increment per ha of volume to 7 cm top diameter, irrespective of age of culmination or of tree species.

Abbreviations

BEAM	Bioeconomic Agroforestry Modelling
BHIP	British Hardwood Improvement Programme
CATIE	Centro Agronómico Tropical de Investigación y Enseñanza
CEC	Commission of the European Communities
CGIAR	Consultative Group on International Agricultural Research
CTFT	Centre Technique Forestier Tropical
DANI	Department of Agriculture for Northern Ireland
DARDNI	Department of Agriculture and Rural Development for Northern Ireland (previously DANI)
EC	European Commission
EU	European Union
GATT	General Agreement on Tariffs and Trade
HRI	Horticulture Research International
ICRAF	International Centre for Research in Agroforestry
ICRISAT	International Crops Research Institute for the Semi-Arid Tropics
IGER	Institute of Grassland and Environmental Research
MAFF	Ministry of Agriculture, Fisheries and Food
MLURI	Macaulay Land Use Research Institute
NNE	National Network Experiment

Printed by Colourgraphic Arts, Bordon, Hampshire.